Insects

of the

Texas

Lost Pines

Number Thirty-three
W. L. Moody, Jr.,
Natural History Series

Insects
of the
Texas
Lost Pines

Stephen Welton Taber & Scott B. Fleenor

Texas A&M University Press · College Station

The paper used in this book
meets the minimum requirements
of the American National Standard for Permanence
of Paper for Printed Library Materials, z39.48-1984.
Binding materials have been chosen for durability.

LIBRARY OF CONGRESS CATALOGING-IN-PUBLICATION DATA

Taber, Stephen Welton, 1956–
    Insects of the Texas lost pines / Stephen Welton Taber,
Scott B. Fleenor.—1st. ed.
        p. cm.—(W. L. Moody, Jr., natural history series ; no. 33)
    Includes bibliographical references (p.   )
    ISBN 1-58544-235-6 (cloth : alk. paper)—
    ISBN 1-58544-236-4 (pbk. : alk. paper)
        1. Insects—Texas—Bastrop Region.   2. Insects—Texas.
I. Fleenor, Scott B., 1962–   II. Title.   III. Series.
QL475.T33   2003
595.7'09764'32—dc21   2002153531

Contents

Insects

of the

Texas Lost Pines

CHAPTER 1

Introduction

The Lost Pines is a forest located on the eastern edge of Central Texas (figs 1, 2). Its alluring name refers to one of its dominant trees and to its isolation from a much larger forest stretching at least historically from eastern Texas to the Atlantic Ocean one thousand miles away. In other words, the pines are "lost" because they grow as a wooded island surrounded by pastures, farms, and scattered trees such as oaks and mesquites. We were drawn to this island ecosystem for several reasons. First among them is isolation itself. Isolation presents the possibility of undiscovered species, a possibility that manifested itself in the form of an animal previously unknown to science. In fact, thirty-five years before our own study drew to a close, two previously unknown green alga species were discovered in this same forest (Milliger 1965). One alga was immediately named *Characium paradoxum.* The other was not given a scientific name at that time.

The Lost Pines also marks the westernmost limit of its namesake species, the loblolly pine (*Pinus taeda,* figs. 3, 4). This primeval-looking tree is endemic to the United States and grows naturally nowhere in the world but in the southern part of the country, from a few miles west of our study site to the Atlantic Ocean in the distant east. No other pine grows naturally in Central Texas. A third factor lending interest to the forest is its encroachment upon an invisible biogeographical line or barrier that passes north and south through the United States. This line is a kind of ecological continental divide long known to separate the country's eastern flora and fauna from its western flora and fauna. The barrier slices through semiarid Central Texas just east of San Antonio, and as a result the forest is a

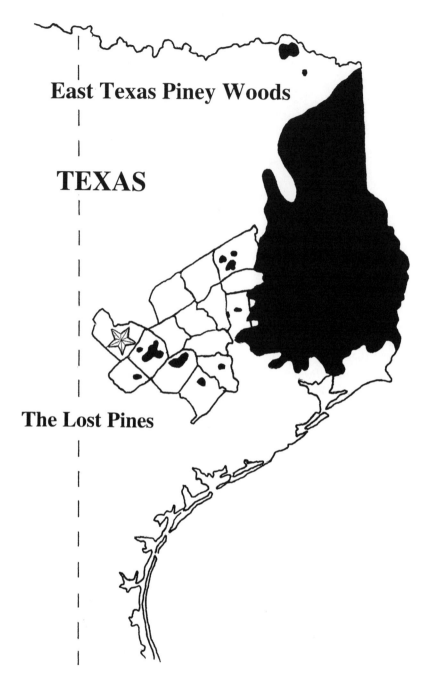

Fig. 1. The Lost Pines of Central Texas. Bastrop County contains the largest stand of isolated loblollies. Immediately to the west is Travis County, including the state capital of Austin (star). Vertical dashed line approximates the biogeographical divide. Map modified from Youngman (1965).

Fig. 2. Seasons in the forest, (A) winter view from little bluestem meadow; (B) summer view from the same point. The bare tree of winter is a black hickory flanked by small eastern junipers. In the distance is a loblolly treeline.

Fig. 3. One of the largest loblollies in the forest, (A) showing diameter near the ground; (B) looking up into the highest branches of the same tree.

challenging habitat of only marginal quality for many of the species living there. The loblolly itself provides a stellar example. It made its original appearance in the humid southeastern corner of the United States before spreading west until the tree's progress was finally halted by the intolerably dry barrier of the invisible line (Schultz 1997).

Fourth, we were attracted to the Lost Pines because we knew that its biodiversity had never been investigated in a comprehensive fashion. This is paradoxical considering the fact that it lies along a short stretch of highway connecting Texas A&M University in College Station with the University of Texas at Austin, a mere one hundred miles to the west. Both schools have a track record of research on environmental topics, from the practical aspects of forestry and agriculture to more basic questions concerning the lives and distributions of plants and animals. Yet the Lost Pines had never been subjected to close scientific scrutiny.

From the perspective of north and south as opposed to the east and west comparison that dominates our work, the Lost Pines lies so deeply within the southern United States that it nearly encroaches upon a part of Texas often described as tropical (the Brownsville area). That part of the country is vastly more diverse in most forms of life than is the northern part of the United States (Danks 1994). In particular, the region defined in the Danks survey as "Texas-Mexico" has a greater insect diversity than any other.

Finally, the remarkable ecosystem of the Lost Pines is at the center of an escalating controversy that pits government agencies against land developers, homeowners, and other private citizens in a bid to save the Houston toad (*Bufo houstonensis*) from extinction (fig. 5). The dwindling amphibian will probably make its last stand in these very woods, and if the Lost Pines itself should someday follow the toad to extinction, we will at least have documented a significant fraction of the plants and animals that disappeared with the ecosystem's namesake

Fig. 4. A loblolly pine (*Pinus taeda*) surrounded by grape lianas.

Fig. 5. Houston toad (*Bufo houstonensis*).

trees. Like the toad, many of these species do not occur in the cultivated and urbanized surroundings of Central Texas. Some that do occur here and in perhaps lesser numbers than the Houston toad have not been recognized until now as currently inhabiting the forest. For example, we found a single spring peeper frog (*Pseudacris crucifer*) and a single red-spotted toad (*Bufo punctatus*) during years of study. In this book we focus on the insects and their relatives, a group collectively known as the invertebrates.

Yet the conventional picture of the Lost Pines as presented here can be somewhat misleading. For one thing, this is a mixed forest where hardwoods such as oaks and hickory comprise about as much of the woodland as the loblolly itself. In addition, though widely conceived of as an island in a savanna, the Lost Pines of Texas is more accurately described as an archipelago with separate stands in Caldwell, Fayette, Colorado, Austin, and Bastrop counties (Youngman 1965). Bastrop County in particular is understood to represent the focus of the forest, and we chose this island above all others as our base of operations.

Even the claim of isolation from the vast pine forest of the southeastern United States has been contested. One student of the subject reported a tenuous connection between the two woodlands (Correll 1966). If he was right, then the Lost Pines is more accurately described as a western, albeit fractured, peninsula than as a distant island or archipelago. And even if the forest truly is isolated, as custom maintains, it need never have been "lost" in the first place. It might have arisen independently of the eastern woodlands from the beginning, as separate as one pine tree from another, with no connection to break.

We are even less sure of the forest's age than of its historical extent. Ancient pollen grains retrieved from bogs nearby suggest that pines have been growing in Central Texas for nearly twenty thousand years (Bryant 1977). More than that we cannot say. Luckily we were not seeking answers to difficult historical questions. Our own interest lies in the present, in the abundance and diversity of life that dwells in the Lost Pines today, regardless of its shrouded past. Our focus became the identification of every apparent species of plant and animal life with the exceptions of house flies, honey bees, and other species that people may identify without recourse to this book. By "apparent" we mean those species readily observed during an inspection of the surroundings. The most abundant species in nearly every natural habitat (e.g., bacteria) will remain unseen without the aid of a hand lens or microscope. Soon we found ourselves searching for rare species too, and all the others that are never encountered without intensive scrutiny and/ or a great measure of good luck. The result is a natural history and inventory of more than seven hundred plant, animal, fungal, lichen, and algal species. When this is combined with the previously published checklist of Lost Pines birds (Freeman 1996), and the Internet list of the Stengl Ranch (www.esb.utexas.edu/philjs/ stengl), the total number of animal and plant species that have been sighted and recorded exceeds one thousand. As already noted, in this book we focus on insects and their relatives.

We found that a small proportion of the insects—nine, to be precise—are Texas endemics as far as current distributional data can tell us (appendix 1). These apparently occur nowhere else in the world, and some are further confined to east-central Texas alone. Two additional animals, Attwater's pocket gopher (*Geomys attwateri*) and the Houston toad (*Bufo houstonensis*), complete the list of endemic species known to us and bring the total to eleven, yet among the denizens of the forest only the Houston toad is known to the public as a native and exclusively Texan species. The single endemic mammal and all nine endemic invertebrates had escaped notice as such. Our newly discovered species is one of these. It is a tiny black and orange beetle of 4.5 mm, presently known from four specimens and recorded only from the Lost Pines and on a single occasion from Kerrville farther west (fig. 6). We named it the Texas long-lipped beetle (*Telegeusis texensis*) for its impressive mouthparts (Fleenor and Taber 2001).

In presenting the known distributions of the invertebrates of the Lost Pines we have emphasized their extent in the east-west direction because the invisible biogeographical barrier (fig. 1) happens to be a north-south line that divides the country into eastern and western realms. Many species are known to reach their

Fig. 6. The
Texas long-
lipped beetle
(*Telegeusis
texensis*), a newly
discovered
species.

limits from one direction or the other near this forest, and we knew that we
would be able to establish new eastern and western records for others. For example, on our first visit to the vast pine forest in far eastern Texas we discovered
that its insects and plants comprise sets of species that are distinct from those of
the Lost Pines despite the fact that the two regions, supposedly connected at one
time, are separated by little more than one hundred miles (Parks et al. 1971).

At this point we conclude the introduction to the Lost Pines with an explanation of our approach to understanding and writing natural history. At our dis-
posal were the Geological and Life Sciences libraries of the University of Texas at
Austin. We perused their journals, studied books written by specialists, accessed
Interlibrary Loan to obtain additional works, looked up scientific names in *Biological Abstracts,* plowed through identification keys constructed by authorities,
and frequently availed ourselves of the Ovid Internet service to carry out these
tasks. This search engine took us from the literature of the year 2002 all the way
back to the journals of the late 1970s. We did see many reports on Internet web
pages but most of these we do not consider as published information because
they have not passed through the fire of peer review that is expected of scientific
work. Hence we were cautious when using the Web. We also faced limitations
with the selection of figures. From an enormous collection of photographs taken
in the field and above the lens of the microscope, we have chosen, for practical
reasons, to emphasize species that have seldom or never been illustrated before.
We have also drawn attention to the need for identification keys in many circumstances when a confident ID is important. These are alerts seldom accompanied

by a citation because they refer to technical works that few but the specialists will wish to deal with, and specialists will know how to track them down.

We are grateful to curators John Oswald and Edward Riley of Texas A&M University for allowing us to spend time among the nearly two million specimens of that institution's insect collection. Texas A&M University is located in College Station, less than one hour's drive from our study site, and its entomology cabinets contain a wealth of species occurring in the Lost Pines. We visited the collection to confirm identifications and to bring to light previously unpublished data. Experts on lesser-known animal groups were frequently consulted from a distance by email, and when identifications proved difficult, specimens were sent to these experts for confirmation.

Finally, we thank David Riskind of the Texas Parks and Wildlife Department for issuing Scientific Study Permit No. 15-00, which made possible the collections necessary for species identifications, and for allowing us to peruse unpublished manuscripts at the headquarters of the TPWD in Austin.

CHAPTER 2

The Lost Pines
as a Setting for Animal Life

C limate is an important factor in the determination of animal distributions. The average annual precipitation in the Lost Pines, coming almost exclusively in the form of rain, is approximately thirty-five inches.
From numbers to words this translates as the dry end of "humid subtropical" and
can be alternately expressed as "dry sub-humid" (Youngman 1965). Precipitation
has two seasonal peaks. One arrives in spring (April, May, June) at a time when
thunderstorms are most prevalent. The second peak is a brief spike in September
in the wake of tropical storms. During peak periods rainfall per month is nearly
double that of other months of the year—four inches rather than roughly two
(Bureau of Business Research 1987).

Just as the Lost Pines may be described as generally dry, it may also be described
as generally warm. In late summer temperatures occasionally soar beyond one
hundred degrees Fahrenheit although mid- and upper nineties are the norm.
Discomfort in summer is balanced to some extent by mild winters with snow
falling only rarely.

Geology and Soil

The Lost Pines grow on sandy soils derived from rocks of Eocene age (55–38 million years ago) and from more recent coarser materials deposited by the Colorado
River in the Pleistocene Epoch (2 million to 10,000 years ago). The ability of

coarse soil to retain water is critical to the survival of this forest, as we later show.

Seven rock formations in particular, all members of the Claiborne group, are exposed here. From oldest to youngest, or equivalently from west to east, they are the Carrizo sandstone, Reklaw formation, Queen City sands, Weches formation, Sparta sandstone, Cook Mountain formation, and the Yegua formation (Rasmussen 1949). Their ultimate origins are tied to the advancing and retreating coastlines of the ancient Gulf of Mexico 40–50 million years ago (Bureau of Economic Geology 1974a, 1974b, 1992).

The most famous of these seven is the Carrizo formation because it lends its name to the aquifer comprised by the sandy formations of the Claiborne group. The rather pure quartz layers of the Carrizo, Queen City, and Sparta formations were laid down by coastal rivers, streams, and creeks, and the formation is thus of continental origin. Formations that alternate with these three were deposited offshore and consist of finer sediments. The Reklaw is one of them. Its structure is complex, consisting of an upper portion of iron-rich shale and an older, lower portion of red to yellow sandstone. The sandstone used for building materials by the Civilian Conservation Corps during the Great Depression era in Bastrop and Buescher state parks was quarried from this formation. For the loblolly pine, sand is the crucial component of these Claiborne layers, in combination with a more recent overlying veneer of Pleistocene river gravels.

Soils derived from these rocks tend to be nutrient-poor, acidic, and rather coarse in the more upland regions of the Lost Pines. In lowlands the soils tend to be finer and richer in clay. They also tend to be nutrient-rich and nearly neutral in pH, in contrast to the strongly acidic soils of uplands.

Why Loblolly Rather Than Some Other Species of Pine?

The presence of loblolly and the absence of any other pine can be explained by a comparison of roots and leaves. Two species occurring in the distant East Texas forest must be included in the comparison. These are shortleaf pine (*Pinus echinata*) and longleaf pine (*P. palustris*). In drier, sandier habitats loblollies have an advantage over shortleaf seedlings because they have longer roots that grow deeper into the soil (Bilan and Stransky 1966). However, longleaf pine can compete with loblolly at this stage of development because its roots are also capable of reaching deep into the soil for water. Loblolly's advantage relative to the longleaf is hinted at in the latter's common name. Long leaves are more prone to lose water to the surrounding air than are short leaves, and of the three Lost Pines candidates, the longleaf pine has the most restricted range in southeast Texas, occurring in regions with the highest rainfall (Critchfield and Little 1966).

Even loblolly seems to have acquired special adaptations for life in the Lost Pines. Compared to more eastern individuals of their own species, the trees here have needles that are shorter and broader and surface layers that resist losing moisture to the air. Furthermore, the Central Texas trees produce larger seeds that allow seedlings to grow root systems faster than plants growing from smaller seeds (Youngman 1965; Schultz 1997).

On the other hand, "lost" pines do show signs of stress. The tallest individuals are stunted compared to more eastern trees, growing to maximum heights of approximately seventy feet (Baker 1979), a full fifty feet shorter than loblollies growing under optimal conditions. Maximum trunk girth does not differ so radically. Individuals with diameters between three and four feet are considered large in any habitat (fig. 3).

In the eighty miles separating the western limit of the loblolly's *continuous* range from the even more westerly Lost Pines itself, the amount of water available for use by plants after allowing for surface evaporation decreases by a rather significant fifteen inches (original calculations from data in Bomar 1995, Larkin and Bomar 1983, and Manogaran 1975). For the loblolly to survive in its challenging outpost this difference must be overcome in one way or another. Once again, the importance of gravelly and sandy soil as a water reservoir becomes immediately obvious. To the west of the forest where even less water is available, the pines are replaced by blackland prairie. On the east, the grassland separating the two loblolly forests has long been known as "the Fayette prairie."

Vegetation Zones

The driest habitats in the Lost Pines are open woods in erosion-resistant deep sands along the crests of hills where the water table is far from the surface. Dominant trees include post oak (*Quercus stellata*), seldom growing to heights above forty feet, and black hickory (*Carya texana*). There is little undergrowth here. Though stunted, some of the post oaks are ancient, craggy specimens upward of three hundred years in age (Stahle 1996), reminiscent of gigantic bonsai trees.

Riddell's sand spikemoss (*Selaginella arenicola riddellii*) grows abundantly along the surface of the sand along with cushions of the southern reindeer lichen (*Cladonia subtenuis*) and many other lichens that festoon the gnarled and twiggy oaks in colors of red, yellow, and gray.

Sandy openings are colonized most conspicuously by bluejack oaks (*Quercus incana*), little bluestem grass (*Schizachyrium scoparium*), yankee-weed (*Eupatorium compositifolium*), queen's delight (*Stillingia sylvatica*), the nettle known as mala mujer (*Cnidoscolus texanus*), and the prostrate prickly-pear (*Opuntia humifusa*).

Loblolly pine makes its appearance on sandy slopes where the water table is closer to the surface than it is beneath the crests of hills. Yet water is scarce enough to stunt these trees at heights of between forty and sixty feet. Post oaks grow taller here than on the crests, and they are more prevalent too. The dense shrub community includes hop-tree (*Ptelea trifoliata*) and fragrant sumac (*Rhus aromatica*). Where thick deposits of Pleistocene river gravels cap the deep sands, loblolly pine and blackjack oak gain ascendance over post oak, with farkleberry (*Vaccinium arboreum)* and yaupon holly (*Ilex vomitoria)* forming an open shrub layer.

Rockier soils can be found on the gentle east-facing slopes, but they vary from deep and gravelly to shallow, with a finer layer of underlying clay in the latter case. In the deeper soils loblolly comes into its own and blackjack oak grows as a scrubby subdominant. Shallow soils turn the tables and give blackjack the upper hand while allowing little bluestem grass to take hold in small openings where clay content is higher. Farkleberry is the dominant small tree or shrub. Post oaks are out of their element here.

Lower slopes and drainages develop a denser shrub cover in response to the greater availability of water. Yaupon holly is more apparent than any other shrub. Next is American beautyberry (*Callicarpa americana*). Where water is most accessible the southern bayberry (*Morella [Myrica] cerifera*) grows in thickets with the former two species and the occasional possumhaw holly (*Ilex decidua*).

The soil in these habitats is complex due to erosion and deposition by water. Slippery elms (*Ulmus rubra*), boxelder (*Acer negundo*), and smooth hackberry (*Celtis laevigata*) grow in abundance along the lower drainage bottoms where fine, silty, recent alluvium has been deposited and the water table is at or near the surface. Oaks and pines occur together higher up where sandy or gravelly material has been washed down and deposited on top of finer alluvium. Along the upper reaches of drainage systems where permanent ground water is available, pines may actually invade the deep sandy stronghold of post oak.

Naturally occurring wetlands are a welcome sight in the Lost Pines because of their rarity and because their appearance refreshes explorers who become hardened to the dry crunch of brown pine needles and oak leaves underfoot. Two types of wetland exist. One is temporary whereas the other is permanent. Temporary wetlands develop in small upland flats and along blocked drainages. During the "wet season" from fall to spring an ephemeral water table may persist long enough to support the insectivorous annual sundew (*Drosera brevifolia*) and the tiny Texas bottle liverwort (*Sphaerocarpos texanus*).

Permanent natural wetlands are the rarest of the rare. They develop where water-bearing rock formations, known as aquifers, contact relatively impermeable formations underneath. Erosion and/or geological faulting can expose these lines of contact, and where this happens, seeps and springs may flow forth. The resulting habitats are swamps and marshes. Many wetland plants reach their western limits in or near the Lost Pines, including narrow-leafed chain fern (*Woodwardia areolata;* Cranfil 1983), and peat or bog moss (*Sphagnum lescurii;* Lodwick and Snider 1980).

Artificial habitats, in the sense that they are provided by our own species, take two general forms: clearings and bodies of water. Artificial clearings are represented by old fields, powerline and pipeline rights-of-way, and roadsides. All are dominated by grasses and wildflowers drawn mainly from the surrounding prairie and by many native and introduced "weedy" species. Mesquite trees (*Prosopis glandulosa*) occur almost exclusively in artificial clearings.

Artificial bodies of water are represented throughout the Lost Pines by catchment tanks and a few lakes. Various floating and submerged aquatic plant species occur only in these habitats, having been dispersed through the activities of visiting humans and other animals. A diverse assemblage of water-loving grasses, sedges, rushes, and forbs crowds the shorelines along with reclining black willows (*Salix nigra*) and the occasional eastern cottonwood (*Populus deltoides*) and American sycamore (*Platanus occidentalis*). At the present time the numerous catchment tanks scattered throughout the sandy uplands are appreciated mostly as the major breeding habitats of the endangered Houston toad (Dr. Andrew Price, pers. comm.). Without these tanks the dwindling amphibian might well become extirpated from the region.

Fire and the Lost Pines

The antithesis of a natural wetland is forest fire, and just as opposite in nature are the reasons for the scarcity of both. Fire has been suppressed by forces usually described as "unnatural," meaning the intervention of our own species. Fire control during the nineteenth, twentieth, and now the twenty-first centuries has sustained an invasion of the Lost Pines by a juniper tree known as eastern red-cedar (*Juniperus virginiana*). Red-cedar has infiltrated nearly all of the habitats described here, though it thrives in moister sites at lower elevations (Anonymous 1990). Fire does an especially good job of ferreting out and destroying red-cedar because the species has shreddy, flammable bark and resinous leaves. Fire also clears the forest floor of thick accumulations of pine needles. If this were allowed to happen, more plant species would take root and greater plant diversity would undoubtedly invite greater animal diversity in turn (Dr. David Riskind, pers. comm.). Animal life of the Lost Pines as it exists at present is of course the focus of this book.

The Future of the Lost Pines

What lies in store for this forest and its denizens? The greatest natural, predict-able threat to the Lost Pines is the annual summer drought of July and August, and the most susceptible trees are those growing in dry upland soils. Indeed, according to one authority, "the frequency and severity of summer droughts are the main factors limiting loblolly pine's western range" (Schultz 1997). If future temperatures do rise, it will not take much to eliminate the loblollies from Central Texas. This might well have occurred time and time again over hundreds of thousands of years during the glacial oscillations of the Quaternary period. Pollen records are available only for the last sixteen thousand of those two million years, and even these exist in trace levels only. They have been retrieved from Boriack Bog thirty miles north of Bastrop State Park and from Soefje Bog and Hershop Bog forty-eight miles south of the same locality (Bryant 1977). The pollen record indicates no significant changes and no expansion into surrounding oak-hickory woodlands or savanna during this short period (Larson et al. 1972).

In addition to poorly known natural forces are the more familiar forces applied by humans. Land development for housing and for business might impact the forest eventually, but at the time of writing this possibility was mitigated by the fact that much of the Lost Pines is contained within state park boundaries and by the fact that one of its denizens, the Houston toad, is protected by federal law under the Endangered Species Act. The largest population of this toad exists here, and without the forest, the species might become extinct.

CHAPTER 3

Butterflies and Moths

Butterflies are among the most apparent or readily observed animals in the Lost Pines. Their beauty ranks them with their fellow fliers the birds as favorite subjects of observation. In contrast, most moths are nocturnal and are not as conspicuous or popular as their brightly colored diurnal relatives. A few moths do fly during the day, and these attractive species make their appearance in spring and summer. Nocturnal moths were among the many visitors to the blacklight traps that aided us when we collected after dark. These consist of an ultraviolet lamp that also glows in the blue end of the visible spectrum and a bucket that flying insects fall into when they come to the light.

Besides the twenty-five species profiled here, an unpublished 1968 document we found in the files of the Texas Parks and Wildlife Department in Austin lists eight additional lepidopteran species for the area. These are the little sulfur (*Eurema lisa*), brown-tailed skipper (*Urbanus dorantes*), gray hairstreak (*Strymon melinus*), Mexican blue (*Hemiargus isola*), dark cloudywing (*Thorybes confusis*), gray skipper (*Lerodea eufala*), dusky little skipper (*Amblyscirtes alternata*), and western swarthy skipper (*Nastra julia*). Records of many other butterflies and moths doubtless await publication. The wingspan measurements reported here are typically conversions from inches to millimeters.

pipevine swallowtail (fig. 7)
Battus philenor

Biology: Adult pipevine swallowtails are common in spring and to a lesser extent in summer when they flit among purple thistles and other wildflowers in search of nectar. Males also fly in search of mates, and once mated the females seek out host plants on which to lay their small orange eggs. Mating pairs seem unconcerned with their surroundings and can be approached and captured by hand (fig. 8). Caterpillars soon hatch from the eggs and become abundant on the sand in their warning colors of red or purplish black (fig. 9). Their color discourages at least some potential predators from eating an animal that contains toxins acquired while consuming leaves of the eerily beautiful pipevine plant, also known as the swanflower (fig. 10). Yet robber flies are undeterred by the poison when feeding on the adult butterfly (fig. 11). A second defense exists in the form of the "osmeterium" structure that is diagnostic for swallowtail caterpillars. This is a yellow, forked organ that appears suddenly from just behind the head when the caterpillar is disturbed. The sight of the osmeterium can startle a foe, as can the odor of an accompanying defensive chemical that stains the skin yellow if the organ is touched. We find the odor rather pleasant, which is not paradoxical because the osmeterium did not evolve as a defense against humans.

Pipevine caterpillars eat knotweed and sometimes one another in addition to swanflower leaves. Both plants are small and neither is common in the meadows of the Lost Pines. This accounts for the fact that big larvae are seldom seen on foliage but are often seen crawling on bare sand, presumably on the move between meals that consume all or most of a single host. In this they are unusual among the caterpillars of the Lost Pines.

Distribution: From the Atlantic Ocean to El Paso, Texas, with isolated populations farther west between New Mexico and the Pacific Coast.

Remarks: Wingspan 102 mm. When the caterpillar creeps across the soil it

Fig. 7. Pipevine swallowtail
(*Battus philenor*).

Fig. 8. Mating pipevine swallowtails.

Fig. 9. Pipevine swallowtail
caterpillar (red phase) on
little bluestem grass.

Fig. 10. The eerie swanflower
(*Aristolochia erecta*).

Fig. 11. A robber fly
with its pipevine
swallowtail prey.

appears to be probing its environment with two large antennae. These are actually fleshy stalks attached *behind* the head and thus are not true antennae at all. The larva's true antennae are too small to be noticed. Other names for the pipevine swallowtail are "blue swallowtail," "green swallowtail," and "Aristolochia swallowtail." The adult is the most common large butterfly of the Lost Pines forest.

Similar species: The pattern of conspicuous orange spots on the lower surface of the hind wing as shown here distinguishes the adult pipevine swallowtail from the similar but less abundant black swallowtail. Black swallowtails have spots too, but they are arranged in a different pattern and include an orange spot on top of each hind wing that the pipevine lacks altogether. It is remarkable that we did not encounter the eastern tiger swallowtail butterfly with its familiar colors of yellow and black. This species is seen occasionally in nearby Austin, Texas.

black swallowtail (fig. 12)
Papilio polyxenes

Biology: Adults sip nectar from wildflowers but we never saw the green and black caterpillar stage that feeds on plants of the parsley family.

Distribution: Black swallowtails range from the Atlantic Ocean to the Rocky Mountains.

Remarks: Wingspan 76 mm. This butterfly flies faster and higher than the pipevine swallowtail, which it closely resembles. It is less common than the pipevine species and less approachable too.

Similar species: *See* pipevine swallowtail.

Fig. 12. Left: Black swallowtail (*Papilio polyxenes*). Right: Giant swallowtail (*Papilio cresphontes*).

giant swallowtail (fig. 12)
Papilio cresphontes

Biology: Adults are very large brown and yellow butterflies that fly high, are difficult to catch with a net, and are seldom seen. They have the look of the tropics about them. The brown and buff caterpillars resemble bird droppings and are known as "orange dogs" or "orange puppies" but not because of any colors they display. They received these common names because they feed on members of the citrus tree family, including the abundant hop-tree of the Lost Pines and the less abundant Hercules-club. The odor of the orange dog's osmeterium is more offensive to humans than that of the pipevine swallowtail. Yet it does not save the larva from every enemy. On one occasion we returned to a hop-tree where we had seen several orange dogs feeding on leaves the previous week. All were gone and had presumably been eaten.

Distribution: From the Atlantic Ocean to Central Texas not far from the Lost Pines, with an isolated population in California.

Remarks: Wingspan 127 mm. This is the largest butterfly in the forest and the last on the list of the three swallowtail species we recorded. It is peculiar in its habit of flitting rapidly through an area instead of lingering, as the other swallowtails often do, and for its tendency to fly too high for capture by a net. The caterpillar is also exceptional for its protective bird-dropping coloration, so unlike that of the other swallowtails when they approach maturity.

Similar species: None.

buckeye (fig. 13)
Junonia coenia

Biology: Adult buckeyes visit wildflowers for nectar, and the caterpillars feed on a wide variety of plants. Males chase other insects that enter their territories.

Distribution: From coast to coast within the United States.

Remarks: Wingspan 51 mm. Prominent eyespots on the upper surface of the wings may serve to startle predators and thus give the adult a head start toward escape. Buckeyes are not as apparent as pipevine swallowtails but they are probably more abundant.

Similar species: None.

red admiral (fig. 13)
Vanessa atalanta

Biology: Adults sip nectar from the purple thistles that flower in clearings and along roadsides. The caterpillar feeds on a wide variety of plants.

Distribution: From coast to coast within the United States.

Fig. 13. Top left: Buckeye (*Junonia coenia*). Top right: Red admiral (*Vanessa atalanta*). Bottom: Variegated fritillary (*Euptoieta claudia*).

Remarks: Wingspan 51 mm. Red admirals have a reputation for perching on humans. This happened to one of us on a single occasion and is indeed unusual among butterflies. At all other times they avoided contact by flying away and were difficult to approach.
Similar species: None.

Hunter's butterfly (fig. 14)
Vanessa virginiensis
Biology: Similar to that of the red admiral and painted lady.
Distribution: From coast to coast within the United States.
Remarks: Wingspan 51 mm. This species, the painted lady, and the red admiral are all known as "thistle butterflies" because those plants figure so prominently in their diets.
Similar species: *See* painted lady.

painted lady
Vanessa cardui
Biology: Similar to that of the closely related red admiral.
Distribution: From coast to coast within the United States.

Fig. 14. Hunter's butterfly (*Vanessa virginiensis*).

Remarks: Wingspan 51 mm. The painted lady is the world's most widely distributed butterfly.

Similar species: Painted ladies have four small eyespots on the lower surface of the hind wing, whereas Hunter's butterfly has two large eyespots in the same area.

variegated fritillary (fig. 13)
Euptoieta claudia

Biology: Adults sip nectar from wildflowers. The caterpillars eat a wide variety of plants, including the violets and passionflowers of the Lost Pines.

Distribution: From coast to coast within the United States.

Remarks: Wingspan 64 mm. This is one of the brush-footed butterflies that do not use their front legs for walking.

Similar species: The Mexican fritillary (*Euptoieta hegesia*) occurs in South Texas, perhaps in the Lost Pines as well, and has less decorative hind wings. We never saw it.

Gulf fritillary (fig. 15)
Agraulis vanillae

Biology: Adults sip wildflower nectar. The caterpillars feed on passionflower leaves.
Distribution: From coast to coast within the United States.
Remarks: Wingspan 71 mm. This is perhaps the most exotic-looking butterfly in the forest. Like the giant swallowtail, it has the look of the tropics about it, as does the closely related black and yellow zebra longwing (*Heliconius charitonius*), which we saw fluttering through the forest on a single occasion and managed to miss with a failed swing of the net. Like the Gulf fritillary, the zebra feeds upon passionflower in the caterpillar stage. We do not know if the zebra actually lives in the Lost Pines or if the one we saw was only passing through.
Similar species: None.

monarch (fig. 16)
Danaus plexippus

Biology: Adults sip nectar from wildflowers, and some individuals take part in an annual migration between Mexico and southern Canada. Many predators avoid monarchs because the attractively striped caterpillars feed on toxic milkweed plants, and as a result poisons accumulate in their tissues.

Fig. 15. Gulf fritillary (*Agraulis vanillae*).

Fig. 16.
Monarch
butterfly
(*Danaus
plexippus*).

Distribution: From coast to coast within the United States.
Remarks: Wingspan 89 mm. The monarch butterfly is the official state insect of Texas, having defeated the red harvester ant for the honor. Though both species occur in the Lost Pines, the red harvester is uncommon because it tends to avoid sandy soil.
Similar species: The monarch has orange wings with thick black veins whereas the closely related queen has brown wings with less prominent veins. The viceroy (*Limenitis archippus*) resembles the monarch even more closely, but it was never seen.

Fig. 17. A queen
(*Danaus gilippus*) on
the forest floor.

queen (fig. 17)
Danaus gilippus

Biology: Similar to that of the monarch.

Distribution: From the Atlantic Ocean to a western limit near the Lost Pines.

Remarks: Wingspan 84 mm. Neither this species nor the monarch is common in the forest. The queen is definitely the commoner of the two. We examined dozens of milkweeds and saw several small, striped caterpillars on one plant that were either queens or monarchs.

Similar species: *See* monarch.

orange sulfur (fig. 18)
Colias eurytheme

Biology: Adults feed on wildflower nectar. The caterpillars feed on leaves of herbaceous legumes such as partridge pea and rattlepod. Both plants are abundant in the Lost Pines.

Distribution: From coast to coast within the United States.

Remarks: Wingspan 51 mm. This species is also known as the "alfalfa butterfly." Adults of summer broods tend to have more orange on their wings than do spring adults.

Similar species: Orange sulfur butterflies vary greatly in appearance. Some females are white. The clouded sulfur (*Colias philodice*) resembles the orange sulfur

Fig. 18. Orange sulfur (*Colias eurytheme*).

and also occurs in the Lost Pines; the two closely related species hybridize, making identification difficult. Smaller sulfurs occur in the forest, but we limited our attention to these two.

goatweed emperor (fig. 19)
Anaea andria

Biology: Adults sip nectar from wildflowers and feign death when handled. The caterpillars eat goatweed leaves (croton).

Distribution: Goatweed emperors are found only between the Appalachian and Rocky Mountains.

Remarks: Wingspan 51 mm. This butterfly has a tail on each hind wing, but it is not a swallowtail. The lower surfaces of its wings resemble dead leaves, and that resemblance earned the goatweed emperor the alternate name of "leafwing." Considering the abundance of goatweed and the occurrence of this plant in thick patches near pond margins, it is remarkable that the butterfly is not more common.

Similar species: None.

question mark (fig. 19)
Polygonia interrogationis

Biology: Adults eschew flower nectar in favor of tree sap, decaying fruit, and dung. The caterpillars feed on elm and hackberry leaves.

Distribution: From the Atlantic Ocean to the Rocky Mountains.

Remarks: Wingspan 64 mm. The lower surface of each wing resembles a dead leaf. The lower surface of the hind wing also bears a small silvery design that has been compared to a question mark.

Similar species: The comma (*Polygonia comma*) is a smaller butterfly that is similar in appearance but does not range as far south as the Lost Pines.

tawny emperor
Asterocampa clyton

Biology: Adults presumably sip nectar from wildflowers. The caterpillars feed gregariously on leaves of the abundant hackberry tree.

Distribution: From the Atlantic Ocean to a western limit near the Lost Pines.

Remarks: Wingspan 64 mm. Though its relative *Asterocampa celtis* has been named the "hackberry butterfly," the closely related tawny emperor has an equally strong claim to the title. Tawny emperors sometimes perch on hats or clothing. One specimen we saw probably had its hind wings nipped by a bird when they were held together in the vertical resting position.

Fig. 19. Top left: Goatweed emperor (*Anaea andria*). Top right: Question mark (*Polygonia interrogationis*). Bottom: Wood nymph (*Cercyonis pegala*).

Similar species: Tawny emperors do not have dark eyespots on the front wing. Hackberry emperors have these spots.

hackberry emperor
Asterocampa celtis

Biology: Similar to that of the tawny emperor.

Distribution: From the Atlantic Ocean to Arizona.

Remarks: Wingspan 61 mm. The caterpillar's head differs from that of the tawny emperor, which has branched horns, whereas the hackberry emperor caterpillar has simple horns.

Similar species: *See* tawny emperor.

wood nymph (fig. 19)
Cercyonis pegala

Biology: Adults sip nectar, decaying fruit, and dung. They flit through broken shade beneath pines and oaks and avoid sunlit meadows where most butterflies are seen. Nevertheless, the caterpillar does feed on grasses, including the abundant purpletop (*Tridens flavus*) that can be seen along roadsides penetrating the forest.

Distribution: From coast to coast within the United States.

Remarks: Wingspan 71 mm. The wood nymph is also known as the "goggle eye" because it bears a pair of large eyespots on each front wing.

Similar species: None.

Texas hairstreak (fig. 20)
Fixsenia favonius

Biology: Like the wood nymph, the Texas hairstreak is remarkable for lingering in wooded areas more than most butterflies of the Lost Pines. The caterpillars feed on leaves of blackjack oak, post oak, water oak, and presumably the rarer oaks as well.

Distribution: Primarily a species of the eastern United States with isolated populations farther west.

Remarks: Wingspan 25 mm. The Texas hairstreak is also known as the southern

Fig. 20. Texas hairstreak (*Fixsenia favonius*).

Fig. 21. Great purple hairstreak (*Altides halesus*).

hairstreak. Hairstreaks are named for the hairlike appendages of their hind wings and for the bands or streaks of color in the same area.

Similar species: There are many hairstreak species, and they can be difficult to identify. Texas hairstreaks have a W-shaped section in one of the lines crossing the hind wing. The orange patches on the upper surface of the front and hind wings and the blue patch on the lower surface of the hind wing are features common to many species. Very distinctive by its green wings is the small olive hairstreak (*Mitoura grynea*), which in the caterpillar stage feeds on eastern juniper. We saw very few adults and noticed no caterpillars.

great purple hairstreak (fig. 21)
Altides halesus

Biology: This is the largest and most beautiful hairstreak in the forest. Adults sip nectar from goldenrods and from other members of the daisy family. While doing so they rub the hind wings together, producing a back and forth motion that makes the "hairs" on those wings resemble the twitching antennae of an insect's head. Perhaps this diverts the attention of potential predators from the butterfly's more vulnerable head at the other end. The caterpillar is exceptional because its sole food is the parasitic mistletoe plant that grows on oaks and hackberries.

Distribution: From coast to coast within the United States.

Remarks: Wingspan 36 mm. The single specimen encountered was mortally injured at the side of a road and was probably a roadkill.

Similar species: None.

colona tiger moth (fig. 22)
Haploa colona

Biology: Adults are attractive day-flying moths that flutter weakly through dense stands of low-growing herbaceous plants such as yankee-weed, grape, and poison ivy. The caterpillars feed on leaves of elm, hackberry, and plum.

Distribution: From the Atlantic Ocean to a western limit somewhere in Texas, perhaps not far from the Lost Pines.

Remarks: Wingspan 51 mm. Colona tiger moths are said to be uncommon (Covell 1984). In the Central Texas forest they appear briefly in spring in large numbers.

Similar species: None.

placentia tiger moth (fig. 23)
Grammia placentia

Biology: Adult males fly to blacklights at night. One female was found beneath a log in the afternoon. The caterpillar stage feeds on legume leaves.

Fig. 22. A diurnal colona tiger moth (*Haploa colona*) resting on an oak leaf.

Fig. 23. Placentia tiger moth (*Grammia placentia*).

Distribution: From the Atlantic Ocean to a western limit near the Lost Pines.
Remarks: Wingspan 41 mm. This tiger moth displays the black and reddish warning colors so prevalent among distasteful insects. It is considered an uncommon species (Covell 1984).
Similar species: None.

tree-of-heaven moth (fig. 24)
Atteva punctella

Biology: This small but very attractive orange and white moth is notable for its nearly cylindrical shape when resting or crawling about on flowers. The caterpillars live in groups in webs on *Ailanthus* trees (tree-of-heaven) and avocados.
Distribution: Tree-of-heaven moths occur from the Atlantic Ocean to a western limit somewhere in Texas.
Remarks: Wingspan 20 mm. We saw the pretty adults nectaring at the flowers of fall boneset in a floral garden at the entrance to Bastrop State Park. Both the animal and the plant are native species. The caterpillars were never seen, nor were their host plants, neither of which would be native to the Lost Pines.
Similar species: None.

io moth (fig. 25)
Automeris io io

Biology: Adults fly to blacklights at night. Caterpillars feed gregariously on a wide variety of plants, including oak, mesquite, and dogwood. They bristle with spines that irritate the skin when handled.

Fig. 24. Tree-of-heaven moth (*Atteva punctella*) on fall boneset.

Distribution: From the Atlantic Ocean to a western extreme near the Lost Pines.
Remarks: Wingspan 64 mm. The io moth is one of several large silk moths that we encountered on rare occasions. The others are the imperial moth and the polyphemus moth.
Similar species: The larger and more thoroughly yellow imperial moth has vaguely similar coloration but does not have huge, dark eyespots on its hind wings.

imperial moth (fig. 25)
Eacles imperialis imperialis
Biology: The caterpillars feed on leaves of oak and juniper and perhaps on the needles of loblolly pine.

Fig. 25. Left: Io moth (*Automeris io io*). Right: Imperial moth (*Eacles imperialis imperialis*).

Distribution: From the Atlantic Ocean to Central Texas, near the city of Kerrville.
Remarks: Wingspan 127 mm. A single adult was seen. It was found in fragments along a trail and had presumably fallen prey to some animal, perhaps a bird.
Similar species: *See* io moth.

polyphemus moth (figs. 26, 27)
Antheraea polyphemus

Biology: Polyphemus caterpillars are said to favor leaves of water oak, a tree present in small numbers in the Lost Pines. Other oaks, hickory, elm, and plum are also accepted.
Distribution: From the Atlantic Ocean to the Rocky Mountains.

Fig. 26. Polyphemus moth caterpillar (*Antheraea polyphemus*) collected on post oak trunk.

Fig. 27. Female polyphemus moth raised from caterpillar of fig. 26.

Fig. 28. Aggregation of redhumped oakworm caterpillars (*Symmerista albifrons*) on oak leaves at night.

Remarks: Wingspan 127 mm. We found a single specimen, a large green caterpillar crawling on a post oak trunk. It transformed in culture to the female pictured here. This is the largest moth or butterfly that we saw. It is notable that while blacklighting in Lost Maples State Park in west-central Texas on a single night we captured this species and the cecropia moth (*Hyalophora cecropia*), but neither appeared at our traps in the Lost Pines. It is possible that populations are being reduced by a fly imported into the United States to control gypsy moths. The fly, *Compsilura concinnata,* was introduced in 1906 for this purpose only, but there is now evidence that it is killing native silk moths as well (Jensen 2000).
Similar species: None.

redhumped oakworm moth (fig. 28)
Symmerista albifrons
Biology: Young caterpillars feed gregariously on oak leaves. If the group is disturbed, each larva responds with jerky movements until the whole aggregation goes into action as one spasmodic mass. This behavior probably wards off parasitic wasps and flies that would otherwise settle and lay eggs on the larvae. A second defense might exist in the form of a false head near the back end of the

body. It is similar in size, shape, and color to the true head, which might not survive attack as readily. The adult moths are known as "white-headed prominents."

Distribution: From the Atlantic Ocean to a western limit near the Lost Pines.

Remarks: Wingspan 38 mm. In early spring when oak leaves are tender there is often a soft pattering in the forest that sounds like a light shower even when the sky is clear. This "fecal rain" is the descent of solid waste falling into the dry leaf litter from countless caterpillars chewing foliage in the canopy above. The redhumped oakworm is one of their number.

CHAPTER 4

Ants, Wasps, and Bees

Among these insects are all those that are capable of stinging. Perhaps it is no coincidence that two are also among the most apparent or readily seen animals in the forest. They are the exotic red imported fire ant and the native Carolina red wasp. Both are in fact wasps from an evolutionist's viewpoint because ants arose from within the wasp family tree with a reduction in flight, just as birds are technically dinosaurs that gained the ability instead.

red imported fire ant (fig. 29)
Solenopsis invicta

Biology: The red imported fire ant is an exotic species from South America that builds large mounds along roadsides and in other disturbed areas. In meadows the mounds are typically smaller and flatter, and nests with no mound at all are the rule within logs and beneath logs and stones. Red imported fire ants are famously aggressive animals that erupt from the nest by the hundreds or thousands to sting all intruders. Stings are painful and usually give rise to white pustules within twenty-four hours.

The fire ant is omnivorous. It eats animals and plants, whether living or dead, as well as secretions and excretions of the same. Winged males and winged queens fly from the nest after rains, mate in the air, and return to earth. The queens dig a new nest and the males die.

Distribution: Within the United States the red imported fire ant occurs from the

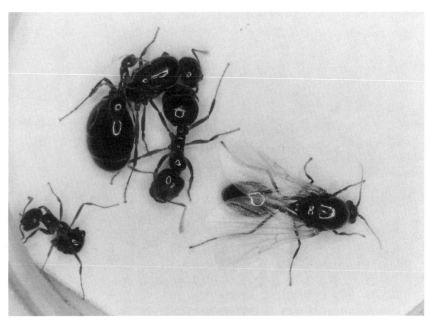

Fig. 29. Red imported fire ants (*Solenopsis invicta*).

Atlantic Ocean to Central Texas, with spot infestations farther north and west, and a major infestation that was developing in southern California at the time of writing.

Remarks: Length 5 mm. The red imported fire ant invaded the Gulf Coast of the United States in the early years of the twentieth century (Taber 2000). This introduced species is now the most apparent insect in the forest and perhaps the most apparent animal of any kind.

Similar species: The tropical fire ant occurs here in smaller numbers. The largest workers have unusually large heads.

tropical fire ant (fig. 30)
Solenopsis geminata

Biology: This possibly native species is similar in habits to the red imported fire ant but it never makes a large domelike mound. Instead it builds low, flat nests that are irregular in shape even when they grow to maximum size. The sting is not as painful and pustules rarely form.

Distribution: Within the United States the tropical fire ant occurs from the Atlantic Ocean to the Pecos River area of West Texas.

Remarks: Length 5 mm. Tropical fire ants are being extirpated in the Lost Pines by the more aggressive and more prolific red imported fire ants.

Fig. 30. Tropical fire ants (*Solenopsis geminata*).

Similar species: The major worker's remarkably large head distinguishes this fire ant from the imported species. The workers are also more orange in color when exposed to bright sunlight.

Comanche harvester ant (fig. 31)
Pogonomyrmex comanche

Biology: This large, red, seed-harvesting native builds its nests in the sandy soil of meadows and along the edges of trails and dirt roads. The structure is a low mound, disk, or crater usually less than one foot in diameter. Comanche harvesters do collect and store seeds as their common name suggests, but they also prey upon other insects, and they scavenge dead animals and excretions as well. Winged males and winged queens fly to trees or other tall objects and mate there rather than on the wing. Mated queens remove their wings and begin a nest as the males begin to die. This ant closes its nest for the night and opens it in the morning. One or two workers often remain outside until dawn.

Distribution: Comanche harvester ants occur within the United States in a central corridor stretching from southern Texas to central Kansas in the north and from Louisiana in the east to the Pecos River area of West Texas.

Remarks: Length 7 mm. Harvester ant workers should not be handled because they can deliver a sting much worse than that of any fire ant.

Similar species: The red harvester ant (*Pogonomyrmex barbatus*) is more robust in build than the Comanche species and tends to build larger nests in less sandy soil

Fig. 31. Comanche
harvester ant
(*Pogonomyrmex
comanche*).

so that pebbles are often seen on the low mound or flat disk. Because the red
harvester tends to avoid sandy soil, it is less common in the Lost Pines. We saw
only two colonies compared to hundreds of Comanche harvester nests.

red harvester ant
Pogonomyrmex barbatus

Biology: Similar to that of the Comanche harvester ant.
Distribution: From the Mississippi River to central Arizona.
Remarks: Length 8 mm. Workers should not be handled because they inflict a
painful sting. This is the consequence of a venom especially adapted to protect
stored seeds from rodents and other small mammals.
Similar species: *See* Comanche harvester ant.

Texas leafcutter ant (fig. 32)
Atta texana

Biology: Leafcutters build huge nests underground, where fungi growing on collected plant material comprises their only food. Long files of workers are often
seen on trails and primitive roads, carrying bits of leaves that they have cut from
a tree with their jaws. In the Lost Pines the favored forage consists of farkleberry
leaves, yaupon leaves and fruits, and the small, berrylike cones of eastern juniper
(red-cedar). The nest is visible at a distance as a large bare patch of sandy hills and
troughs, typically located near the edge of a clearing. Occasionally one sees a

Fig. 32. Mounds of the Texas leafcutter ant (*Atta texana*) in a deep-sand clearing.

small dome composed of dried bits and pieces of rejected stems and leaves. This too is the work of the fungus-growing leafcutter.

Distribution: The Texas leafcutter ant occurs within the United States only in a narrow southern corridor stretching from the Big Bend of Texas in the west to Louisiana in the east.

Remarks: Length of larger workers 8 mm. Leafcutters are active night and day but are most likely to be seen on cloudy days after a rain. Hundreds are sometimes observed in the act of defoliating a tree, or thousands along a trail in what appears at first to be a column of marching leaf fragments. These lines of returning foragers can be more than one hundred feet long.

Similar species: Workers are red and resemble harvester ants, but they have spines above and beyond the single pair that Lost Pines harvesters display near the waist.

Hyatt's ant (fig. 33)
Pheidole hyatti

Biology: This is an omnivorous species. Big-headed workers process seeds for the colony and defend the large, volcano-shaped nest built in the pure sand of meadows and other clearings.

Distribution: Hyatt's ant is one of the relatively few western animals of the forest, occurring from the Pacific Ocean to an eastern limit in or near the Lost Pines.

Remarks: Length 3 mm. The scarcely known biology could be worked out in the Central Texas forest, where the animal is reliably abundant and easy to locate.

Populations within these colonies appear to be quite large. We have not seen Hyatt's ant beyond the forest.

Similar species: The volcano-shaped mound, several inches in height, is a useful key to identification. Workers are small and honey-colored.

dusky carpenter ant (fig. 34)
Camponotus festinatus

Biology: This is a large amber and blackish ant that builds its nests without soil in standing trees, in soil beneath stones and logs, and even in open ground. One colony living beneath a small rock shared its space with a red imported fire ant colony situated at the edge of the same rock. The diet is omnivorous and includes the insect prey that we saw being carried into a nest. A juvenile broad-headed bug (*Hyalymenus tarsatus*) that we captured on frostweed bears a great resemblance to the minor worker of *Camponotus festinatus,* even under a microscope at low power.

Distribution: The dusky carpenter ant is one of the relatively few western animals of the Lost Pines, ranging from Arizona to an eastern limit in or near the Central Texas forest.

Remarks: Length 10 mm. The large black Pennsylvania carpenter ant so common in the homes and forests of the eastern United States has not colonized these

Fig. 33. The volcano-shaped mound of Hyatt's ant
(*Pheidole hyatti*), in deep sand.

Fig. 34. Dusky carpenter
ants (*Camponotus
festinatus*); queen
at top, worker
at bottom.

semiarid woods as far as we know, though we saw it regularly a mere one hundred
miles to the east, in the mixed pine forest near Huntsville, Texas, and farther
south in the Ottine swamp of Gonzales County, where there are no pines at all.
Similar species: Several orange or amber carpenter ant species are likely to occur
in the Lost Pines. Carpenter ants in general are notoriously difficult to identify. A
microscope, the proper keys used by specialists, and much patience are needed.

toothed ant
Pheidole dentata

Biology: Toothed ants are omnivorous. They make their nests beneath stones
and especially beneath and within decomposing logs, dwelling under the loose
bark as well as within the wood itself. Big-headed workers are recruited by smaller
colony members when foraging fire ants approach the nest. A battle ensues and
the fire ants are cut to pieces before they can return to their own nest where they
might recruit others to attack the toothed ant colony.
Distribution: From the Atlantic Ocean to New Mexico.

Fig. 35. The trap-jaws of the jumping ant (*Odontomachus clarus*).

Remarks: Length 4 mm. At first glance, the aggressive response mounted by disturbed colonies and the small size and brownish color of the workers suggest that this is a fire ant. But when allowed to run over one's skin, toothed ants do little or no harm.

Similar species: Darker color, slightly smaller size, and especially the spines on the workers' backs serve to distinguish this Texas native from all fire ants.

jumping ant (fig. 35)
Odontomachus clarus

Biology: Jumping ants live beneath stones and logs in colonies of no more than a few hundred individuals. They capture arthropod prey with spectacular jaws that function like a bear trap, springing shut when long sensory hairs are touched by the victim. The resulting force is great enough to dismember or decapitate. If the jaws are closed on a hard object that cannot be pierced, the force of their collision sends the jumping ant flying through the air for a distance of several inches or more, with an audible clicking sound. Hence the jumping ant jumps with its jaws, not with its legs.

Distribution: From the Atlantic Ocean to southern Arizona.

Remarks: Length 6 mm. This ant is one of several Lost Pines species considered to be of a primitive type. The others are Montezuma's ant and the slender ponerine ant. None of them should be handled because of their potent stings.

Similar species: None.

Fig. 36. Slender ponerine ant (*Leptogenys elongata*).

slender ponerine ant (fig. 36)
Leptogenys elongata

Biology: This sleek brown predator makes its nest beneath logs and stones, and its specialized diet consists of the small terrestrial crustaceans known as pillbugs. These prey are not as common in the forest as one might imagine. Perhaps the semiarid climate is responsible for the scarcity of moisture-loving pillbugs. Slender ponerine ants are also notable for the absence of a winged queen. Instead, the egg layers look much like ordinary workers. Colonies are small and consist of less than one hundred individuals.

Distribution: In the United States this species might be restricted to Texas, though it likely occurs in Louisiana too (Creighton 1950).

Remarks: Length 6 mm. *See* jumping ant.

Similar species: None.

Montezuma's ant (fig. 37)
Pachycondyla harpax montezumia

Biology: Montezuma's ant is a large black nocturnal species that makes its nest beneath logs and stones. Colonies consist of no more than two hundred individuals. The predatory diet includes millipedes and other arthropods. Some egg layers in the colony resemble typical ant queens but others bear a greater resemblance to workers.

Distribution: In the United States this species occurs only in southern Texas and Louisiana.

Remarks: Length 8 mm. William Morton Wheeler studied Montezuma's ant in or near the Lost Pines at the beginning of the twentieth century and noted that the workers bear a peculiar resemblance to tiny rats in their manner of peeking out of cracks and crevices in the ground.

Similar species: The large size, black color, and forest habitat predispose Montezuma's ant for misidentification as the black carpenter ant (*Camponotus pennsylvanicus*). However, as far as we can tell, the black carpenter ant does not occur here, and it surely cannot sting.

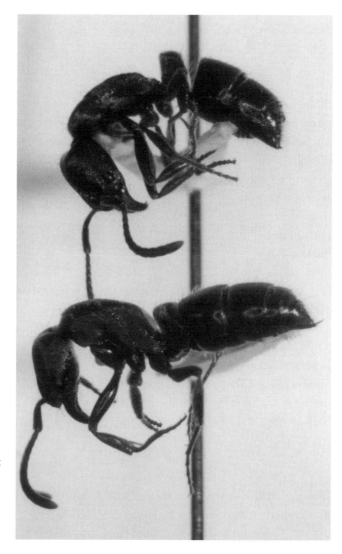

Fig. 37.
Montezuma's ant
(*Pachycondyla harpax montezumia*).

little black ant
Monomorium minimum

Biology: This is a tiny, shiny black ant that lives beneath the loose bark of de-composing logs. Though small, the omnivorous little black ant is aggressive, and sometimes it succeeds in driving fire ants from disputed food. Several wingless queens are often seen in a single colony. One nest discovered beneath willow bark in nearby Victoria, Texas, stretched across the trunk for thirty feet (Mitchell and Pierce 1912).

Distribution: From coast to coast within the United States.

Remarks: Length 1 mm. Workers are the smallest ants that visitors are likely to see in the forest. They often appear at picnic tables, where they favor peanut butter.

Similar species: None.

Treat's ant (fig. 38)
Aphaenogaster treatae

Biology: The diet of Treat's ant is poorly known, but it is omnivorous to some extent because it eats mushrooms as well as insects. Nests are built in logs, in the soil beneath stones, and beneath piles of pine needles that completely obscure the colony from view. In the eastern United States crater-shaped nests have been reported on open ground, but we never saw the species in such obvious circum-stances. The preferred habitat of Treat's ant appears to be sandy black oak wood-lands like those of the Central Texas forest.

Distribution: From the Atlantic Ocean to Texas with a western limit in or near the Lost Pines.

Remarks: Length 6 mm. We saw Treat's ant on very few occasions and made our first contact unexpectedly when workers visited a test tube baited with hot dog meat. The nest itself could not be found. On another occasion they were seen on a trail struggling with a moth pupa that a large number of workers dragged off to a nest shielded from view by pine needles. Baits are used to monitor fire ant invasions and to detect cryptic species.

Similar species: Treat's ant resembles the harvester ants and to a lesser extent the leafcutter ant but is slender and readily distinguished with a hand lens by a pecu-liar widening of the antenna near its base.

dark army ant (fig. 39)
Neivamyrmex nigrescens

Biology: These true army ants are nomadic predators that house their huge colo-nies temporarily in decomposing logs as they wander through the forest in search of food. They hunt both above ground and below, mainly at night, and have very

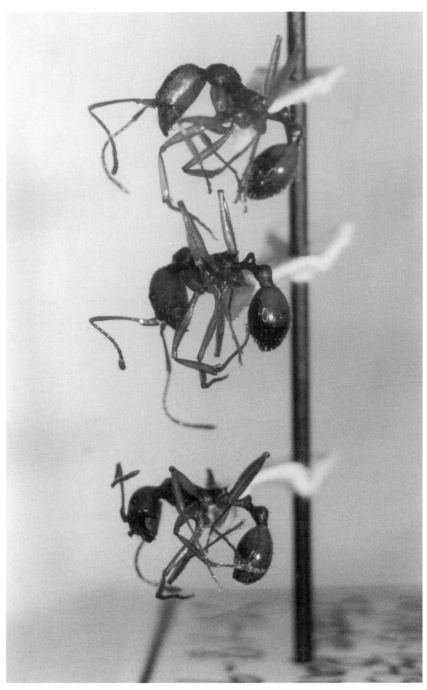

Fig. 38. Treat's ant (*Aphaenogaster treatae*).

Fig. 39. Dark army ants (*Neivamyrmex nigrescens*); queen on left, worker on right.

small eyes. On a summer evening at dusk one of us encountered a seemingly endless column crossing the Lost Pines hiking trail. The queen eventually appeared within the protection of a racing bulge in the column. Males resemble thick-bodied wasps and fly to blacklights at night.

Distribution: The dark army ant occurs in the United States from West Virginia to the Pacific Ocean.

Remarks: Length of typical worker 5 mm. The small size and ordinary-looking jaws of this army ant are likely to disappoint those who expect a Neotropical giant with ice-tong mandibles. One curious feature of the workers is their distinctive meaty or musky odor.

Similar species: Several army ants that might occur in the Lost Pines bear a great resemblance to this species. Microscopic examination and the proper keys are necessary for confident identification.

red army ant
Labidus coecus

Biology: Similar to that of the dark army ant. We found two colonies, both of them ensconced in decomposing pines. One pine was a huge log and the other was a small stump. In Central America, and presumably in the Lost Pines as well, the red army ant wars underground with the tropical fire ant.

Distribution: Within the United States this species is confined to the region between the Mississippi River and the Big Bend of Texas.

Remarks: Length of larger worker 6 mm. We never saw the red army ant exposed to daylight. It appears to be more subterranean than the dark army ant.

Fig. 40. Carolina red wasp
    (*Polistes carolina*).

Similar species: Reddish color and shinier body distinguish this species from the other army ants, which are brown and dull.

red wasps (figs. 40, 41)
Polistes carolina, P. metricus, P. apache

Biology: Adult females build gray paper nests with exposed cells. These typically hang in the hollows of snags and logs or even unprotected from the branch or trunk of a tree. Colonies often consist of only a few dozen individuals. The paper is made by chewing wood and herbaceous vegetation and mixing the substance with saliva. Excursions into forest and meadow for building materials are supplemented by forays into green vegetation for caterpillars and other insects to feed the grubs back at the nest. Each grub lives in one of the exposed cells, which give the nest a honeycomb appearance. Queens overwinter beneath the bark of logs or in hollow spaces within logs.

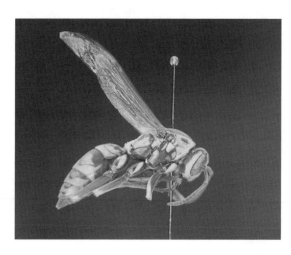

Fig. 41. Apache red wasp
    (*Polistes apache*).

The Apache red wasp differs greatly in coloration from the others. It has enough yellow in its striped pattern to resemble a large yellowjacket. When accidentally introduced into California from Texas around 1920, the Apache wasp became a pest of the fig industry because it nested in branches and stung workers who harvested figs by shaking the trees.

Distribution: The Carolina red wasp and *Polistes metricus* occur from the Atlantic Ocean to the Lost Pines region of Texas. The natural range of the Apache red wasp in the United States is limited to the central part of the country with its inland eastern limit near the Lost Pines. Along the coast of Texas it ranges farther east.

Remarks: Typical lengths for these wasps are a little over 20 mm. Carolina red wasps are the commonest of the three. During the hottest summer afternoons when nothing else seems to be stirring on the ground or in the air, these relentless animals are undaunted by searing heat. They fly to the shrinking artificial ponds and float on the surface with widespread legs as they drink water for themselves and other members of the colony. Sometimes a few workers fail to reach the nest before nightfall. These spend the hours of darkness clinging to vegetation. Once by headlamp we saw four workers clinging to the leaves of a single *Sesbania* plant in a meadow. All red wasps are feared for their potent sting.

Similar species: These three are the only red wasps that we have noted in the woods. Viewed from a little distance with the unaided eye, the Carolina red wasp is almost entirely red with shiny black wings, whereas *Polistes metricus* has a much darker general color.

southern yellowjacket (fig. 63)
Vespula squamosa

Biology: The gray paper nest of the yellowjacket differs from that of the red wasp. It is larger, the combs are covered over with a paper shell, the nest is usually built underground, and it is populated by thousands rather than dozens. Worker yellowjackets can be a nuisance at picnics because they scavenge lunch meats for protein to feed the grubs. Natural prey includes caterpillars plucked from green vegetation.

Young queens yet to establish a nest of their own overwinter beneath the bark of logs, snags, and even living trees. They are unmistakable for their large size and especially for the orange color so different from that of the yellow and black workers. When spring arrives the queens emerge and buzz about in search of a nesting site. Sometimes the southern yellowjacket does not build her own nest but invades and usurps that of the eastern yellowjacket. Such queens are called "social parasites." Southern yellowjackets are at home in the Central Texas forest because their preferred habitat is piney woods.

Distribution: From the Atlantic Ocean to West Texas.

Remarks: Length of queen 20 mm. We never saw a yellowjacket nest or evidence of a nest with the exception of the remains of two small, incipient structures left uncompleted due to the queen's death or desertion. One of these was under a small rock. The other was found in a decomposing oak. We were never bothered by either of the two yellowjacket species occurring in the Lost Pines.

Similar species: Workers are smaller than the Apache red wasp and their striping is yellow and black, not yellow and red. Eastern yellowjackets have a black mark in the shape of a mushroom or anchor on the first segment of the rounded abdomen.

eastern yellowjacket
Vespula maculifrons

Biology: Similar to that of the southern yellowjacket. Colonies tend to be more populous.

Distribution: From the Atlantic Ocean to the Rocky Mountains, though according to the standard map (Akre et al. 1981), the Lost Pines itself was not previously known to be within the range of the species.

Remarks: Length of worker 11 mm. We visited a small pond and stood in the midst of hundreds of flying eastern yellowjackets that were visiting the pond for water. They did not bother us.

Similar species: *See* southern yellowjacket.

potter wasp (fig. 42)
Eumenes fraternus

Biology: Female potter wasps build remarkable pot-shaped nests fashioned from mud. In the wild the little vessels, less than one inch wide, are built on twigs or under stones (fig. 42), and in urban areas they appear on brick or stone in shaded

Fig. 42. Potter wasp nest found beneath a stone.

places. When the structure is ready the female searches for caterpillars, stings them into paralysis, stores them in the nest, and plugs the vessel (Ashmead 1902). Apparently some potter wasps lay the egg before bringing caterpillars to the pot whereas others lay the egg after the provisions have been stored. In either case, when the larva hatches it eats the living but helpless prey.

Distribution: From the Atlantic Ocean to a western limit in Central Texas not far from the Lost Pines, with a questionable record from Colorado.

Remarks: Length 16 mm. In mid-July we found dozens of potter wasps flying in and out of lush vegetation in the shade along the shore of a pond that was drying out in one-hundred-degree heat. They often rested motionless on leaves.

Similar species: Other potter wasps occur in the area and it is quite difficult to identify them to species.

Klug's cowkiller wasp (fig. 43)
Dasymutilla klugii

Biology: The hairy, wingless female races over sandy soil in search of an insect's nest in which to lay her eggs. It is believed that Klug's cowkiller invades the burrows of the huge cicada-killer wasp. An egg is laid near the offspring of the killed, ejected, or outmaneuvered adult wasp, and when the Klug's grub hatches, it consumes the resident grub. Though the usurper is much smaller than the cicada-killer, she has a panoply of weapons that make up for the difference in size. These include a huge and highly mobile sting, a defensive chemical secretion, great speed, and a tough, slippery exoskeleton (Schmidt and Blum 1977). Red and black warning colors combined with an ability to squeak by rubbing body parts together help to ward off potential enemies that might interfere with her

Fig. 43. Klug's cowkiller wasp (*Dasymutilla klugii;* male).

search above ground. Male cowkillers have wings (fig. 43) and spend much of their time flying low over the sand in search of mates. Sometimes they are seen at flowers. They often fly to blacklights at night.

Distribution: This is one of the few western insects of the forest, occurring from Arizona to an eastern limit near the Lost Pines of Texas.

Remarks: Length 20 mm. Cowkillers are active, attractive animals with a fuzzy, endearing look, but females should never be handled because, as their common name emphasizes, they can deliver a very painful sting. Among wasps of the United States the pain caused by these stings is exceeded only by the stings of certain giant tarantula-hunting species. Nevertheless, the common name of "cowkiller" overstates the sting's potency against large mammals. When caught in net or hand the male also makes stinging motions with its abdomen, but this is of course all bluff, because no male insect can sting. Another common name is "velvet-ant."

Similar species: The large size, in combination with the particular arrangement of red and black colors shared by both sexes, distinguish this common cowkiller from other species.

golden-haired cowkiller wasp
Sphaeropthalma auripilis

Biology: Similar to that of Klug's cowkiller. In this case the host (or at least one of its hosts) is the organ-pipe mud dauber wasp. We found a single specimen, a dead male, still inside the cocoon of the young organ-pipe wasp that it had devoured, and this cocoon was itself inside a chamber of the host species' nest. The cowkiller was completely developed as far as the eye could tell, and the cause of its death was unclear.

Distribution: Found only in Texas and Oklahoma.

Remarks: Length 14 mm. It appears that this is the first record of the golden-haired cowkiller from the nest of the organ-pipe mud dauber.

Similar species: The Lost Pines with its sandy soil and arid climate is ideal for cowkillers. There are many species here, including a variety of tiny ones, and confident identification usually requires the proper keys and much patience.

organ-pipe mud dauber wasp (fig. 44)
Trypoxylon politum

Biology: Females build vertical mud nests in protected areas such as a large scooped-out irregularity in the trunk of a loblolly pine. These nests are shaped like organ pipes, and the effect is heightened when the wasp builds three or four side by side. Mud is retrieved from a pond or creek and applied to the lower, open edge of the growing pipe in a manner that produces a stack of chevron-shaped

Fig. 44. Organ-pipe mud dauber (*Trypoxylon politum*) nest built on loblolly trunk near ground level.

layers. An entire five-inch pipe can be completed in less than one day. Males are unique or nearly so among wasps because they remain in the nest and guard it while the female is away. Several cells comprise each pipe. These are stocked with spiders paralyzed by the female's sting, and the spiders are consumed by the grubs that live in the cells. When they become adults they chew a hole through the pipe and make their exit.

Distribution: From the Atlantic Ocean to a western limit near the Lost Pines.

Remarks: Cowkiller wasps parasitize the organ-pipe mud dauber. *See* the golden-haired cowkiller for details.

Similar species: The unique nest is unmistakable. The wasp itself is dark with dark wings, but the extremities of its legs are light in color.

black and yellow mud dauber
Sceliphron caementarium

Biology: This is a large, familiar, slender wasp with a thread-like waist. The female collects mud to build her nest and is most often seen in the act of doing so near a pond, or flying about in a meadow in search of wildflower nectar and pollen for herself and for spiders to feed her young. The largest nests are stacks of slender mud tubes an inch or so long, each stack constructed as if to form a loose pile of cordwood. Sometimes there is a single cell and thus a single tube. The wasp provisions the tubes with spiders that it paralyzes with its sting, and the grubs eat them.

Distribution: From coast to coast within the United States.

Remarks: Length 22 mm. Nests are most often seen in protected areas of structures built by humans. A good place to find the yellow and black mud dauber itself is among the *Sesbania* plants growing along the margins of artificial ponds. Here it flies and crawls in search of prey. Sometimes the wasps spend the night on the same plants.

Similar species: *Sceliphron assimile* is a tropical mud dauber that is closely related to *S. caementarium*. It is known from Texas but probably does not occur as far north as the Lost Pines.

cicada-killer wasp (fig. 45)
Sphecius speciosus

Biology: The huge female hunts cicadas in the boughs of pines and oaks, paralyzes them with a sting, and flies back to her burrow in the sand with the prey slung upside down beneath her body. Nests have one primary tunnel, several secondary branches, and a cell at the end of each branch that is stocked with one to several cicadas. The wasp lays an egg in each cell, and when the grub hatches it eats the living but helpless prey animal.

Fig. 45. Cicada-killer wasp (*Sphecius speciosus*).

Distribution: From the Atlantic Ocean to the Rocky Mountains.
Remarks: Length 37 mm. This is the largest wasp in the forest as far as we know. Reports differ as to the severity of its sting. Humans rarely feel its effects in any event because solitary wasps are less likely to use this defense than are social wasps such as the easily irritated yellowjackets and red wasps.
Similar species: None.

blue sand wasp (fig. 46)
Chlorion cyaneum

Biology: The blue sand wasp is a large and attractively metallic species that excavates a nest in the sand, seeks out and stings Boll's cockroach, drags the paralyzed prey into the burrow, lays an egg on it, and leaves the grub to hatch and devour the living but helpless roach.
Distribution: This is one of the few western insects of the Lost Pines, ranging from Arizona to an eastern limit near the Texas loblolly forest.
Remarks: Length 28 mm. The prey was unknown until Dr. Allan Hook of Austin, Texas, discovered this wasp's preference for cockroaches shortly before our own encounter with the wasp.
Similar species: One close relative might occur in the area. A hand lens or microscope must be used to distinguish the two. The female of the species treated here is wrinkled on the side of its thorax. The relative, *C. aerarium,* is smooth.

Fig. 46. Blue sand wasp
(*Chlorion cyaneum*).

golden digger wasp (fig. 47)
Sphex ichneumoneus

Biology: A beautiful red and gold solitary wasp with a life history much like that of the blue sand wasp except that its prey consists not of roaches but of katydids, including the Texas bush katydid. Several prey items are buried within each nest.

Distribution: From coast to coast within the United States.

Remarks: Length 26 mm. Other green, long-horned grasshoppers are selected as prey by the golden digger. In the Lost Pines the thread-legged katydids might be among their number.

Similar species: None. We found the much smaller species *Tachytes distinctus* and its shallow nest near the shore of an ephemeral pond. This wasp also differs from the golden digger in its choice of prey, selecting immature short-horned grasshoppers instead of long-horned species. The nest contained two paralyzed, juvenile hoppers belonging to the genus *Melanoplus*. *Tachytes distinctus* occurs from coast to coast.

Fig. 47. Golden
digger wasp
(*Sphex ichneumoneus*).

Fig. 48. Sand-loving caterpillar wasp (*Ammophila procera*).

black and red grasshopper wasp
Prionyx atratus

Biology: Much like that of the blue sand wasp and golden digger except that the prey are short-horned grasshoppers such as the destructive differential grasshopper. Each nest is provisioned with a single prey item.

Distribution: From coast to coast within the United States.

Remarks: Length 27 mm. This predator has its own enemy in the red bee-eater assassin bug.

Similar species: None.

sand-loving caterpillar wasp (fig. 48)
Ammophila procera

Biology: This slender black and pinkish wasp is a solitary species. Females dig a nest in the soil, provision it with a single caterpillar for the grub to eat, close the burrow, and tamp the soil down with a pebble held between the jaws. The redhumped oakworm that is so abundant in these woods is one of the species chosen as prey by this wasp. Both sexes "sleep" at night in a characteristic fashion. They grip the stem of a herbaceous plant between the jaws and hang on until sunrise, the stalklike abdomen projecting from the body almost at a right angle.

Distribution: From coast to coast within the United States.

Remarks: Length 27 mm. The female's use of a pebble while sealing the nest is a form of tool-using behavior.

Similar species: There are perhaps 30 different *Ammophila* species that might occur in Texas, and because the 1934 keys to identification are outdated and contain numerous errors, it is difficult to identify these wasps with confidence.

scarab beetle parasites (fig. 49)
Campsomeris plumipes, Trielis octomaculata

Biology: The male *Campsomeris* shown here is a remarkably slender yellow and black wasp that visits flowers. In the grub stage both sexes feed as external parasites on the grubs of scarab beetles. Some species live in the soil and others live in wood rat nests. We have not noticed these uncommon wasps beyond the confines of the sandy forest.

   Campsomeris plumipes males are unusual because they burrow into the sand, a behavior usually associated with female wasps that dig nests or seek out prey underground. Males that dig probably do so to avoid approaching storms or to hide from predators at night (Kurczewski and Spofford 1986).

Distribution: *Campsomeris plumipes* occurs from the Atlantic Ocean to a western limit somewhere in the Rocky Mountains. *Trielis octomaculata* occurs from coast to coast within the United States.

Remarks: Length of *C. plumipes* 26 mm; length of *T. octomaculata* 17 mm. The males have three distinctive points at the tip of the abdomen that call to mind the tines of a pitchfork, and these might be mistaken for a trio of stingers.

Similar species: Little recent work has been done on the North American members of the family Scoliidae, and the papers of the early specialists are so poor that it is nearly impossible to identify these wasps with confidence.

Fig. 49. Adult scarab beetle parasite (*Campsomeris plumipes*, male).

poison ivy sawfly (fig. 50)
Arge humeralis

Biology: Gregarious grubs of this wasplike insect feed on poison ivy foliage, which is extremely abundant in the shade of the Lost Pines. This is their only food plant, and no other wasp or sawfly in the United States is known to eat it. Females lay their eggs inside the tissues of the leaf. Defoliation in some parts of the country occurs on a scale large enough to earn the animal consideration as a biocontrol agent.

Distribution: From the Atlantic Ocean to the Rocky Mountains.

Remarks: Length 12 mm. Despite the enormous poison ivy ground cover and its occurrence as thick vines wrapped around loblolly trunks, we saw only one plant infested by the caterpillar-like grubs.

Similar species: None.

crown-of-thorns wasp (fig. 51)
Megischus bicolor

Biology: The rare crown-of-thorns wasp is a parasite in its grub stage. Its hosts are woodboring beetles. We encountered two specimens, both males, and both on a wounded mulberry tree—itself an uncommon species in the forest. When the wasp takes to the air its flight is weak and fluttering, like that of the adult antlion. When resting on bark it appears to have no wings at all. The circlet of five spines surrounding the middle eye gives the animal its common name. These head-spines probably aid young adults as they exit the wood wherein they developed.

Distribution: From coast to coast within the United States.

Remarks: Length 20 mm. Records have been kept of the host trees of the beetles that these wasps parasitize. This is the first record of the wasps occurring on mulberry and suggests that the beetle species they parasitized as juveniles, whatever species that might be, is not currently known as a host of the wasp.

Similar species: None.

humpbacked pincer wasp (fig. 52)
Gonatopus cyphonotus

Biology: The spectacular scissors-shaped appendages at the tips of the rare, wingless female's front legs are used to grasp a leafhopper bug long enough to lay an egg on it. A grub hatches from the egg and consumes its host from within. A sign of an infected leafhopper is a cyst or sac of accumulated shed skins that forms around the wasp grub as it grows. The scissors, or more accurately the forceps, evolved when an outgrowth of the lower leg began working in unison with a claw

Fig. 50. Poison ivy sawfly (*Arge humeralis*).

Fig. 51. The tiny crown-of-thorns wasp
(*Megischus bicolor;* male).

Fig. 52. Humpbacked pincer wasp (*Gonatopus cyphonotus;* female).

of the same leg that grew much larger than normal. The remaining claw degenerated until the little vestige lost all function as far as we know. The modifications force the female to "walk in a peculiar way" (Richards 1939).

Distribution: This is the first record of the species from Texas, according to our literature search. Until now it was known from Canada coast to coast but nowhere in the United States closer to Texas than Florida.

Remarks: Length 2.5 mm. We discovered a single specimen while sweeping roadside vegetation with nets. This tiny wasp resembles an ant, as do many other pincer wasps. The resemblance might help them to infiltrate herds of small bugs that certain ants tend for their sugary excretions.

Similar species: Rare and very small, pincer wasps require microscopic examination and the proper keys for confident identification (Olmi 1984).

Pennsylvania bumblebee
Bombus pennsylvanicus

Biology: This big, hairy, yellow and black bee lives above or below ground, in both cases favoring abandoned mouse nests. One large nest contained a single queen, fifty-three workers, and twenty-three males (Franklin 1912). The developing grubs live in wax cells and are fed with pollen and honey obtained from a variety of plants.

Distribution: From coast to coast within the United States.

Remarks: Length 22 mm. Though bumblebees are famous for a potent sting, they are no match for the powerful wheel bug that we saw feeding upon this formidable prey when both were captured by our net.

Similar species: Several bumblebee species occur in Texas. The Pennsylvania bumblebee is by far the most common, but confident identification requires a microscope and the proper keys.

splendid green bee
Agapostemon splendens

Biology: These beautiful solitary bees visit a variety of flowers for nectar and pollen. The female constructs a multicelled nest in sandy soil and provisions it with pollen for grubs that will hatch from eggs placed with the food. Males visit flowers for their own sustenance and for mates.

Distribution: From the Atlantic Ocean to Utah.

Remarks: Length 12 mm. These metallic green bees might be described as living jewels.

Similar species: The Texas green bee (*Agapostemon texanus*) and the angelic green bee (*Agapostemon angelicus*) may also occur in the Lost Pines, but if they do, they are likely to be less common because both species nest in loam rather than sand. The wings of these two are clear rather than the transparent brown of the splendid green bee's wings.

eastern stone bee
Lithurge gibbosus

Biology: The eastern stone bee might just as well have been called the "cactus bee" because females collect pollen from these plants, to the apparent exclusion of other plants, and provision their nests with the resulting "bee-bread" for the sustenance of their larvae or grubs. Nests are commonly built within decaying logs. Adults of both sexes visit a variety of additional flowers for nectar that they imbibe as their own food.

Distribution: From the Atlantic Ocean to a western limit somewhere in Texas, perhaps not far from the Lost Pines.

Remarks: Length 15 mm. Stone bees are among the less common of the native bees. One male specimen was collected in a yellow flower of an *Opuntia* cactus.

Similar species: Other stone bees occur in Texas and their identification is a difficult matter that requires a microscope and the proper keys.

leafcutter bee (fig. 53)
Megachile policaris

Biology: Leafcutter bees visit flowers for nectar, and females in particular collect pollen. They carry it to the nest among hairs located on the lower surface of the abdomen, whereas honey bees and bumblebees carry pollen on specialized legs.

Fig. 53. A leafcutter bee (*Megachile policaris*) on ironweed.

The leafcutter's nest is constructed in the soil or in wood and is lined with circular pieces of cut leaves. The female lays her eggs, and when the grubs hatch they eat the stored pollen gregariously.

Distribution: From coast to coast within the United States.

Remarks: Length 13 mm. Leafcutters are among the more common native bees and are seen on wildflowers such as Texas ironweed. The lighter-colored honey bee, an introduced species, is not as apparent in the Lost Pines as one might expect.

Similar species: Several similar leafcutter bees are likely to live in the area and confident identification requires a microscope and the proper keys.

Mexican leafcutter-parasite
Coelioxys mexicana

Biology: The remarkable shape of the female's abdomen hints at an unusual life history, for it tapers at the end until it resembles a gaping bird's beak. This structure is adapted for poking into the cells of leafcutter bees and for depositing an egg there. When the grub hatches from the egg it develops an armored head, and before long "the tips of its long and sharp mandibles appear on top of the bee-bread in the vicinity of the host egg (or young host larva), opening and closing in rhythmical sequence" (Graenicher 1927). The leafcutter egg or grub is soon killed and partially eaten, and the parasite is free to consume the pollen provisions meant for the other. The fighting period of its life over, the grub discards its armor and the weapons of its head with the shedding of its skin and soon resembles a more typical juvenile bee.

Distribution: From the Atlantic Ocean to Texas and south into Mexico, as the common name suggests.

Remarks: Length 10 mm. The tapering abdomen of the female is easily seen without the aid of a hand lens.

Similar species: Like most native bees, these parasitoids are difficult to identify to the species level, and because similar relatives occur in Texas, confident identification requires a microscope and the proper formal keys.

Norton's bee (fig. 54)
Nomia nortoni

Biology: Norton's bee is a large native species that builds its nest in soil. The nest is irregular in shape and contains as many as fourteen cells, which are not lined with leaves (Ribble 1965). The cells are provisioned with pollen for developing grubs. A wide variety of flowers are visited by both sexes for nectar and by the female for pollen.

Fig. 54. Norton's bee (*Nomia nortoni;* male).

Distribution: From the Atlantic Ocean to Arizona.

Remarks: Length 22 mm. The male has a large and remarkable swelling on each of its hind legs that is partially translucent and probably functions as a vessel to carry some substance. Perhaps the unknown substance is attractive to potential mates.

Similar species: Several species of the genus *Nomia* occur in Texas and confident identification requires microscopic examination and the proper keys.

CHAPTER 5

True Flies

The most apparent flies in the Lost Pines are large predatory species seldom seen in Central Texas beyond the confines of the forest. Relatively few fly species of any kind are evident, and the small but bothersome biting flies that make life miserable in boreal forests are no problem here. Even horse flies and mosquitoes are rarely a nuisance.

spine-tailed robber fly (fig. 55)
Proctacanthus arno

Biology: The spine-tailed robber fly is a substantial predator that frequents clearings, spends much time resting on the sand, and preys upon other insects as large as red wasps and grasshoppers, including its own kind. It captures its prey with long legs, stabs the victim with a sharp beak, flies about with the prey slung beneath its body, and drinks it dry.

When approached the spine-tailed robber fly escapes in a manner similar to that of the tiger beetles that share its sandy habitat. Both animals fly up from the ground, land a short distance away, and sometimes turn to face their pursuer. The common name of the species derives from a set of tiny spines located at the tip of the abdomen. These are thought to aid the female as she lays her eggs in the sand. An even larger robber fly, the bee-killer, preys upon the spine-tailed species.
Distribution: This is one of the relatively few western insects of the Lost Pines. This spine-tailed robber fly ranges from the Pacific Ocean to a new eastern record in the forest as established here.
Remarks: Length 35 mm. Robber flies are large and abundant and are the most

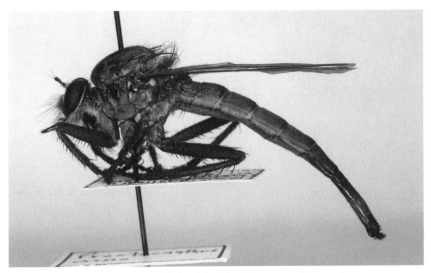

Fig. 55. Spine-tailed robber fly (*Proctacanthus arno*).

apparent flies of these woods. They should never be handled because they can deliver a painful stab with the beaklike mouthparts.

Similar species: Gray is a common color among robber flies. A number of smaller species of the genus *Efferia* share this feature with the spine-tail. Some have a silvery patch on the abdomen that calls to mind the light of a firefly beetle, though in this case the brightness is due to reflection rather than emission. *Efferia argentifrons* is one of these species.

bee-killer robber fly (fig. 56)
Diogmites symmachus

Biology: The bee-killer is a big, orange-brown, slow-flying predator with bright green eyes and long legs that dangle beneath the tubular body like grappling hooks as the fly cruises about the meadows in search of food. It pounces on other insects including fellow robber flies and the assassin bug known as the black bee-eater (*Apiomerus crassipes*). When tackling dangerous prey such as the big red paper wasps, the bee-killer robber fly uses its six gangly legs to hold the probing stinger at arm's length until exhaustion overcomes the prey. Then the beak delivers the coup de grace with a stab in the eye or in the soft membrane between hard exoskeletal plates. A toxin is injected and body fluids are sucked out.

Distribution: The bee-killer has an unusual range within a narrow corridor of the United States, including only Texas and Louisiana in the south but extending north across the plains to Canada.

Fig. 56. Bee-killer robber
fly (*Diogmites
symmachus*).

Remarks: Length 26 mm. Long ago an authority on this animal and its relatives declared Texas to be the state with the greatest diversity of robber flies in the entire country (Bromley 1934).

Similar species: Hook's mydas fly (*Nemomydas hooki*) bears some resemblance to the bee-killer. It is smaller and does not have conspicuously pointed mouthparts.

Texas bumblebee robber fly (fig. 57)
Laphria macquartii

Biology: This is a large, hairy, yellow and black predatory fly resembling a bumble-bee so greatly that we had to examine it close up to confirm our suspicions that it was something else. We thought it might be a fly by the manner in which it

Fig. 57. Texas bumblebee robber fly (*Laphria macquartii*).

alighted on an oak leaf. Its resemblance to the bee gives it protection against animals that steer clear of a potent stinger, and perhaps it allows the fly to maneuver close enough to the bee itself to capture and kill the mimic's model. This is called "aggressive mimicry." Several specimens were carrying tiny pseudoscorpions on their abdomens. Through the glass of a hand lens, the miniature clawed arachnids looked as if they nestled in a mammal's fur rather than in the hairlike covering of an insect's body.

Distribution: This is a Texas endemic species found nowhere else in the world.

Remarks: Wingspan 46 mm. The bumblebee robber fly provides a fine example of nature's imperfection. Random mutation and natural selection placed the fly's beelike "pollen basket" on its middle leg, not on the hind leg where it occurs on a real bee. The fly also mimics a plant, for the yellow "pollen" is a mere imitation conjured up from a patch of yellow hair.

Similar species: We saw no mimics as large as this one.

Cole's robber fly (fig. 58)
Stichopogon colei

Biology: Unknown except for our observation of two individuals mating in early October. When seen, this robber fly is usually resting on bare sand, often on the

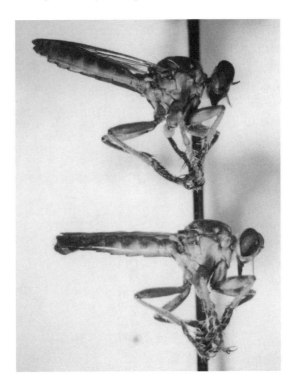

Fig. 58. Cole's robber fly
   (***Stichopogon colei***).

clearing of a Comanche harvester ant nest. Perhaps the ants are among their unknown prey.

Distribution: This is one of the eleven endemic Texas animals we encountered in the Lost Pines. The species was previously reported from only three Texas counties: Bexar and Milam in Central Texas and Brewster in the far west.

Remarks: At a length of only 7 mm, Cole's robber fly is by far the smallest robber fly noticed in our survey. It is a mere one third of an inch in length.

Similar species: None.

Hook's mydas fly (fig. 59)
Nemomydas hooki

Biology: Unknown beyond the fact that one of two specimens (both males) was visiting flowers of the daisy family. It has been assumed that adult mydas flies are generally predatory in their feeding habits. The presumably predatory maggot probably lives in decomposing logs or in sand.

Distribution: Hook's mydas fly was first made known to science from Texas specimens that included one male from Bastrop State Park in the Lost Pines (Welch and Kondratieff 1990). We would have treated it here as a Texas endemic were it not for a single male specimen collected in Vera Cruz state, Mexico (Fitzgerald and Kondratieff 1998).

Remarks: Length 16 mm. This interesting and little known species was named for Dr. Allan Hook of St. Edward's University in Austin, Texas, who was instrumental in its discovery. Mydas flies in general are uncommon, and there are few species to begin with, though the largest fly in the world appears to be a Brazilian species that exceeds two inches in length.

Similar species: Hook's mydas fly resembles a small version of the bee-killing robber fly *Diogmites symmachus*.

Fig. 59. Hook's mydas fly (*Nemomydas hooki*).

Fig. 60. Sand bee fly (*Exoprosopa* of undetermined species).

sand bee fly (fig. 60)
Exoprosopa, undetermined species

Biology: The sand bee fly is a large and powerful flier that hovers above wildflowers as it sips nectar and pollinates plants. Its maggot stage is a sand-dwelling predator that feeds upon other insects.

Distribution: Unknown until the species has been identified. Perhaps it is new to science.

Remarks: Length 16 mm. The sand bee fly is unusual because it becomes abundant in late fall rather than spring.

Similar species: None.

scaly bee fly (fig. 61)
Lepidophora lepidocera

Biology: Sun-loving adults appear briefly in spring and feed on wildflower nectar. They resemble predatory robber flies in size and shape, and they resemble bumblebees in color. This might give them double protection because the former model bites and the latter model stings. The maggot stage lives in wasp nests, eating provisions gathered by the wasp for its own young. These include paralyzed caterpillars, cockroaches, and spiders (Hull 1973).

Distribution: From the Atlantic Ocean to a western limit in Texas, perhaps not far from the Lost Pines.

Remarks: Length 20 mm. No other large, harmless flies appear to be as interested in human activity as these. Our first encounter was disturbing: scaly bee flies

Fig. 61. Scaly bee fly
(*Lepidophora lepidocera*)

buzzed our faces repeatedly as we photographed wildflowers in a meadow. At the time we did not know what they were.

Similar species: None.

little white bee fly (fig. 62)
Systoechus solitus

Biology: This is a small, round, white, and very fuzzy denizen of meadows and clearings. The little white bee fly and its golden and brown relatives are endearing to behold as they hover above flowers and sip nectar with remarkably long tongues. When caught in a net they buzz like a true bee. The maggot stage is thought to live in the soil as a predator of grasshopper eggs.

Distribution: This is a species of the eastern United States that has not been reported from Texas until now, according to the results of our literature search.

Fig. 62. Little
white bee fly
(*Systoechus
solitus*).

Fig. 63. Left: Two southern yellowjacket queens (*Vespula squamosa*).
Right: Yellowjacket hover fly (*Milesia virginiensis*).

Remarks: Length 7 mm. Bee flies bloom with the wildflowers they feed upon, and they have been described as "the hairy and handsome harbingers of spring" (Cole 1969).

Similar species: The snowy color of the little white bee fly distinguishes it from darker relatives.

yellowjacket hover fly (fig. 63)
Milesia virginiensis

Biology: Hover fly adults resemble bee flies in their behavior. Both sip nectar and pollinate plants in the process. This particular species resembles the orange southern yellowjacket queen that also inhabits the Lost Pines. The fly derives protection from its similarity. Our single specimen was found near a pond margin, where it might have developed in moist soil before emerging as an adult.

Distribution: From the Atlantic Ocean to a western limit near the Lost Pines.

Remarks: Length 18 mm. This is arguably the most attractive fly in the forest, though the Halloween colors of the smaller feather-footed fly are also beautiful. In the Florida piney woods the yellowjacket hover fly is "the largest and most striking syrphid in the region" (Dozier 1920). Syrphid is another name for hover fly.

Similar species: None.

feather-footed fly
Trichopoda pennipes

Biology: This is an exotic-looking orange and black fly with black wings and feathery legs. Adult females lay their eggs on stink bugs and squash bugs. When the maggot hatches it burrows into the bug, which is then devoured from within. From time to time we saw one of the scurrying largid bugs with an egg on its back and wondered if this had been put there by a feather-footed fly.

Distribution: From coast to coast within the United States.

Remarks: Length 7 mm. Feather-footed flies attack pestiferous bugs and have been widely introduced as biocontrol agents.

Similar species: None. The closely related *Trichipoda lanipes* also occurs in the forest but it is much larger, uniformly dark in color, and apparently less common.

June beetle tachinid fly (fig. 64)
Microphthalma disjuncta

Biology: The maggot stage of this large black and gray fly is a parasite of June beetle grubs (Aldrich 1926). As such one might expect it to be more abundant or at least more apparent in the forest than it is.

Distribution: From coast to coast within the United States.

Remarks: Length 15 mm. We usually saw this fly resting on loblolly trunks, but there is no demonstrated biological association between the animal and the plant.

Similar species: None.

gray horse fly (fig. 65)
Tabanus longus

Biology: Essentially unknown. The females are biting, blood-sucking flies that presumably feed on small mammals and perhaps birds. The male is certainly harmless but remains unknown to science. Maggots probably live in the sand and feed on other insects. They too are unknown.

Distribution: From the Atlantic Ocean to a western record in the Lost Pines as established here.

Fig. 64. June beetle
tachinid fly
(*Microphthalma
disjuncta*).

Fig. 65. Gray horse fly (*Tabanus longus*).

Remarks: Length 10 mm. The gray horse fly appears briefly in spring. We have seen only a few, and these in only one or two years. The fly might bite if allowed to settle on skin or clothing. We never saw the alarmingly huge black horse fly (*Tabanus atratus*) that also occurs in Central Texas.

Similar species: None.

inornate mosquito
Culiseta inornata

Biology: The natural hosts of the biting female are forest mammals, and not surprisingly, these mosquitoes bite humans too. They are capable of transmitting the agent of western equine encephalitis and are known to fly on cold nights. One specimen arrived at our blacklights after dark on a chilly November evening. Winter is indeed the breeding season (Bohls 1944).

Mosquito larvae are aquatic creatures known as "wrigglers." Wrigglers of this species in particular tolerate very polluted water and occur in ponds, ditches, artificial containers, and especially in shaded, leaf-filled forest pools.

Distribution: From coast to coast within the United States.

Remarks: Length 5 mm. We were never plagued by this or any other mosquito through years of fieldwork in the Lost Pines.

Similar species: The inornate mosquito is one of the largest species in the woods, but confident identification requires a microscope and the proper keys.

CHAPTER 6

True Bugs

M any apparent and colorful true bugs make their homes in the Lost Pines, and prominent among them are the predatory assassin bugs. Yet several well-known species are conspicuous only for eluding our scrutiny. For example, we never saw ambush bugs (a type of assassin bug that lurks in flowers), nor did we see the famous and widespread kissing bug *Triatoma sanguisuga* or any of its closest relatives, though they appear to the north in nearby Austin from time to time at porch lights in the center of the city, and to the south in the Ottine swamp. Similarly, the black masked-hunter *Reduvius personatus* made no appearance at our lights. It is unclear why these widely distributed species escaped our detection.

red bee-eater (fig. 66)
Apiomerus spissipes

Biology: This assassin bug preys upon bees and other insects that visit flowers and foliage in open areas. Sometimes it perches high on a cactus pad or bloom, waiting to pounce on pollen-eating insects that fly into the yellow, cup-shaped flower below. At other times it waits within the flower itself. Red bee-eaters eat one another too. Mating pairs are often seen on vegetation.

Distribution: From the Atlantic Ocean to Arizona.

Remarks: Length 14 mm. This sit-and-wait predator is the most conspicuous of the true bugs in the forest, with the possible exception of the exceedingly active but herbivorous largid bug (see species account). The red and black bee-eater's

Fig. 66. The red bee-eater (*Apiomerus spissipes*) on queen's delight.

bright colors warn of a painful stab delivered by its piercing mouthparts should the assassin bug be handled.

Similar species: The black bee-eater is more black than red.

black bee-eater
Apiomerus crassipes

Biology: Similar to that of the red bee-eater, though it spends more time in the trees than its close relative.

Distribution: From coast to coast within the United States.

Remarks: Length 14 mm. Bee-eaters sometimes fly away when approached. Occasionally they rear back in a threat posture that calls to mind the praying mantis.

Similar species: *See* red bee-eater.

wheel bug (fig. 67)
Arilus cristatus

Biology: Like all assassin bugs, this animal is a predator that stabs its prey and sucks juices from its body. The wheel bug is the largest of its kind in the forest and there are few terrestrial or flying insects that it cannot capture and kill. Wheel bugs perch on oak leaves, hide among the needles of loblolly pine, and lurk in rank vegetation along the shores of artificial ponds.

Fig. 67. The
wheel bug (*Arilus
cristatus*) feeding
on female giant
walkingstick.

Distribution: From the Atlantic Ocean to New Mexico.

Remarks: Length 25 mm. The wheel bug is named for the remarkable cog-wheel structure on its back. Its function is unknown, and because both sexes bear wheels of similar proportions, it probably has not evolved to its current large size by female choice or by combat between competing males. This insect can deliver a painful stab if handled, with effects lasting for weeks. Considering the wheel bug's size and power, it is perplexing to discover that its color is dull gray rather than the bright red and black of warning.

Similar species: None.

black May beetle-eater (fig. 68)
Melanolestes abdominalis

Biology: This black and red assassin bug lurks beneath rocks in the daytime and preys upon May beetle adults and their grubs (Readio 1927). When attacking adults the bug mounts the beetle from behind and pierces the neck with its beak. Spongy pads on the predator's legs stick to the prey much like suction cups.

Males have fully developed wings but adult females appear to be juveniles at first sight because their wings are tiny and probably useless. The mating process is very similar to the capture of prey. Males mount females from behind and place the beak in the same neck area that is pierced when killing May beetles. The female makes scraping sounds during copulation by rubbing her beak against her body. When mating is concluded the female lays eggs one at a time by pushing them into the soil beneath a rock. According to the literature, this species flies to blacklights at night. We seldom saw it at our own lights, though the bug is common in the forest and our blacklights logged hundreds of hours of use.

Distribution: From coast to coast within the United States.

Remarks: Length 15 mm. The bite of the May beetle-eater is painful, and when the bug strikes a human face while flying it is apt to bite immediately (Blatchley 1926).

Similar species: Some authors recognize *Melanolestes abdominalis* (with red on the abdomen) and *M. picipes* (which is entirely black) as two different species. Others believe that there is only one species that varies in color. Here we consider them as two different species and assume that the biology of both is essentially identical. Red and black individuals are more common in the forest than those that are entirely black. In the Lost Pines we know of no other assassin bug similar enough to cause confusion.

cruciate assassin bug (fig. 69)
Rhiginia cinctiventris

Biology: Unknown except for the few observations reported here. Males fly to blacklights at night during a brief period in spring and occasionally arrive in numbers. A single female was discovered beneath a large decomposing log. No males were seen under natural conditions and no individuals at all were seen in broad daylight. Cruciate assassin bugs thus appear to be nocturnal animals, and if so, their striking red and black warning colors presumably function to deter predators that encounter them while the bug is inactive and hiding during the day.

Distribution: This is one of the few primarily tropical insects of the Lost Pines. It ranges north into the southern United States but is confined to a central region from Louisiana to Arizona.

Fig. 68. Black May beetle-eater (*Melanolestes abdominalis*).

Fig. 69. Cruciate assassin bug
(*Rhiginia cinctiventris*).

Remarks: Typical length 19 mm. There are no published prey records for this beautiful, rarely seen insect that rivals the wheel bug in size.
Similar species: None.

corsair (fig. 70)
Rasahus hamatus

Biology: Corsairs are colorful but nocturnally active assassin bugs that fly to blacklights at night and are seldom seen under other circumstances. Like all assassin bugs they are predatory in habit.
Distribution: This is a tropical species ranging as far north as the southern United States. The distribution is disjunct, with separate populations occurring in Texas, Florida, Oklahoma, and Missouri.
Remarks: Length 17 mm. The corsair is said to occur under rocks and boards and in vegetation along wet lowlands. We never saw the big, attractive bug in such places and it was never seen during the day. It delivers a painful bite when handled.
Similar species: All three of the corsair's closest U.S. relatives occur in Texas, and confident identification requires a microscope and the proper keys.

spined assassin bug
Zelus luridus

Biology: This predator, variable in color but often apple-green in life, prefers shaded areas in woodlands and feeds on a wide variety of insects (Readio 1927).

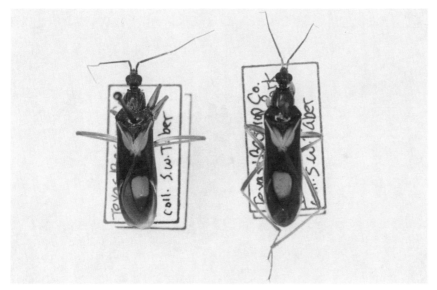

Fig. 70. Corsair assassin bug (*Rasahus hamatus*).

Farther north, in Kansas, the nymphs have the peculiar habit of spending the winter in curled leaves, up to thirteen individuals sharing the same leaf. It is not clear how they cope with the milder winters of Central Texas.

Distribution: Spined assassin bugs occur at least sporadically from coast to coast within the United States.

Remarks: Length 16 mm. The common name of this insect refers to the long sharp spine projecting from each hind corner of the front portion of the thorax.

Similar species: Other *Zelus* species probably occur in the forest but we did not see them.

horned assassin bug (fig. 71)
Repipta taurus

Biology: Unknown.

Distribution: Discontinuously distributed within the United States, with records from Colorado, Florida, Illinois, Louisiana, Pennsylvania, and Texas.

Remarks: Length 11 mm. The horned assassin bug has all the marks of warning. Its red and black colors are supplemented by six spikes, four of them on its back and most spectacularly of all, two on its head just in front of the eyes. We found a single specimen in the Lost Pines.

Similar species: Two close relatives occur in Texas but neither has the distinctive red and black coloration of this one.

Fig. 71. The head of the horned assassin bug (*Repipta taurus*).

bark-dwelling assassin bug (fig. 72)
Microtomus purcis

Biology: Little known except for our confirmation of a previous report that the red, black, and white predator lives beneath loose bark. We found one adult beneath the bark of a decomposing bluejack oak and one juvenile beneath the bark of a decomposing loblolly pine.

Distribution: From the Atlantic Ocean to a western limit somewhere in Texas, perhaps within the Lost Pines forest.

Remarks: Length 24 mm. The bark-dwelling assassin bug's prey species are unknown or at least unreported.

Similar species: White patches on the animal's back distinguish this species from all other assassin bugs in these woods.

thread-legged assassin bug
Emesaya brevipennis

Biology: This is a peculiar, straw-thin killer that swings its body back and forth and up and down while it clings to twig or leaf. It seizes its prey mantis-style with spined forelegs that pierce and hold the victim in a tight, viselike grip. Known prey include mosquitoes, small flies, other thread-legged bugs, and reportedly even stinging insects. These assassin bugs have the ability to walk across spider webs without becoming entangled as they pirate the spider's own prey. Adults can fly, but the wings are small and the bugs are very slow when moving through the air. Females lay their eggs on bark after matings that appear to be forced upon them by the males.

Distribution: The thread-legged assassin bug occurs from the Atlantic Ocean to Texas and is also recorded from California.

Remarks: Length 32 mm. This bug is said to be gregarious but we found only a very few and never in groups.

Similar species: None.

Carolina stink bug (fig. 73)
Brochymena carolinensis

Biology: Carolina stink bugs occur on and under loblolly bark. The protective coloration of this plant feeder matches the tree's bark so closely that the insect is likely to be overlooked despite its large size. It is said to feed upon the pine's

Fig. 72. Bark-dwelling assassin bug (*Microtomus purcis*).

Fig. 73. Carolina stink bug (*Brochymena carolinensis*).

viscous resin rather than the sugary sap, and if so it is truly an exceptional diet, because resin is one of the tree's *defenses* against insect attack. The diet and the barklike color suggest a long and close relationship with pine. Generally speaking, the Carolina stink bug is considered a rare species.

Distribution: From the Atlantic Ocean to a western limit in or near the Lost Pines.

Remarks: Length 15 mm. At one time this bug was believed to be a species endemic to Texas, but that view is no longer favored. The Texas populations are now considered members of a single widespread species. Like most stink bugs this one emits a defensive odor when handled.

Similar species: A related species is *Parabrochymena arborata,* which is lighter in color and at least slightly smaller in size. It occurs from the Atlantic Ocean to a western limit near the Lost Pines with the exception of a southern arc that stretches from Brownsville to Arizona.

elm stink bug (fig. 74)
Menecles insertus

Biology: This gregarious, nocturnal animal has a remarkable daily schedule that includes migration up and down the trunk of a tree. It hides on the ground beneath leaf litter during the daylight hours, and when darkness falls the bark-colored creatures begin crawling up the trunk in large numbers. After feeding on the trunk throughout the night they descend once more into the leaves, where their brown, mottled coloration continues to provide camouflage against potential predators (Balduf 1945). Known hosts occurring in the Lost Pines include elm, hickory, and hackberry.

Our own experience with the elm stink bug was confined to a single group of slippery elms growing on high ground near an artificial lake. We found adults and nymphs in small groups after dark feeding on the bark at least as high as eye level, and near the base of the trunk in the morning. At least some individuals appeared to be feeding on their way back to the leaf litter.

Distribution: The elm stink bug has one of the most unusual distributions among the insects in the Lost Pines. Though occurring coast to coast within the United States, it is entirely absent from the southeast, with the exception of a single possible record from Florida. A search of the literature, including a web search with the OVID service, suggests that our record from the Lost Pines is the first report of the elm stink bug from Texas.

Remarks: Length 13 mm. This bug is widely distributed "but nowhere abundant" (Van Duzee 1904), and is not common enough to earn a place in one of the standard works on the true bugs of the United States (Slater and Baranowski 1978). It is curious that we never found the animal on hickory or hackberry, though both trees are common in the Lost Pines.

Fig. 74. Elm stink bug (*Menecles insertus*).

Similar species: Only two species of this genus occur in the United States and there is little chance for confusion because the elm stink bug's close relative is the Texas endemic *Menecles portacrus,* which is restricted to the Big Bend country hundreds of miles west of the Lost Pines. The brown stink bug (*Euschistus servus*) is a crop pest that occurs from coast to coast. With a hand lens the margin of the brown stink bug's body just behind and on either side of the head can be seen to display an array of tiny teeth. If these are present on the elm stink bug, they are not obvious at such low magnification.

rice stink bug
Oebalus pugnax

Biology: The rice stink bug is an important pest of various grains including corn, wheat, sorghum, and of course rice. The animal is at least occasionally beneficial for it has been seen in the guise of predator, feeding upon the Alabama cottonworm (*Alabama argillacea*). Though there is a long list of recognized host plants, our discovery of this pest on little bluestem in the Lost Pines appears to be the first record of the rice stink bug from that plant species. It must be quite suitable, for we saw hundreds feeding on little bluestem in a meadow in September.

Distribution: From the Atlantic Ocean to Arizona.

Remarks: Length 9 mm. We did not see the rice stink bug on any of the various panic grass species in the forest. Elsewhere these are known to be suitable hosts.

Similar species: The narrow body, yellow-white underside, and especially the large and forwardly curved spines on the shoulders separate the rice stink bug from all other bugs in the Lost Pines.

pine seed-bug (fig. 75)
Tetyra bipunctata

Biology: In some parts of the United States this bug becomes a pest when it feeds on pine seeds that are still attached to the cone. In the Lost Pines we often saw the species on pine, but the individuals were usually dwelling beneath bark and were never observed on a cone. We did see groups of pine seed-bugs feeding at night on the green fruits of American beautyberry. This appears to be the first record of this bush as a host plant. Occasionally a specimen was found hibernating on the ground in duff or on a rock beneath a covering of dry pine needles, and once a mating pair was observed on beautyberry. In flight the pine seed-bug buzzes like a bee. Other modes of defense include the release of an odorous chemical and noises made by rubbing the hind legs against the lower surface of the abdomen.

Distribution: From the Atlantic Ocean to a western limit in or near the Lost Pines.

Fig. 75. Pine seed-bugs (*Tetyra bipunctata*) feeding on American beautyberry.

Remarks: Length 11 mm. This species is considered rare (Slater and Baranowski 1978), but it is abundant in the isolated pine forest of Central Texas.
Similar species: None.

giant spine-headed bug (fig. 76)
Acanthocephala declivis

Biology: This big plant-feeder probably sucks sap from oak trees. We never saw it in the act. On one occasion a group of individuals was found clustered and active beneath a piece of sheet metal, where they presumably overwintered. Spine-headed bugs possess curious hind legs that bear spines and flat dilations. The shapes of these structures have earned the animal the alternate name of "leaf-footed bug." Individuals of both sexes use their specialized legs to seize and pinch one another in battles over food and reproduction (Eberhard 1998).

Distribution: From the Atlantic Ocean to Arizona and south into the tropics.

Remarks: Typical length 30 mm. This is the largest terrestrial bug in the Lost Pines, rivaled only by the predatory wheel bug. Both are much smaller than the aquatic electric light bug. The resemblance to the big assassin bug extends even to shape and color, but the giant spine-headed bug is a sap feeder that will not bite if handled. Instead it releases a pleasant-smelling chemical that melted our plastic collecting containers.

Similar species: Two additional spine-headed bugs occur in the Lost Pines, none

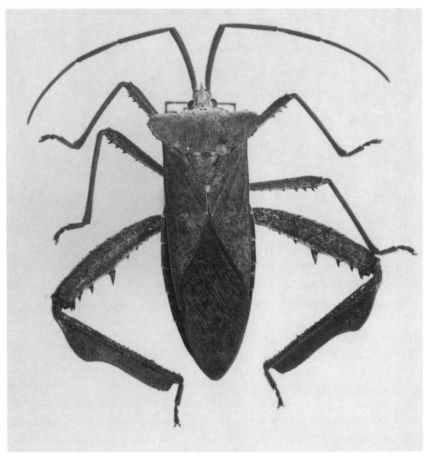

Fig. 76. Giant spine-headed bug (*Acanthocephala declivis*).

as large as this one and none having the distinctive shoulder bulges. They are *Acanthocephala femorata* and *A. terminalis*. The male of *A. femorata* has swollen hind legs with strong spines and is easily recognized. The other species is best identified by the process of elimination.

leaf-footed thistle bug
Leptoglossus phyllopus

Biology: These bugs feed on a wide variety of plants and often become pests when they attack crops. In Central Texas they are common in wild areas on large thistles, where they are often seen while mating.

Distribution: From the Atlantic Ocean to Texas with records from California in the far west.

Remarks: Length 18 mm. One of our specimens was not captured on thistle but on a tall legume growing in a meadow near a treeline. Another individual was captured after alighting on yaupon in the shady undergrowth of a creek bed.

Similar species: Several closely related leaf-footed bugs occur in Texas. The nearly straight yellowish white line across the back, the unusually broad leaflike dilations of the hind legs, and the white spots on those dilations separate this very common species from the others.

largid bug (fig. 77)
Largus succinctus

Biology: In the Lost Pines the largid bug feeds on the tender apical shoots of oak trees. Elsewhere it also feeds on cotton, various seeds, and at least one member of the potato family. It is abundant and is often seen scurrying across trails and over the leaf litter as if it were in a great hurry to get somewhere. On two occasions we saw groups attracted to fresh mammalian feces, but it was not clear if they were drinking. Perhaps they supplement their plant diet with animal waste, as has been recorded for the species by other observers. Some adults carry a small tan object about on the back, presumably the egg of a parasitic enemy. The young are different enough from the adults to be misidentified as a different species altogether. They are metallic blue with an orange spot on the back.

Distribution: From the Atlantic Ocean to a western limit near the Lost Pines.

Fig. 77. A largid bug (*Largus succinctus*) feeding on a blackjack oak leaf.

Remarks: Length 15 mm. Like the loblolly pine, the pine seed-bug, the Carolina stink bug, and the false mealworm beetle, the largid bug is a fixture of the forest that one is unlikely to see in Central Texas beyond its borders.

Similar species: None.

larger milkweed bug (fig. 78)
Oncopeltus fasciatus

Biology: Adults and juveniles suck juices from milkweed pods, seeds, leaves, and flowers. Red and black colors warn potential predators of a distastefulness acquired by feeding on a host plant that is toxic to many animals. Willow and goldenrod might be occasional food plants (Blatchley 1926), but our observations in Central Texas suggest a strict association with milkweed. We have never seen the attractive bug on other plants.

Distribution: From coast to coast within the United States.

Remarks: Length 13 mm. This is the first report of the large milkweed bug from the host species *Asclepias asperula,* the most apparent milkweed in the forest.

Similar species: None.

smaller milkweed bug (fig. 78)
Lygaeus kalmii

Biology: This pretty seed-bug is more diminutive than the larger milkweed bug and is accordingly known as the "smaller milkweed bug." Its common name reflects its usual host plant, and that is where we found our few specimens. One of these was feeding on a large pod.

Fig. 78. (A) The larger milkweed bug (*Oncopeltus fasciatus*) on a milkweed pod; (B) the smaller milkweed bug (*Lygaeus kalmii*).

Distribution: From coast to coast within the United States.

Remarks: Length 11 mm. This bug has also been recorded from blueberry. East of the hundredth meridian, the smaller milkweed bug has two white spots as shown here. West of the invisible barrier they are merged into a single large spot.

Similar species: None were noticed in the forest.

cactus bugs (fig. 79)

Chelinidea vittigera, Narnia femorata

Biology: The two cactus bug species feed only on cactus. The larger and more common *Chelinidea vittigera* leaves small yellow and brown scars on the pad. When approached too closely the adults defecate and scuttle out of sight to the opposite side of the plant. After mating on the pads beginning in early March, the females lay their eggs on the sharp cactus spine, a behavior that suggests extreme specialization for this host plant beyond the level of diet. However, few cacti in the Lost Pines bear the familiar long spines, and it is not known where eggs are laid on these plants. Perhaps they are laid among the smaller glochidial spines that occur in bunches on every pad. Young bugs live in dense herds and are much darker than adults. Less is known about the biology of *Narnia femorata*. which resembles a miniature version of the big spine-headed bug *Acanthocephala femorata*.

Fig. 79. (A) The large cactus bug (*Chelinidea vittigera*) on its host; (B) the small cactus bug (*Narnia femorata*).

Distribution: *Chelinidea vittigera* occurs from coast to coast within the United States. *Narnia femorata* is a western species that meets its eastern limit in the United States in or near the Lost Pines, as established here.

Remarks: Length of both species 13 mm though the "large" species is bulkier. Cactus bugs are not as common as one might expect given the abundance of cactus in open areas. In other parts of the United States *Chelinidea vittigera* has been intentionally introduced to control cacti growing as weeds.

Similar species: None.

stilt bugs (fig. 80)
Jalysus spinosus and *J. wickhami*

Biology: In late summer and early fall spined stilt bugs can be seen standing on their slender, hairlike legs among the nodding flowers of purpletop grass (*Tridens flavus*). Until now this plant was not known to be a food plant, though it is the bug's most apparent host in the Lost Pines forest. Wild millet (*Panicum*) is the favored host in spring and in the earliest days of summer before purpletop makes its appearance.

Adult stilt bugs fly off at the slightest provocation. A closer look at the flowers will reveal tiny green nymphs, wingless and incapable of flight. Both stages of the life cycle feed upon flowers as well as tiny aphids that suck juices from the same plant. With the approach of winter adults move into the insulating layers of dead leaves and await the arrival of spring.

Distribution: The spined stilt bug is an eastern species meeting its western limit near the city of San Antonio, Texas.

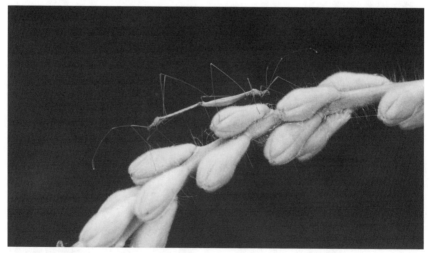

Fig. 80. Wickham's stilt bug (*Jalysus wickhami*); mating pair with male on left.

Remarks: Length 7 mm. These small, spindly insects resemble tiny walkingsticks, and their legs and antennae are so thin that appendages appear to be missing altogether until the animal is inspected at very close range.

Similar species: Wickham's stilt bug (*Jalysus wickhami*) is very closely related and must be distinguished from the spined stilt bug with the aid of hand lens or microscope. It occurs throughout the southern United States and feeds upon a wide variety of herbaceous plants.

round-headed ant mimic bug
Hyalymenus tarsatus

Biology: Adults are rarely seen, nocturnally active herbivores that feed on members of the daisy family (Oliveira 1985). Juveniles not only resemble ants in their appearance and behavior, but as they molt from one stage to the next they change models from one ant species to another. We saw one of these on a frostweed leaf in late October. It bore an uncanny resemblance to the minor worker of the carpenter ant *Camponotus festinatus.*

Distribution: This is a tropical species that ranges just far enough north to occur in Texas, Arizona, and California.

Remarks: Length 9 mm. The round-headed ant mimic is the only member of its family (Alydidae) we noted in the Lost Pines. Individuals fly to blacklights at night but are rare visitors. Adults may be recognized by a curiously curved and strongly flattened segment of the hind leg.

Similar species: None.

granular flat bug (fig. 81)
Mezira granulata

Biology: Granular flat bugs feed on fungus beneath the bark of decomposing snags and logs. We found them on oaks but never on loblolly pine.

Distribution: From the Atlantic Ocean to Texas with a curiously disjunct population farther west in Arizona.

Remarks: Length 6 mm. These tiny bugs are dark, rough-textured, and extraordinarily flat. The flat shape is clearly adaptive for living under bark, but the color and texture appear to be adaptations for living on its *surface* instead.

Similar species: None.

four-toothed water scorpion (fig. 82)
Ranatra quadridentata

Biology: This lanky aquatic predator resembles a praying mantis in shape, size, means of capturing its prey, and in its diet of other insects, but it differs from the

Fig. 81. Granular flat bug (*Mezira granulata*).

land dweller by the inclusion of fishes and tadpoles among its prey. The tail-like structure responsible for the water scorpion's common name is actually a harmless tube used for breathing air when the rest of the bug hangs head-down just beneath the surface. The long, slender, dark body and a tendency to feign death when disturbed provide excellent camouflage at the bottom of a dip-net dripping with muddy pine needles dredged from the bottom of a pond.

This is not a swimming bug but one that gets around underwater by walking. On land it is very clumsy. In the air it is a good flier. Flight is seldom witnessed and might only occur when drying ponds require dispersal to new waters. Females lay their distinctive eggs in a wet log. The eggs have filaments that aid in the acquisition of oxygen for the young bug developing inside.

Distribution: This is another of the relatively few western insects of the Lost Pines, ranging from southern California to the piney woods of East Texas.

Remarks: Typical lengths for these animals are in the range of 65 mm. Water

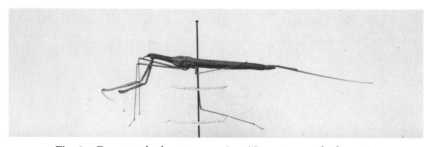

Fig. 82. Four-toothed water scorpion (*Ranatra quadridentata*).

scorpions cannot sting but they can deliver a painful stab with the piercing mouth-parts. They also discourage capture by rubbing the front legs against the body to make squeaking noises. Under the microscope this submariner's body is often seen to be covered with algae, parasitic mites, and sundry debris that evoke an image of seaweed and barnacles growing on a ship's hull. More exaggerated names than "water scorpion" are "alligator flea" and "water dog."

Similar species: Four or five species of slender water scorpions creep about in the ponds of the forest. Reliable identification requires the proper keys (Sites and Polhemus 1994). The remaining species are the southern water scorpion (*R. australis*), dark water scorpion (*R. nigra*), Bueno's water scorpion (*R. buenoi*), and Texas water scorpion (*R. texana*). It is disappointing that the one species we never saw is the only water scorpion endemic to Central and southern Texas, named for the state where the Lost Pines grow (Sites and Polhemus 1994). The southern water scorpion, dark water scorpion, and Bueno's water scorpion all occur from the Atlantic Ocean to a western extreme in or near the Lost Pines. Our record from this forest is now the westernmost record for Bueno's water scorpion.

Howard's water scorpion (fig. 83)
Curicta scorpio

Biology: Similar to that of the five larger, more elongate, and more tubular water scorpions.

Distribution: Found nowhere else in the United States but in southern Texas and southern Louisiana.

Fig. 83. Howard's water scorpion
(*Curicta scorpio*).

Remarks: Length 26 mm. Howard's water scorpion is generally considered to be a rare or uncommon species. It is locally abundant in the artificial ponds of the Lost Pines.

Similar species: None.

giant electric light bug (fig. 84)
Lethocerus medius

Biology: This formidable aquatic creature is a powerful, air-breathing water bug that eats other insects, small fishes, salamanders, tadpoles, and even snakes. It is the largest true bug in the forest, and its ambush strategy is aided by such great resemblance to a dead leaf that its unsuspecting prey sometimes seek shelter beneath the bug's body. Once when we were seeking a particular individual seen the previous week in a water hole, one of us stared directly at it, passed it off as a submerged leaf, and continued looking elsewhere. That individual was camouflaged even beyond its normal state by a rust-red covering of the iron-rich minerals of Copperas Creek. Its vision was surely diminished (fig. 84).

Female giant electric light bugs lay their eggs above the water line on emergent vegetation. The male crawls out of the pond to guard them, and when approached by a human it spreads the powerful front legs and postures in defiance (Smith and Larsen 1993).

Distribution: Within the United States this species occurs from west-central Arizona to an eastern limit near Houston, Texas, not far from the Lost Pines.

Remarks: Length 60 mm. Electric light bugs can inflict a painful stab if handled. The common name reflects a habit of flying in large numbers to streetlights. The

Fig. 84. A giant electric light bug (*Lethocerus medius*) covered with iron from Copperas Creek.

Fig. 85. A male toe-biter carrying eggs on its back.

spectacle is not as common as it was in former times. One of us can remember as a boy seeing an occasional giant electric light bug wheeling about the streetlights in College Station, Texas, but has not witnessed this in Central Texas for decades. A dead specimen of a related species found at the time of this writing on the sidewalk beneath a streetlight on the busy and highly developed University of Texas campus in Austin demonstrates that the namesake spectacle is not yet a thing of the past.

Similar species: Several giant electric light bug species might occur in the Lost Pines, but every individual we identified was *Lethocerus medius.* The species do resemble one another closely and keys must be consulted for confident identification.

toe-biters (fig. 85)
Belostoma lutarium, B. confusum, B. fusciventre

Biology: Similar to that of the much larger electric light bug. The toe-biters do indeed appear to be miniature versions of their larger relative. One difference is the manner of guarding the eggs, which is perhaps unique in the animal kingdom. The female deposits her clutch on the male's back (fig. 85), sometimes in the face of resistance from her mate. This has two potential benefits. First, the eggs are aerated more efficiently when moved about through the water with the swimming male. Second, they are protected at least to the degree that the adult protects itself. This leads one to wonder why the behavior is not more widely adopted.

Distribution: *Belostoma lutarium* occurs from the Atlantic Ocean to the Lost Pines area of Texas, *B. confusum* occurs only in southern Texas and in southeastern Arizona, and *B. fusciventre* is limited to central and southern Texas and Louisiana.

Remarks: Typical lengths range from 17 to 25 mm. The common name of these aquatic predators reflects their habit of biting the toes of people who venture barefoot into ponds.

Similar species: The toe-biters are treated here as a group precisely because they are so similar in nearly every way. Confident identification requires microscopic examination and the proper keys. Yet as a group they do not resemble any other bugs save the much larger electric light bug.

creeping water bug (fig. 86)
Pelocoris biimpressus

Biology: This is a small, green, turtle-shaped aquatic predator similar in life history to the larger water bugs but not nearly as well known.

Distribution: Within the United States this species is found only in Central and southern Texas.

Remarks: Length 10 mm. Though small, the bug can inflict a painful bite.

Similar species: A similar (and much better known) creeping water bug occurs near the Lost Pines and perhaps within the forest as well. Microscopic examination is needed for confident identification (Sites and Polhemus 1995a, 1995b; Davis 1996).

giant backswimmer (fig. 87)
Notonecta irrorata

Biology: Backswimmers are unique among water bugs for their habit of swimming on their backs using hind legs that look and act like oars. Keel-forming wings combine with the rest of the anatomy to make an upside-down bug built like a boat. They are predatory and feed upon other insects.

Distribution: From the Atlantic Ocean to Texas with a few curious records from Arizona.

Remarks: Length 14 mm. This average-sized bug is only a giant with respect to other backswimmers. Regardless of their size they can inflict a painful stab that has earned them pest status in public swimming pools and the alternate name of "water-bee."

Fig. 86. Creeping water bug (*Pelocoris biimpressus*).

Fig. 87. Giant backswimmer (*Notonecta irrorata*).

Similar species: The pale backswimmer *Notonecta indica* occurs from coast to coast and rows alongside the giant backswimmer in the ponds of the Lost Pines. At a length of 11 mm it is smaller, and the white phase of this species in particular is easily distinguished from its larger, darker relative.

water strider
Limnoporus canaliculatus

Biology: Water striders are aquatic, surface-dwelling, predatory bugs that resemble spiders with their long outstretched legs as they skate across pond or creek in search of prey and mates. Waves made by potential prey are picked up as signals just as an owl detects the activity of a rodent. Males generate similar waves to call to prospective mates.

Distribution: From the Atlantic Ocean to a western limit in Texas, perhaps not far from the Lost Pines.

Remarks: Length 11 mm. Water striders are among the few aquatic insects readily seen from shore because their habitat happens to be the surface. They are also known as "good luck bugs" or "wherrymen." Some can fly, some cannot, and the development of their wings can vary within a single species.

Similar species: Several water strider species are likely to occur in the forest. A microscope and the proper keys must be used to distinguish one from another.

Fig. 88. Martin's water measurer (*Hydrometra martini*).

Martin's water measurer (fig. 88)
Hydrometra martini

Biology: This is a tiny, surface-walking, aquatic scavenger that is also predatory in the sense that it sucks fluids from weak and dying insects, occasionally feeding in groups on a single victim. Water measurers remain close to shore and their slender shape is very difficult to detect among the pine needles and detritus at the margin of a pond. Some individuals can fly but others cannot.

Distribution: Martin's water measurer occurs from the Atlantic Ocean to Texas with a disjunct population in Arizona.

Remarks: Length 10 mm. This dark green dwarf resembles a tiny walkingstick and creeps along very slowly.

Similar species: At least one additional water measurer species probably occurs in the forest. Confident identification is difficult and requires a microscope and the proper keys.

smooth water boatman (fig. 89)
Hesperocorixa laevigata

Biology: Water boatmen are unusual among aquatic bugs because they have a highly modified beak that allows them to eat entire microscopic organisms, and thus they do not necessarily drink the fluids of an individual animal or plant as

Fig. 89. Smooth water boatman
(*Hesperocorixa laevigata*).

other true bugs typically do. They move about by rowing through the water with their legs.

Distribution: From coast to coast within the United States.

Remarks: Length 9 mm. Water boatmen are among the few aquatic bugs that do not bite when handled. At night they fly to blacklights in large numbers.

Similar species: These insects comprise a very successful group of aquatic animals, and many species are likely to occur in the Lost Pines. Some are quite small. A microscope and the proper keys are required for confident identification.

resh cicada (fig. 90)
Tibicen resh

Biology: Adults feed on oak sap, females lay their eggs in twigs, and juveniles feed underground on the roots of the same trees, for we have seen this cicada among the oaks in nearby Austin where loblollies do not grow. Male cicadas sing loud and long in summer to voiceless females, but despite the racket neither sex is likely to be seen because adults hide on branches high above ground. When young cicadas hatch from the eggs placed in twigs that have been slit open by the female's swordlike ovipositor, they drop to the ground, burrow into the soil, and feed on roots for a year or more before emerging to transform into the winged adult on the bark of a tree.

Distribution: The resh cicada occurs from Alabama to a western extreme somewhere in Texas.

Remarks: Wingspan 104 mm. The species is named for a mark on its back that resembles the Hebrew letter resh. The empty, dry, brown husks of cicada nymphs are often seen on tree trunks. This cast-off skin is likely to be the visitor's only glimpse of the animal. Its shrill song, however, is diagnostic for late spring and summer in the forest. In fact, east-central Texas was once described as "a veritable cicada paradise" (Bromley 1933).

Similar species: Several smaller species occur in the Lost Pines, including the hieroglyphic cicada, but none can be confused with this one. Identification of the others is a daunting task, and a key to the cicadas of Texas would be a desirable addition to the entomological literature. The famous periodical cicadas with their thirteen- and seventeen-year life cycles do not occur in Central Texas. Here we have annual and perhaps biennial species instead. As a class these are better known as "dog day cicadas" because they appear reliably in the heat of every summer. The most abundant of their number among the oaks in Central Texas is the superb cicada (*Tibicen superba*), which we did not notice in the Lost Pines.

hieroglyphic cicada (fig. 90)
Neocicada hieroglyphica

Biology: This species is much smaller than the resh cicada and it appears to be more abundant as well. The broken greenish pattern of its upper surface allows it to blend in with lichens that grow on post oaks and blackjacks, trees in which the

Fig. 90. Top: Resh cicada (*Tibicen resh*). Bottom: Hieroglyphic cicada (*Neocicada hieroglyphica*); female on left, male on right.

silent female "delights to make her nests" (Beamer 1929). This preference, combined with the preference of the underground larval stage for sandy soils, and the cicada's presence in the piney woods of New England, suggests that the Lost Pines is an ideal habitat for the hieroglyphic cicada.

Remarks: There is a remarkable and uncommon beetle exceeding one inch in length that feeds parasitically on juvenile cicadas when the beetle itself is in the grub stage. We never saw this animal, *Sandalus niger* though it has been recorded from Texas and Indiana. A weather eye should be kept out for it. The creature resembles a small prionus beetle but with much shorter antennae (see fig. 43.1, Downie and Arnett 1996, page 721). According to these authors *Sandalus niger* is attracted to backyard laundry during the months of autumn. The attractant might be the odor of bleach. Elsewhere the cicada parasite has been seen on hickory trees, and these are common enough in the uplands of the Central Texas forest.

Distribution: The hieroglyphic cicada occurs from the Atlantic Ocean to a western limit in or near the Lost Pines.

Remarks: Wingspan 63 mm. Males are noisy singers but the shed skins of the larvae left behind on tree trunks are likely to be the only glimpses of any cicadas to be found in the forest.

Similar species: None.

CHAPTER 7

Beetles

eetles are among the most apparent insects in the Lost Pines. One of them
is a species new to science. We call it the Texas long-lipped beetle (*Telegeusis
texensis*) because of the remarkably long and ribbonlike mouthparts (fig. 6).
Every aspect of the animal's biology remains unknown, and it appears to be found
nowhere else in the world but in Central Texas. A single specimen landed on the
junior author's leg at dusk and might have been squashed with a slap if it had
been mistaken for a mosquito instead of a new species. As we mention it now and
in chapter 1, we give no separate entry for the species among the other beetles
presented here.

The forest is home to more than fifty better known beetle species that are
readily observed, particularly interesting, or both. We were unsuccessful in our
efforts to find the giant eastern Hercules beetle (*Dynastes tityus;* fig. 91) that occurs in these woods near the western edge of its range (Edward Riley, pers. comm.).
This striking animal exceeds two inches in length and flies to blacklight traps but
must be very scarce indeed. A battered, dusty, preserved female specimen we saw
in a back room of the park headquarters in South Llano River State Park more
than one hundred miles west of the forest suggests that the species finds its western limit there.

noble tiger beetle (fig. 92)
Cicindela formosa

Biology: Beautiful purple adults run rapidly across the sand in clearings and
along trails and primitive roads. When approached they fly a short distance be-

Fig. 91. Eastern Hercules beetle (*Dynastes tityus*); male collected in Maryland.

fore setting down again, and while airborne they resemble wasps or flies. Tiger beetles in both the adult and grub stages are predators with large, powerful jaws. The grubs live in burrows in the sand, where they anchor themselves to the wall with a hooklike structure and snatch up passing insects. Both the burrow and the predatory behavior are similar to those of a trap-door spider, but in this case the door to the dwelling is the predator's own head.

Fig. 92. Noble tiger beetle (*Cicindela formosa*).

Fig. 93. Six-spotted tiger beetle
(*Cicindela sexguttata*).

Distribution: From coast to coast within the United States but spottily distributed in the far West.

Remarks: Length 17 mm. We never saw the larva or burrow of any tiger beetle. They must be abundant and well hidden.

Similar species: The large size and especially the purple or deep red color distinguish this tiger beetle from all others that occur in the forest.

six-spotted tiger beetle (fig. 93)
Cicindela sexguttata

Biology: Similar to that of the noble tiger beetle.

Distribution: From the Atlantic Ocean to a western limit, in the southern part of its range, almost precisely in the vicinity of the Lost Pines.

Remarks: Length 12 mm. This is the most common of our tiger beetles. It is said to emit a fragrant aroma, though we never noticed it.

Similar species: The metallic green or blue color distinguishes the six-spotted tiger beetle from the rest of the species considered here. However, the number of white dots on its wing covers ranges from zero to ten, so that "six" is more like an average than an absolute.

red-rumped tiger beetle (fig. 94)
Cicindela rufiventris

Biology: For over one hundred years the red-rumped tiger beetle has been known to have exacting habitat requirements. It favors sloping ground in forests of stunted pines and oaks in New Jersey and Indiana (Leng 1902; Blatchley 1910), and indeed our first encounter with a small population of this animal was on a short stretch of sloping ground extending less than one hundred feet in length at the edge of a powerline cut. A lone specimen flew to a blacklight at night. Neither the noble tiger beetle nor the six-spotted tiger beetle ever flew to our lights, though they are much more common species.

Distribution: The red-rumped tiger beetle occurs from the Atlantic Ocean to at least as far west as Arizona.

Remarks: Length 10 mm. An observer in Massachusetts said of the adult "When flying in the sunshine its crimson and nearly transparent abdomen appears like a drop of blood suspended to its tail" (Leng 1902). We never saw the six- to eighteen-inch burrows made by tiger beetle grubs, but according to Schaupp (1883), the grubs can be "easily extracted by introducing a fine straw or grass down the holes to which they cling tenaciously."

Similar species: The red tip of the lower surface of the abdomen easily distinguishes this species from all others we saw in the forest.

Fig. 94. Red-rumped tiger beetle (*Cicindela rufiventris*).

Fig. 95. Ornate
tiger beetle
(*Cicindela
trifasciata*).

ornate tiger beetle (fig. 95)
Cicindela trifasciata

Biology: The habitat preferred by this species contrasts sharply with that preferred by the red-rumped tiger beetle. Ornate tiger beetles frequent the low, moist
ground of shorelines and mud flats. We found one population along the shore of
a large artificial pond, where they scrambled and flew about beneath low-growing *Sesbania* plants. One specimen flew to a blacklight at night. In Florida swarms
of a thousand or more occur along riverbanks in spring.

Distribution: From the Atlantic Ocean to at least as far west as Central Texas.

Remarks: Length 11 mm. This tiger beetle has also been known as *C. tortuosa*
because of the long, winding white line on each wing cover.

Similar species: The winding line on the wing covers can be faint, but the red-
rumped tiger beetle also differs by the red abdominal rim for which it is named.
Five additional tiger beetles have been reported above and beyond our total of
four. These are *Cicindela scutellaris,* C. *punctulata,* C. *splendida,* C. *obsoleta,* and
C. *ocellata* (Schultz 1989). Tiger beetles are apparent species of open ground, and
we do not know why we missed several species listed in the earlier study. We did
see several of these in nearby Austin, Texas.

Fig. 96. Fiery searcher (*Calosoma scrutator*), (A) adult; (B) larva.

fiery searcher (fig. 96)
Calosoma scrutator

Biology: The beautiful metallic green, red, and blue adults and the blackish, armored grubs are voracious predators of caterpillars and other insects. Adults exceed one and one half inches in length, have big, scissors-shaped mouthparts, and will kill and eat other adult beetles as large as themselves. Because of their impressive size and great speed they are often heard scrambling across dry oak and pine litter like small mice before they are seen. Even the wormlike grub stage is capable of climbing into the trees in search of prey. And they are cannibals too. On one occasion we placed two grubs, roughly equal in size, into the same vial. An hour later one had completely devoured the other. The survivor had nearly doubled in size.

Distribution: This caterpillar hunter occurs sporadically from coast to coast within the United States.

Remarks: Length 30 mm. Fiery searchers and their relatives are widely used for biocontrol of destructive caterpillars. Adults appear briefly in April and May in large numbers, but by summer they are few and far between. When picked up they release an unpleasant defensive odor much worse than that of a stink bug. We found one adult beneath a rock in a cell it had constructed, perhaps when it was yet a grub or perhaps when it was overwintering. Adults fly and crawl to blacklights at night.

Similar species: Other caterpillar hunters probably occur in the forest, but we have identified dozens of specimens and they were all fiery searchers. Bombardier beetles comprise a related group of ground beetles that we never saw in this usually dry habitat. Yet they, and several caterpillar hunters, are common in the Ottine swamp of Gonzales County, a mere fifty miles south of the Lost Pines.

black woodland beetle (fig. 97)
a species near *Cyclotrachelus brevoorti*

Biology: We found a mating pair beneath the shelter of a sandstone rock after a lengthy rainy period in November. Little is known about the biology of these animals and their close relatives. They are probably omnivorous, including ants, weevils, and fungi in a broad diet. Neither sex can fly, for the wing covers are fused shut, and the flight wings underneath are vestigial. It has long been known that this species or at least its relatives are creatures of the forest floor, and some are restricted to piney woods in particular.

Distribution: Because the identification is uncertain, the distribution must remain uncertain as well.

Remarks: Length 15 mm. The genus to which these animals belong is better known as *Evarthrus*. We have followed the nomenclatural change recommended by Bousquet (1984).

Similar species: We were unable to identify these animals with confidence even while using the standard key to the large number of very similar species (Freitag 1969). This might be due to our own confusion, to a problem with the key itself, or to the presence of an undescribed species in the Lost Pines.

Fig. 97. Black woodland beetle (a species near *Cyclotrachelus brevoorti*).

black-horned tumble beetle
Canthon nigricornis

Biology: This species is the only beetle treated here that rolls small balls of dung away from piles of animal droppings. One male and one female cooperate in the effort, and it saves the larva that will eat the dung from the many scavengers and predators that assemble at the droppings of white-tailed deer and other mammals. After the pair push and pull the dung to a suitable distance, they bury it and the female lays an egg inside.

Distribution: Black-horned tumble beetles occur from the Atlantic Ocean to a western limit near the Lost Pines.

Remarks: Length 8 mm. Although this is the most commonly encountered dung beetle of daylight hours, it never flew to our blacklight traps, whereas the lined dung beetle and African dung beetle (*see* species accounts) often did. Tumble beetles occasionally steal dung balls from other tumble beetles.

Similar species: The small size and dull black color combined with the habit of rolling dung away rather than burying it on the spot separate this beetle from all other dung-feeding species dealt with here.

lined dung beetle
Onthophagus striatulus

Biology: Lined dung beetles dig a hole beneath animal droppings and carry the dung into the burrow instead of rolling it away. Adults prefer fungi and rotten watermelons to the food that they provide for their own grubs. They fly to blacklights at night, and this is the best way to capture them in numbers.

Distribution: Lined dung beetles occur from the Atlantic Ocean to a western limit near the Lost Pines.

Remarks: Length 8 mm. Males vary greatly in size and often have a pair of horns on their head. An Australian relative does not wait for the dung to fall to the ground. Individuals hang by the hundreds from the hair of a wallaby and compete for the resource as it exits the animal's body.

Similar species: The smaller size distinguishes this native from the otherwise similar African dung beetle (*see* species account).

African dung beetle
Onthophagus gazella

Biology: Similar to that of the native lined dung beetle. It flies to blacklights in greater numbers.

Distribution: This is an African scavenger released from coast to coast within the United States to control, by competition, the dung-breeding flies that pester cattle.

Remarks: Length 13 mm. Males have a pair of horns on the head. Populations can grow large enough to remove an entire cow pat in two days.

Similar species: This exotic species is larger than the otherwise similar native lined dung beetle.

Blackburn's dung beetle (fig. 98)
Geotrupes blackburnii

Biology: Blackburn's dung beetle does not roll dung for its grubs. It buries the dung at its source, sometimes to the incredible depth of three feet. If the male lags behind the female during excavations, she stimulates him by making rasping noises with her hind legs. If this fails, she tracks him down and claws her mate until he returns to work (H. Main in Howden 1955).

Distribution: From the Atlantic Ocean to a western limit in Texas, perhaps not far from the Lost Pines.

Remarks: Length 17 mm. This is a robust, tanklike beetle with conspicuous grooves on its wing covers. Specimens are occasionally seen on the hiking trails and primitive roads. We found one individual in a spider web, stridulating loudly as a spider swathed it in silk.

Similar species: Blackburn's dung beetle resembles the opaque dung beetle, which has smoother wing covers. The similarly large but much more beautiful metallic green species of the genus *Phanaeus* are more strongly associated with cow pastures and thus are not evident in the forest, though they are abundant in the surrounding fields of Central Texas.

Fig. 98. (A) Blackburn's dung beetle (*Geotrupes blackburnii*);
(B) opaque dung beetle (*Geotrupes opacus*).

opaque dung beetle (fig. 98)
Geotrupes opacus

Biology: Similar to that of Blackburn's dung beetle. On a rainy November day we collected one individual in flight and observed nearby a mating pair that had arrived at fresh mammal feces. They and a third individual were already digging alongside the excrement. On a cool day in February a pair of adults were dug up approximately two inches beneath the excrement of a carnivorous mammal. Their presence underground was indicated by a small hole and a bit of loose soil.

Distribution: From the Atlantic Ocean to Colorado.

Remarks: Length 15 mm. Like its close relative Blackburn's dung beetle, this species is seen most often along hiking trails and dirt roads.

Similar species: The smoother wing covers separate this scarab from Blackburn's dung beetle.

false mealworm beetle (fig. 99)
Alobates pennsylvanica

Biology: Adults are nocturnal omnivores that feed on other insects and fungi. During the day and when overwintering in groups they hide beneath the coarse bark of loblolly pines and to a lesser extent beneath the finer bark of oak trees. If handled they secrete a defensive odor that we found pleasant rather than noxious. They also draw in their legs and feign death. The grub stage lives within decaying logs and feeds upon other insects.

Fig. 99. A false mealworm beetle (*Alobates pennsylvanica*) on loblolly pine.

Distribution: From coast to coast within forested regions of the United States.
Remarks: Length 22 mm. If the loblolly is the botanical symbol of the Lost Pines, then the seemingly ubiquitous, pine-dwelling, false mealworm beetle would be a good choice as its symbolic animal.
Similar species: None.

lined darkling beetle
Eleodes tricostatus

Biology: The grubs of the lined darkling beetle's close relatives, and presumably this species as well, feed on the roots of grasses. Some of them achieve pest status as a result. Adults are said to prefer open, sandy areas, near shrubs or trees (Lago 1988; Maxwell and Young 1998), and this characterization is entirely supported by our own findings in Central Texas.
Distribution: The animal occurs west of the Mississippi with sporadic occurrence east of the river, including central Wisconsin (Maxwell and Young 1998).
Remarks: Length 18 mm. The lined darkling beetle is uncommon in the Lost Pines, according to our experience.
Similar species: None.

pine darkling beetle (fig. 100)
Uloma punctulata

Biology: The small and reddish brown pine darkling beetle occurs under the loose bark of decomposing loblolly logs. Little else is known about its biology.
Distribution: The animal occurs at least sporadically from the Atlantic Ocean to

Fig. 100. Pine darkling beetle (*Uloma punctulata*).

a western limit somewhere in Texas, presumably near or within the Lost Pines.

Remarks: Length 8 mm. Pine darkling beetles are more abundant in the humid piney woods of East Texas than in the drier forest of Central Texas.

Similar species: Two additional species of this genus are reported from Texas, though we have not identified them in the Lost Pines.

blind click beetle (fig. 101)
Alaus myops

Biology: Adults and grubs are predators that feed upon other insects. The adults have two dark patches resembling eyes that are located just behind the head, and individuals are occasionally seen on pines and oaks in summer. The grubs live in decaying loblollies and reach lengths of two inches.

Distribution: The blind click beetle occurs in the eastern and southern United States with its precise limits undetermined. The Lost Pines is probably at or near the western limit of its range.

Remarks: Length 31 mm. One dead adult was discovered with its head protruding from the wood of a loblolly snag. It was lodged tightly in a tunnel and presumably died while attempting to escape after completing the grub stage inside the tree.

Click beetles in general earn their name by the clicking noise they make when they are captured in hand or overturned on their backs. They regain their feet by

Fig. 101. Blind click beetle
(*Alaus myops*).

Fig. 102. Male ox beetle (*Strategus antaeus*).

employing a mechanism on the thorax that makes the clicking sound as it flips the animal into the air. After one or more tries it lands catlike on all six legs.
Similar species: The blind click beetle might easily be confused with the much better known eyed click beetle (*Alaus oculatus*) if the latter occurred in the forest. We never saw it there, though in nearby Austin the eyed click beetle and not the blind click beetle was the only species we encountered (usually on a sidewalk). Simulated eyes in addition to real ones are common to both species. They are merely smaller on the "blind" click beetle.

ox beetle (fig. 102)
Strategus antaeus

Biology: The big, tanklike, mahogany brown adults exceed one inch in length and reportedly hide beneath fallen, decaying logs during the day. Their grubs live inside the logs and presumably eat the wood itself or the fungi growing on it. We never saw living adults under natural conditions, and we saw only one grub large enough to be this species. The few adults we did see were individuals of both sexes that flew to our blacklights at night.

One of our male specimens was glued together after being found dead and in pieces in the web of the giant orb weaver spider (*Araneus bicentenarius*), an animal of comparable size. The beetle had flown into the huge web during the previous night.
Distribution: Occurs from the Atlantic Ocean to a western limit near the Lost Pines.

Fig. 103. Profound May beetle (*Phyllophaga profunda*).

Remarks: Length 42 mm. Males have three enormous, exotic-looking horns that rise from a plate just behind the head. Females have one small horn instead. When these monsters fly into a plastic light trap at night, the crash can be heard from one hundred feet away.
Similar species: None.

May beetles (fig. 103)
Phyllophaga profunda and others
Biology: Adult May beetles are nocturnal leaf eaters capable of defoliating small blackjacks and post oaks when they appear in hundreds on a single tree. Yet they manage to remain hidden from view during the day by digging into the soil until nightfall. The larvae, widely known as "white grubs," eat the roots of grasses underground. As a result both stages of the life cycle are known as pests.
Distribution: The profound May beetle in particular is a species of the eastern United States that reaches its western limit near the Lost Pines.
Remarks: Length 20 mm. May beetles of various species are famous in the South for buzzing about porch lamps in spring and early summer. They are also known as "June beetles" or "June bugs."
Similar species: More than one hundred May beetle species occur in the United States, and they are too similar to identify on sight. A male is required for certain identification, and it must be dissected and viewed under a microscope so that features of its reproductive tract become visible.

green June beetle (fig. 104)
Cotinis nitida
Biology: All active life cycle stages feed on plants. The attractive adults can become pests above ground because they eat fruits and flowers, whereas grubs de-

stroy turfgrass roots underground and out of sight. They do this in a most un-usual fashion by crawling on their backs instead of on their legs.

Distribution: From the Atlantic Ocean to a western limit near the Lost Pines.

Remarks: Length 22 mm. The metallic green and bronze adults fly mostly at night. When flying during the day they look and sound like bees. Another common name is "fig-eater."

Similar species: None.

nettle scarab (fig. 105)
Hypothyce mixta or undetermined or new species

Biology: Unknown, except for the fact that we found the winged males on nettle plants from time to time; no similar association was noted for any other beetle. According to Edward Riley, assistant curator of the Texas A&M University insect collection, the females are flightless.

Distribution: We are aware of only two records in addition to the Lost Pines specimens we and others collected. These are males from Nacogdoches in far eastern Texas and from Anderson County between that location and the Central Texas forest.

Remarks: Length 13 mm. We were unable to find any information on these interesting animals despite an extensive literature search.

Similar species: None. The general appearance is quite distinctive.

Fig. 104. A green June beetle (*Cotinis nitida*) on loblolly pine.

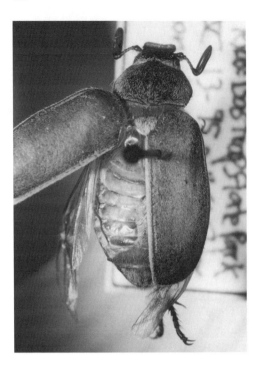

Fig. 105. Nettle scarab
(*Hypothyce* of undetermined
species).

black tumbling flower beetle (fig. 106)
Mordella melaena

Biology: Adults feed on pollen and are often seen in numbers within the bowl-shaped yellow cactus flowers of spring. When disturbed the small, slender, hump-backed creatures tumble off the flower to the ground. Based upon published studies of related species, the poorly known grubs could be predators, parasites, or even herbivores.

Distribution: From coast to coast within the United States.

Remarks: Length 6 mm. Anyone who has searched beneath a leaf or flower where beetles have employed the widely used tumbling escape strategy can attest to its effectiveness, even when it is clear that the animal landed directly below the plant.

Similar species: The various tumbling flower beetles are small and similar enough to require a microscope and the proper keys for confident identification. Some false darkling beetles resemble tumbling flower beetles, but they live on and under bark where they feed on fungi.

eight-spotted wedge-shaped beetle (fig. 107)
Macrosiagon octomaculatum

Biology: The life cycle of the wedge-shaped beetle is complex and fantastic. It begins when an adult female visits a flower where suitable host wasps will later

Fig. 106. Black tumbling flower beetles (*Mordella melaena*).
(A) on flower, upper and lower left; (B) magnified.

appear to feed on pollen and nectar. The beetle lays an egg, and from it hatches an active larva that attaches itself to a visiting wasp. By this means it is carried back to the host's nest, where it burrows into a grub. After feeding within the creature for some time, it erupts onto the skin and feeds externally until the time comes to metamorphose into an adult. We found only two wedge-shaped beetles, both of them females, and both on flowers of spotted beebalm (*Monarda punctata*). Elsewhere these beetles have been collected on milkweeds, wild buckwheat, and members of the daisy family.

Potential wasp hosts in the Lost Pines include the species *Trielis octomaculata* and *Campsomeris plumipes* (*see* scarab beetle parasites species account, chapter 4). Ironically, these wasps are parasites of beetles, but they do not attack their own enemy in kind. They feed on May beetle grubs instead.

Fig. 107. Eight-spotted wedge-shaped beetle (*Macrosiagon octomaculatum;* female).

Distribution: The eight-spotted wedge-shaped beetle occurs from the Atlantic Ocean to Arizona.

Remarks: Length 15 mm. Adults have tiny heads and resemble cows when viewed from the side.

Similar species: None.

Texas flower scarab (fig. 108)
Trichiotinus texanus

Biology: Adults eat the pollen of cactus, mint, poppy, winecup, thistle, milkweed, and many other flowers. The unknown grub stage probably lives within the trunks of decaying trees.

Distribution: Nearly endemic to Texas, according to one authority (Hoffman 1935). A more recent checklist suggests a range from the Atlantic Ocean to New Mexico, but no details are provided (Arnett 1983).

Remarks: Length 11 mm. In size, shape, color, hairiness, dusting of pollen, wariness of approach, and buzzing flight, this scarab resembles a bee, and it presumably derives some protection from the similarity. It is briefly common in spring.

Similar species: The Texas flower scarab has black wing covers, whereas those of the dark flower scarab are brown.

metallic green flower scarab (fig. 109)
Trichiotinus lunulatus

Biology: Similar to that of the Texas flower scarab.

Distribution: From the Atlantic Ocean to a western extreme in or near the Lost Pines.

Fig. 108. Texas flower scarab (*Trichiotinus texanus*).

Fig. 109. Metallic green
flower scarab
(*Trichiotinus lunulatus*).

Remarks: Length 10 mm. This is the prettiest of the flower-visiting beetles and is common for a brief period in spring.

Similar species: The green June beetle is much larger, not as shiny, and has bronzy areas in addition to metallic green.

dark flower scarab (fig. 110)

Euphoria sepulcralis

Biology: In more northern regions of the United States the adults eat goldenrod pollen; we did not see this in the southern forest. Instead they gnaw on young twigs of shrubby blackjack oaks as the leaf buds prepare to unfold in spring, and they do considerable damage to the tree in the process. Their brown coloration hides them well despite the fact that they are much wider than the little stems where they perch to feed. These scarabs defend themselves by releasing a foul odor and by feigning death, and they do not open their wing covers in flight. A groove on each side of the body allows the wings simply to slip out from underneath the covers. The grub stage probably lives in decaying wood.

Distribution: From the Atlantic Ocean to a western extreme in or near the Lost Pines.

Remarks: Length 14 mm. The bark-gnawing habit we observed is especially in-

Fig. 110. Dark flower scarab (*Euphoria sepulcralis*) feeding on
young blackjack oak twig.

teresting because it has not been reported before and because the jaws of this
species are said to be weak and even partly membranous (Dillon and Dillon
1961).

Similar species: The plains bumble scarab is more colorful, with some degree of
orange on its wing covers.

plains bumble scarab
Euphoria kernii

Biology: Adults eat flower pollen in the forest and a close relative becomes a pest
elsewhere when it feeds upon corn, peaches, grapes, and apples. The grubs probably live in decomposing logs, leaf litter, and dung.

Distribution: From the central Great Plains to at least as far south as Central
Texas.

Remarks: Length 12 mm. Adults defend themselves with a foul-smelling odor
that has been compared to chlorine. When flying they buzz like bees, and like the
dark flower scarab they fly without opening their wing covers.

Similar species: The Plains bumble scarab has orange on its wing covers but the
dark flower scarab does not.

Texas stillingia beetle (fig. 111)

Typocerus lunulatus texanus

Biology: The Texas stillingia beetle is a pollen-eating longhorned woodborer that has never been reported from stillingia flowers until now. This is worth noting because in the eastern United States adults feed on a variety of flowers, while in the Lost Pines they seem strongly tied to this single food source and never appear in numbers until *Stillingia sylvatica* (queen's delight) blooms in the meadows and powerline cuts. At that time nearly every plant seems to have one or more of the active black and yellow animals clambering about in search of pollen and mates. Whether coupled or alone the beetles are wary and fly off like wasps when approached. The host plant of the grub stage is unknown, but it probably lives in stumps of oak and pine.

Distribution: Texas stillingia beetles occur from the Atlantic Ocean to a western limit in or near the Lost Pines.

Remarks: Length 10 mm. Specimens from this forest were among those studied when the Texas subspecies was originally made known to science.

Similar species: None.

Fig. 111. A Texas stillingia beetle (*Typocerus lunulatus texanus*)
on stillingia (queen's delight).

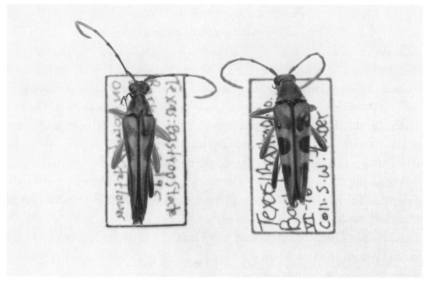

Fig. 112. Virile strangalia beetle (*Strangalia virilis*); male on left, female on right.

virile strangalia beetle (fig. 112)
Strangalia virilis

Biology: This is a longhorned woodborer that feeds on flower pollen in the adult stage. The wasplike red and yellow beetle is usually found on red and yellow *Coreopsis* flowers when these plants bloom in May and June. The grub stage lives within the trunks of oak trees.

Distribution: Known only from Texas and Oklahoma.

Remarks: Length 18 mm. Adult virile strangalia beetles rise in red and yellow clouds when they are disturbed while visiting the abundance of wildflowers growing along the roadsides of the forest.

Similar species: One or two closely related species may occur in the Lost Pines, but the male virile strangalia beetle is identified by the strongly swollen tip of its abdomen. No other species has this feature.

clown weevils (fig. 113)
Eudiagogus pulcher, E. rosenschoeldi

Biology: These two pink and black weevils are abundant on *Sesbania* plants that grow along roadsides and especially along pond margins and in floodplains. The hosts of *E. pulcher* are *Sesbania vesicaria, S. macrocarpa* (which we did not see in the forest), and *S. drummondii*. Rosenschoeld's clown weevil feeds on the first two species but not the last. Adults of both weevil species feed on foliage and can

Fig. 113. (A) A clown weevil
(*Eudiagogus pulcher*); (B) Rosenschoeld's
clown weevil (*E. rosenschoeldi*) defoliating
its *Sesbania* host plant.

occur in numbers great enough to strip the plant of its leaves. Females lay their eggs on the lower parts of the shoot. When the grubs hatch they move underground and feed on root nodules where these legumes harbor symbiotic nitrogen-fixing bacteria (Kovarik and Burke 1989).

Distribution: *Eudiagogus pulcher* occurs from coast to coast within the United States. *Eudiagogus rosenschoeldi* occurs from the Atlantic Ocean to Texas, perhaps not far west of the Lost Pines.

Remarks: Length 7 mm. These beetles are conspicuous on their host plants and are seen as mating pairs more often than any other animal in the forest. In the rich growth of *Sesbania vesicaria* along the shores of the small artificial lake in Bastrop State Park both species were often found just inches apart on the same plant.

Similar species: None. *Eudiagogus pulcher* has black, even-margined patches of color on its pinkish back, whereas the black patches of *E. rosenschoeldi* have highly irregular outlines.

goldenrod blister beetle
Epicauta pennsylvanica

Biology: This slender black beetle is named for its habit of feeding on the pollen of goldenrod flowers, and appropriately enough we encountered the animal for the first time in a small patch of goldenrods consisting of only a few dozen plants. There were no other goldenrods in sight, and we seldom saw the flower elsewhere in the forest. Later we did observe a few goldenrod blister beetles on other wildflowers in a powerline cut. Adults become pests beyond the confines of the forest when they feed on potatoes and beets. The grub stage lives in the soil and eats grasshopper eggs. The grubs do this after crawling out of the soil nest where the female beetle laid her eggs. Upon finding a pod of grasshopper eggs, also laid in the soil by a parent, the beetle grubs pierce one egg after another with sicklelike jaws and consume up to twenty-seven eggs during their development. If two grubs find themselves positioned at the same place on a pod of hopper eggs, they bite one another with their sharp jaws until one is dead or both (Horsfall 1941).

Distribution: The goldenrod blister beetle occurs from the Atlantic Ocean to the Rocky Mountains.

Remarks: Length 11 mm. Blister beetles are named for an ability to raise blisters on human skin when the disturbed animal releases a defensive fluid from the joints of its legs.

Similar species: Black is a common color for blister beetles. Confident identification requires a microscope and the proper keys.

elm leaf beetle
Calligrapha scalaris

Biology: Adults feed on the leaves of slippery elm (*Ulmus rubra*) and do much damage in the process. They overwinter in a bark crevice or underground. Their grubs also feed on elm leaves, and as a result the tree must bear an assault from both stages of the insect's life cycle.

Distribution: From the Atlantic Ocean to Texas, perhaps with a western limit somewhere near the Lost Pines.

Remarks: Length 9 mm. The elms of the Lost Pines grow near water, and this is where the beetle will be found. The species is reportedly uncommon, but in Central Texas it is abundant both within the forest and beyond its borders in the city of Austin thirty miles to the northwest.

Similar species: None.

pollen-eating beetle (fig. 114)
Heliocis repanda

Biology: Previously unknown. Because the animal is locally abundant in the Lost Pines (but apparently uncommon elsewhere), we are able to say that the adults feed on the pollen of wildflowers, shrubs, and trees. The hop-tree is a favorite. In spring a single plant may play host to dozens of the little purple and red "false blister beetles" crawling and flying over its green leaves and white flowers. The grub stage is unknown but probably lives in decaying wood or beneath the bark of a living tree.

Distribution: Very unusually distributed, with isolated records from Texas, Florida, Washington, D.C., Arizona, and Utah.

Remarks: Length 7 mm. The Lost Pines would be a fine place to uncover the

Fig. 114. Pollen-eating beetle
(*Heliocis repanda*).

details of this interesting animal's biology because it occurs reliably in huge numbers in spring.

Similar species: Other small purple and red beetles are easily confused with this one; we nearly mistook it for other species on several occasions. Confident identification requires a microscope and the proper keys.

fern soldier beetle (fig. 115)
Malthinus difficilis

Biology: Apparently unknown. We found the tiny species on bracken fern in April and at no other time and on no other plants, though its closest relatives have been found on oak, juniper, and elm. Perhaps they prey upon even smaller insects in the manner of many other soldier beetles.

Distribution: From the Atlantic Ocean to a western limit somewhere in Texas.

Remarks: Length 3 mm. The short wing cover tipped with sordid yellow swellings is a distinctive feature. If we had not beaten green bracken ferns in spring with our nets we would never have seen this cryptic animal.

Similar species: *Malthinus occipitalis* and *M. difficilis* are closely related and have a similar range, making the two species difficult to separate (Wittmer 1980). Perhaps the Lost Pines species is the former rather than the latter. Keys do not allow as much confidence in the ID as one would like.

Fig. 115. Fern soldier beetle
(*Malthinus difficilis*).

spotted cucumber beetle
Diabrotica undecimpunctata

Biology: The small green and black adults fly so slowly that their extended wing covers are visible and they seem at first glance to be parachuting rather than engaging in powered flight. They eat leaves whereas the grubs, known as "southern corn rootworms," eat the roots of various plants. Outside the forest this beetle is ranked among the ten worst insect pests in the United States (White 1983) and does its damage in both active stages of the life cycle. Leaves of melons and cucumbers are among the adult's favorite foods. In fall it appears on goldenrod.

Distribution: Spotted cucumber beetles occur from coast to coast within the United States.

Remarks: Length 7 mm. The abundance of the spotted cucumber beetle in the Lost Pines is especially noteworthy because we saw only a single individual of the cucumber family during our exploration of the forest, and that sole representative, possibly introduced, was growing in a highly disturbed garbage dump.

Similar species: None.

zebra longhorned borer (fig. 116)
Typocerus zebra

Biology: Adults feed on the pollen of various flowers and fly off when approached. They are found on leaves more often than most other pollen feeders. The grub stage probably feeds within dead loblolly pines, the first record of a host species for this insect.

Distribution: From the Atlantic Ocean to East Texas, according to the standard reference (Linsley and Chemsak 1976). Our Lost Pines record appears to be the westernmost locality reported to this date.

Remarks: Length 13 mm. A nearly identical borer has been partly responsible for the devastation of a beloved shade tree in the eastern United States. The damage it does to the chestnut's bark allows the spores of a blight fungus to enter and kill the tree. No chestnuts grow in the Lost Pines forest.

Similar species: Other beetles have similar beautiful color patterns but none are likely to be confused with this one.

Texas milkweed beetle
Tetraopes texanus

Biology: This red and black longhorned beetle is more strongly tied to a single type of plant in all active stages of its life cycle than are most members of the huge woodborer family. That fact is all the more remarkable because the plants are herbaceous milkweeds that are toxic to most animals by way of defensive chemicals contained in milky latex exuded when the plant is damaged by feeding. Adult beetles eat leaves and flowers; eggs are laid in dry, dead stems of a previous year's growth; and the newly hatched grubs eat milkweed roots after dropping from the stem to the ground below. The inactive pupa lies in the soil and is the only stage of the life cycle with no direct connection to the host.

Distribution: The Texas milkweed beetle was known only from Texas and Oklahoma until disjunct populations were reported as far east as Missouri (Rice 1988) and Mississippi and Alabama (Schiefer 1998).

Fig. 116. A zebra longhorn borer (*Typocerus zebra*) on black willow.

Remarks: Length 14 mm. The milkweed *Asclepias asperula* is reported here for the first time as a host of the Texas milkweed beetle. The insect is not immune to the plant's defensive latex but avoids it by snipping a leaf vein to bleed the toxins away while it moves aside to feed on a portion of the leaf now incapable of receiving the fluid's protection. If the latex should befoul the beetle's jaws, it dries to a clear rubber and the animal starves to death (Dussourd and Eisner 1987).

Texas milkweed beetles display the red and black warning colors so common among insects that sting animals or feed upon toxic plants. Another interesting feature is the four-eyed appearance caused by the position of its antennae, which divide the two true compound eyes into sections.

Similar species: This animal can easily be confused with the western milkweed beetle (*see* species account), but the tips of the Texas species' antennae are sharply pointed whereas those of the western species are blunt.

western milkweed beetle (fig. 117)
Tetraopes femoratus

Biology: Similar to that of the Texas milkweed beetle. We found the western milkweed beetle in spring, summer, and fall. The autumn discovery was a group of about half a dozen adults feeding on the foliage of an unidentified milkweed that was not flowering at the time. Most of the beetles were near the base of the plant and nearly hidden by foliage.

Distribution: This is one of the relatively few western insects of the forest, ranging from the Pacific Ocean to a new eastern record for Texas in the Lost Pines. In more northern states the animal occurs as far east as Tennessee and Ohio (Ode 1980).

Fig. 117. A western milkweed beetle (*Tetraopes femoratus*) on its host plant.

Remarks: Length 14 mm. This is the first record of the western milkweed beetle from the milkweed species *Asclepias asperula*.

Similar species: The blunted antenna tips distinguish this species from the Texas milkweed beetle with its pointed antennae.

red and black sumac borer
Oberea ocellata

Biology: The grub stage of this slender and brightly colored longhorned beetle bores in a wide variety of plants, including flowering dogwood, red mulberry, oak, perhaps blackberry, at least three sumac species (*Rhus copallina, R. glabra,* and *R. typhina*), and poison sumac (*Toxicodendron vernix*) (Linsley and Chemsak 1995). The last three plant species do not occur in the forest. Dewberry is a possible host because the insects were once swept from related blackberries in the eastern United States. Some of the trees on this list are abundant in the Lost Pines and we are puzzled by the fact that we encountered only a single specimen of the borer. This was a female snatched from the air as she flew through a powerline cut.

Adult females girdle the growing tips of sumac stems and lay an egg there. The grub hatches out, bores into the stem, and moves down into the root system, girdling the plant near the ground. Eventually the stem is cut off, plugged with frass (insect solid waste), and used as a pupation site (Craighead 1950).

Distribution: From the Atlantic Ocean to Texas, perhaps not far west of the Lost Pines.

Remarks: Length 13 mm. The red and black warning colors may be associated with life in sumac species, some of which could be toxic to the beetle's predatory enemies.

Similar species: None.

fire-collared longhorned beetle (fig. 118)
Batyle ignicollis ignicollis

Biology: This is a beautiful red and metallic blue beetle that arouses interest because its different subspecies use host plants as distantly related as pine and sumac (Linsley 1962). We found only the nominate subspecies in the Lost Pines, but we did manage to collect both sexes. Grubs of this type bore in the stems of sumac and other herbaceous plants, whereas those of a different subspecies bore in pine branches (Yanega 1996). Our specimens were adults found in early April on the leaves of scrubby blackjack oaks in a powerline cut.

Distribution: The subspecies treated here has an unusual inland distribution from the Rocky Mountains in the west to Missouri in the east.

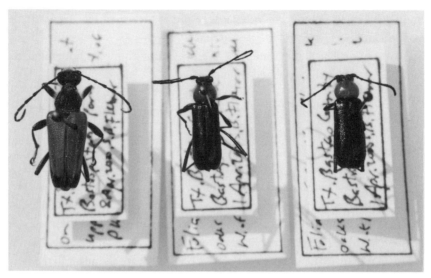

**Fig. 118. Left: Little hickory borer (*Trigonarthris proxima;* female).
Center and right: Fire-collared longhorned beetle (*Batyle ignicollis*);
male at center, female on right.**

Remarks: Length 11 mm. We found only a very few individuals. The female has a more thoroughly red collar than the male.
Similar species: None.

red and black oak borer (fig. 119)
Leptura emarginata
Biology: The adults are large, attractive, longhorned beetles that resemble big spider wasps in size, color, and even in the manner of their flight. They presumably eat wildflower pollen if they feed at all, but this is one species that seems to stay within the timber, never straying to the meadows and powerline cuts where wildflowers grow in abundance. The grub stage bores in the wood of dead oak trees, including the black oaks native to the Lost Pines (Proceedings 1914), and the elms that grow along the artificial ponds. A female was seen by another observer in a different part of the country in the act of laying eggs in the wood of a living beech tree, but this borer is too rare to be ranked as a pest of any tree.
Distribution: From the Atlantic Ocean to a western limit in or near the Lost Pines.
Remarks: Length 32 mm. We saw only three of these impressive animals. They were all caught while flying among the trees and were never seen at rest.
Similar species: Only one beetle resembles this one enough in both color and

size to cause confusion. *Leptura gigas* is known in the United States from Texas and from no other state, and the few specimens taken elsewhere by others were captured in flight, just as we captured all of our *L. emarginata* specimens in flight. *Leptura gigas* chooses willow rather than oak and should occur in the Lost Pines, according to a published distribution map, but we never saw it flying or crawling among the black willows of the artificial ponds. Others wishing to attract these two rare species might try applying a concoction of fermenting syrup-bait to the bark of trees. Confident separation requires close examination and the proper identification keys.

A much smaller and similarly scarce beetle resembles *Leptura emarginata* in shape and color but it is less than one inch long. We found a single female of this species, the little hickory borer (*Trigonarthris proxima,* fig. 118; length 12 mm), on black willow flowers in early April. It has been reported from dogwood and chestnut but not from willow before now, and not from a month as early as April. Adults also fly to blacklights, though we never saw one at ours. The grub stage feeds within decaying hardwoods including hickory (Yanega 1996). This attractive little animal occurs from the Atlantic Ocean to a western limit somewhere in Texas, perhaps in or near the Lost Pines.

gray and black longhorned beetle
Acanthocinus nodosus

Biology: Details of the attractive adult's biology seem to be unknown. The grub stage is actually a *bark-feeding* "woodborer" that lives in dead or dying pines. This is the first record of the species from loblolly.

Fig. 119. Red and black oak borer (*Leptura emarginata*), an apparent wasp mimic.

Distribution: From the Atlantic Ocean to a western limit in the Lost Pines.
Remarks: Length 23 mm. Males have enormously long antennae that can exceed three times the length of the body.
Similar species: Each wing cover bears a distinct, velvety black, arrowhead-shaped patch displayed by no other beetle in the forest.

southern pine sawyer
Monochamus titillator

Biology: Adults eat pine needles and twigs. Females are attracted to loblollies that have been attacked by bark beetles (Dodds and Stephen 2000). They lay eggs in bark tissue and upon hatching, the grubs bore in dead and dying pines and in doing so they become pests of lumber.
Distribution: Southern pine sawyers occur from the Atlantic Ocean to Texas where the Lost Pines seems to mark the new western record for the species.
Remarks: Length 25 mm. The common name "sawyer" refers to the sawing sound made by the grubs as they chew away inside the pine tree's trunk.
Similar species: The robust oak borer (*see* species account) is similar in appearance, and a reference should be consulted to distinguish them (Yanega 1996).

robust oak borer
Enaphalodes atomarius

Biology: The adult's biology appears to be unknown. Grubs bore within dead oaks, hickories, hackberries, and perhaps plum, all of which grow in the Lost Pines.
Distribution: From the Atlantic Ocean to Arizona, though more common in the East than in the West.
Remarks: Length 24 mm. This and many of the other woodborers treated here were encountered by good fortune and might have been missed altogether but for a forest fire that damaged a small section of the Lost Pines in the spring of 1999. Woodboring beetles in particular appeared in greater numbers than usual because they lay eggs in damaged, dying, and dead trees. They might have been too few and far between for us to encounter by chance under any other circumstances. The fire was generally considered a minor disaster for the usual reasons, but for our biodiversity survey it was good fortune indeed.
Similar species: *See* southern pine sawyer.

spined twig girdler (fig. 120)
Psyrassa pertenuis

Biology: This small, red-brown, and very attractive longhorned woodborer presumably spends its larval life tunneling in twigs of hickory and perhaps oak, but

Fig. 120. Spined twig girdler (*Psyrassa pertenuis*).

this presumption is based upon scant knowledge of its close relatives. The biology of the spined twig girdler itself appears to be largely unknown. Our single specimen was attracted to a blacklight trap at night.

Distribution: The Lost Pines apparently marks the western limit of a range that extends east to the Atlantic Ocean (Yanega 1996).

Remarks: Length 10 mm. The identification of the beetle proved difficult even when illustrations and the formal, published keys were consulted.

Similar species: Several species of the genus *Psyrassa* occur in the United States, and some are quite similar in appearance. Formal keys are necessary to separate one from another. We thank Dr. John Chemsak for confirming our identification.

pine bark runner
Xylotrechus sagittatus

Biology: The agile adult beetles crawl at night on the bark of fire-damaged or fire-killed loblolly pines. Sometimes they crawl or fly to blacklight traps. Females lay their eggs in the bark and the grubs feed in sapwood before tunneling deeper into the tree. Once there they tend to confine their activities to a single annual ring. The pupal stage is also passed in the tree rather than in the soil below. Newly formed adults leave the pine by chewing their way to the surface (Gardiner 1957). Pine bark runners are known from spruce, fir, hemlock, and a variety of pines; this appears to be the first record of the species from loblolly.

Distribution: From the Atlantic Ocean to Arizona. The animal has apparently not been reported from Central Texas until now.

Remarks: Length 17 mm. *Xylotrechus* means "wood runner." These insects are indeed quick on their feet, and they are the fastest longhorned beetles we encountered in the Lost Pines. When running at night they may at first glance be mistaken for crickets.

Similar species: None.

Fig. 121. Texas short-winged woodborer (*Methia constricticollis*).

Texas short-winged woodborer (fig. 121)
Methia constricticollis

Biology: Our single specimen flew to a blacklight trap in late August. The previously recorded host plants for the Texas short-winged woodborer are *Celtis pallida* (desert hackberry), *Prosopis glandulosa* (honey mesquite), and *Zanthoxylum fagara* (Linsley and Chemsak 1997). Of these three species only the mesquite occurs in the Lost Pines. However, the forest is home to three plants closely related to the other two known hosts. These are the smooth hackberry, *Celtis laevigata;* rough hackberry, *C. reticulata;* and Hercules-club, *Zanthoxylum clava-herculis.*

Distribution: This is a rare Texas endemic previously known only from Brownsville and perhaps neighboring areas in the extreme southern part of the state (Linsley 1962). It may also occur in Mexico across the Rio Grande. Our Lost Pines record thus marks the northern limit of the animal's range as currently understood.

Remarks: Length 7 mm. This tiny longhorned beetle with its remarkably short wing covers is a rarely encountered species. We are unaware of any previous photographs of it or of any of the other members of its genus, with the exception of *M. pusilla* (Yanega 1996). All are considered to be quite uncommon.

Similar species: None in the area according to our experience. We thank Dr. John Chemsak for help in identifying this interesting animal.

tile-horned prionus beetle (fig. 122)
Prionus imbricornis

Biology: Huge, drooping, antlerlike antennae and a dark brown body distinguish this big impressive beetle from all others in the forest. Adult females lay

Fig. 122. Tile-horned prionus beetle
(*Prionus imbricornis*).

their eggs near the base of a plant and the grubs that hatch from those eggs are roundheaded borers that typically tunnel their way through the living roots of oaks, chestnuts, grape, pear, and corn (Yanega 1996). Of these plants only oaks and several grape species occur in the Lost Pines. Several years of feeding and tunneling culminate in transformation to the adult stage in oval pupation cells near the surface of the soil.

Distribution: The tile-horned prionus ranges from the Atlantic Ocean to a western limit in or near the Lost Pines of Texas.

Remarks: Length 36 mm. We encountered a single specimen of this exotic-looking creature. It was crawling on the sandstone wall of one of the Depression era cabins of Bastrop State Park. We never saw it under natural conditions.

Similar species: A closely related species (*Prionus debilis*) is smaller and paler and probably occurs in the forest, though we never saw it.

banded checkered beetle
Cymatodera undulata

Biology: Adult banded checkered beetles are attractive, nocturnal, predatory animals that crawl on the bark of pines and oaks and sometimes fly to blacklights at night. If what is known about certain related species applies to this one as well, then they probably roam stems and trunks where they prey on gall wasps (Dillon and Dillon 1961). Based upon our frequent sightings we assumed that banded checkered grubs develop only in trees, and elsewhere they have been collected on maples (Blatchley 1910). Yet according to the old but standard reference on the identification of *Cymatodera* species in the United States, this species was once reared from stems of *Bidens bipinnata* in Missouri (Wolcott 1922). This is a herbaceous plant.

Distribution: The banded checkered beetle occurs from the Atlantic Ocean to Arizona.

Remarks: Length 10 mm. This is the only adult checkered beetle that we noticed in the Lost Pines. It has a very elongate, nearly cylindrical body.

Similar species: At least twenty-one closely related species occur in Texas. We have seen only this one, and the three dark bands of each wing cover are useful guides to identification. The Texas A&M University insect collection contains similar specimens from the Lost Pines identified as *Cymatodera balteata*.

bronze woodborer
Chalcophora virginiensis

Biology: At more than one inch in length this beautiful bronzy beetle is the largest member of the flatheaded woodborer family occurring in the United States. The color and the sculptured body provide camouflage when adults mate and perch on loblolly pines, where the female lays her eggs in wounds and cracks in the rough bark. When the grubs hatch they mine for several years within the trunk to depths as great as the heartwood.

Distribution: Bronze woodborers occur from the Atlantic Ocean to a western limit in Texas, perhaps in or near the Lost Pines. There is a questionable record from Idaho.

Remarks: Length 25 mm. Adults buzz loudly as they fly among the pines, and they perch like sunning lizards on the loblolly's bark.

Similar species: None. The close relatives of this beetle are all easily distinguished by their smaller size and different coloration. They include the lined buprestid (*Buprestis lineata*), the yellow-spotted buprestid (*Buprestis maculipennis*), the smaller flatheaded borers (*Chrysobothris dentipes, C. floricola*), the yellow flower buprestids (*Acmaeodera pulchella, A. obtusa, A. neglecta, A. ornata*), the oak leaf-mining buprestid beetle (*Brachys ovatus*) and its relatives *Brachys tessellatus* and *B. aerosus,* and finally the tick clover leaf-mining buprestid beetle (*Pachyschelus laevigatus*), which at a length of a mere two millimeters is the smallest of all.

More than thirty close relatives of these beetles, all members of the flatheaded woodborer family, are known to occur in Texas. Confident identification requires a microscope and formal keys. One infamous pest species is the apple tree borer (*Chrysobothris femorata*) that is said to attack virtually all fruit, shade, and forest trees. We never saw it in the Lost Pines.

Haldeman's ironclad beetle (fig. 123)
Zopherus haldemani

Biology: Essentially unknown. We and other workers have collected adults on dead oak trees. Adults, grubs, and pupae were once found on a pecan tree, but pecans do not occur at our forest study site.

Distribution: This is a Texas species found nowhere else in the United States but in the central and eastern part of the state between Kerrville and Houston, with one outlying record farther west (Triplehorn 1972). Because it also occurs in Mexico it cannot be described as a Texas endemic. This limited range is shared by several grasshoppers, mantids, and cockroaches and suggests a history of grassland expansions and contractions associated with ice ages and the evolution of the Great Plains.

Remarks: Length 25 mm. The ironclad is named for an exoskeleton so tough that entomologists sometimes drill a small hole in a wing cover to accept an insect pin that otherwise might bend or break but never penetrate. This raises a second interesting fact. Though the ironclad has wing covers as seen in other beetles, it has no wings beneath them to protect, and the covers are locked shut. In 1976 this beetle was chosen as the official mascot of the Southwestern Entomological Society, and it has appeared on the covers of the society's journal ever since.

Similar species: No other animal in the Lost Pines has a color pattern resembling the ink blots of a Rorschach personality test.

Fig. 123. Haldeman's ironclad beetle (*Zopherus haldemani*); mating pair.

horned fungus beetle (fig. 124)
Bolitotherus cornutus

Biology: Adults are nocturnal consumers of the fungi growing on decomposing oak logs. They resemble little chips of bark and might be mistaken for the same. Males have two small horns on the head. Females lack horns altogether. Both sexes protect themselves by hiding in bark crevices and by feigning death when disturbed. The grub's diet is the same as that of the adult.

Distribution: From the Atlantic Ocean to a western limit in or near the Lost Pines.

Remarks: Length 11 mm. We found a single specimen, a female, in a decomposing oak log.

Similar species: None.

patent leather beetle (fig. 125)
Odontotaenius disjunctus

Biology: The patent leather beetle's life history is remarkable because this very large species lives in loose societies within decomposing logs of post oak and blackjack. All stages of the life cycle are present: eggs, grubs, pupae, and adults. Members of the society communicate by making vibrations that we perceive as sound. The adults generate creaking, hissing noises when they rub the abdomen against the overlying wings, which in turn lie beneath protective covers. The covers seldom open because this beetle rarely uses its large, well-developed wings

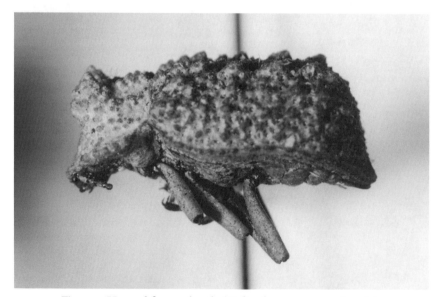

Fig. 124. Horned fungus beetle (*Bolitotherus cornutus;* female).

Fig. 125. Patent leather beetle (*Odontotaenius disjunctus*), (A) adult; (B) grubs collected from decomposing hardwood log.

to fly and usually walks wherever it goes. Grubs are of course forced to use a different set of organs for making sounds. The third pair of legs is reduced to a pair of stumps that scratch against the more typical legs just in front. These stumps are shaped like tiny bear paws. Stridulation also deters predation by crows (Buchler et al. 1981).

Female patent leather beetles carry their eggs in their jaws while searching for a suitable place to set them down if human investigators create unnatural conditions in the laboratory. Both sexes feed the grubs indirectly by plastering tunnels inside the log with chewed-up pieces of wood. Grubs eat the pulp as they crawl about, and both they and the adults eat termites and cannibalize injured juveniles.

When the grub is ready to become an adult it makes a depression in the soft wood of a tunnel floor by rolling back and forth like a buffalo in its wallow. Then it crawls into the depression and is covered over with wood and/or mud by the adults. This protects the soft, vulnerable pupa from being trampled or eaten by other members of the society. Grubs will accept a hollow made by the pressure of a human thumb (Gray 1946). When metamorphosis is complete, the insect appears in beautiful but temporary colors of orange and white that soon change to shiny black as the exoskeleton hardens. Every adult seems to harbor numerous mites that crawl about on the undersurface and cling to the mouth area.

Distribution: Patent leather beetles range from the Atlantic Ocean to a western limit near the Lost Pines.

Remarks: Length 34 mm. Our experience suggests that loblolly pines are never colonized in Central Texas, though these are obviously abundant and the beetle occasionally colonizes them in the eastern United States. Dispersal from one log to another presumably occurs by overland march since the wings are seldom used for flight. In fact, there are only two reports of flight in this species. One of them was a mating flight with both sexes united (Macgown and Macgown 1996).

Midwestern children of bygone days amused themselves with the black beetle known to them as "the horn" in reference to the small tubercle which all adults bear on the head. One end of a string was tied to the horn and the other end to some object for the beast of burden to tow. Experiments later showed that patent leather beetles can haul seven pounds, or three thousand times their own weight (Hinds 1901). Other common names for the patent leather beetle are "pegbug," "Betsy beetle," "Bess beetle," and "horned passalus."
Similar species: None.

spotted grapevine beetle (fig. 126)
Pelidnota punctata
Biology: Adults eat grape leaves and become pests in the eastern United States where the plants are grown commercially. They also feed on Virginia creeper, which is a close relative of the grape and is plentiful in the Lost Pines. Though we never saw adults during the daylight hours, they are said to fly during the day from vine to vine, making a loud buzzing sound (Saunders 1874). The grubs are not harmful because they live in stumps and decaying roots of oak, hackberry, and elm.

Fig. 126. Spotted grape-vine beetle (*Pelidnota punctata*).

Fig. 127. A loving scarab
(*Phileurus truncatus*).

Distribution: From the Atlantic Ocean to a western limit along the Rio Grande River near Del Rio, Texas.

Remarks: Length 21 mm. This large and attractive beetle is curiously scarce considering the abundance of grapes in the forest and the fact that elsewhere it becomes a pest when the vine is plentiful. We never saw them under natural conditions but only when a total of a mere half dozen or so flew to our blacklights at night over the years. The same was true of our experience in the Ottine swamp of Gonzales County. Living specimens should be handled with care because the sharp claws can pierce the skin like fishhooks.

Similar species: None.

loving scarabs (fig. 127)
Phileurus truncatus, P. valgus

Biologies: Little is known about the biologies of these rare and rather exotic scarab beetles except for the fact that *P. valgus* has been found beneath the bark of decomposing trees (Blatchley 1910) and *P. truncatus* in dead oaks (Glaser 1976). Both sexes of both species can exceed one inch in length and each individual has three small horns, two projecting from the head and one just behind. They probably make noises by rubbing certain body parts together because they bear structures known to have this function in other beetles. We never saw either species under natural conditions. A few specimens flew to our blacklights at night.

Distribution: Both loving scarabs occur between the Atlantic Ocean and a western limit in or near the Lost Pines.

Remarks: Typical length of *P. valgus* 20 mm; length of *P. truncatus* 32 mm. So poorly known are the loving scarabs that they do not appear in the various modern books dedicated to the beetles of the United States, and we coined the common name ourselves from a translation of the scientific name. *Phileurus valgus* is usually smaller than its close relative, and it has more obvious lines on its wing covers.

Similar species: None.

firefly
Photinus pyralis

Biology: In late May these half-inch beetles fly at dusk, emitting greenish yellow light from the abdomen. Males of this species have a dipping flight consisting of alternating climbs and drops. The light is lowest at the peaks and brightest in the valleys, thus increasing in intensity as the beetle drops and decreasing as it climbs. Females have a smaller light, fly more slowly, and often lie in vegetation, where they answer the flying male's courtship light with their own. The grub is a luminous "glowworm" that emits light near the end of its lower surface. It crawls along with pushes of its abdomen (McDermott 1910).

Distribution: From the Atlantic Ocean to Texas.

Remarks: Length 12 mm. This species, though large, is not a good one to collect in a jar for the traditional light display. Unlike some others, it stops flashing in captivity.

Similar species: The color of the flash, the flight pattern, and the large size are useful aids in the identification of this species. Other fireflies occur in the forest.

little Texas glowworm (fig. 128)
Distremocephalus texanus

Biology: Poorly known. In 1881 J.L. LeConte, the greatest nineteenth-century authority on American beetles, wrote one of the few reports on this species. By lamplight a male ran across a table, twisting its wings in a peculiar fashion as if trying to straighten them out. When we captured several specimens at our blacklights on two occasions nearly 120 years later, we saw the same phenomenon. But we did not see any light shining from within the head, nor did we see any at the back end of the little animal, as LeConte reported. However, we did see this exactly as LeConte described it while examining a specimen from the Ottine swamp in south-central Texas. The grub also shines with a weak light, and it eats snails (apparently in captivity; LeConte 1881).

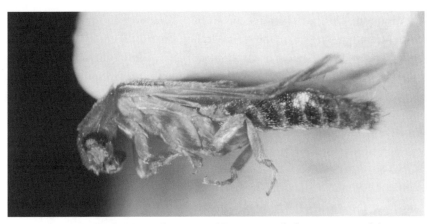

Fig. 128. Little Texas glowworm (*Distremocephalus texanus*, male).

Distribution: In the United States the little Texas glowworm has been reported only from Texas and Nevada (Zaragoza 1986), though we saw mention of it in a webpage devoted to New Mexico beetles. Specimens in the Texas A&M University insect collection suggest that the range of the species in Texas extends from the Panhandle area to the extreme south and then on into Mexico.

Remarks: Length 6 mm. If LeConte's remark of 1881 still holds then the female sex remains unknown.

Similar species: None.

Texas rain beetle (fig. 129)
Scaptolenus ocreatus

Biology: Entirely unknown. Its close relatives are called rain beetles because males fly in search of mates during heavy downpours (Werner 1969). The habits of this species are presumably similar, though it was not raining when all but one of the few living specimens that we collected flew to our blacklights at night. The single exception flew during a rainy period but at a time when it was misting lightly at best.

Fig. 129. Texas rain beetle (*Scaptolenus ocreatus*, male).

Distribution: This rare species seems to be a Texas endemic and has been reported from nowhere else in the world. In fact, our Lost Pines record appears to be the first and only report of a specific collection locality beyond the simple mention of "Texas" when the animal was first made known to science in 1881. With this in mind we visited the Texas A&M University insect collection and found specimens from Bexar County, Hidalgo County, San Patricio County, and Victoria County. All these counties are in the southern part of Texas, and our own records represent the northernmost limit of the species as currently known. It thus appears that the Texas rain beetle is confined not just to Texas but to its southern region in particular. Several rain beetles from southern Arizona are also housed in the A&M collection in a box labeled "*Scaptolenus ocreatus*," but the validity of that identification is unclear. The yet unidentified specimens from Brazos County, where the collection itself is located, might well be *Scaptolenus ocreatus*.

Remarks: Length 15 mm. All of our specimens are males. The female sex remains unknown. Several individuals came to our blacklight traps at night, but a similar number were found already dead and in pieces. One dead beetle was hanging from a spider's web and another was lying beneath a decomposing branch on the forest floor.

Male rain beetles are remarkable in appearance as well as behavior. They have ominous-looking jaws shaped like tongs and patches of "hair" resembling mammal fur.

Similar species: LeConte's rain beetle (*Scaptolenus lecontei*) occurs in nearby Austin. We never saw this rare species in the Lost Pines, nor have we seen the Lost Pines species in the city. LeConte's rain beetle is reddish brown in sharp contrast to the very dark brown of the Texas rain beetle, and males do fly in the rain as expected.

glowworm (fig. 130)
Phengodes ?frontalis

Biology: Glowworms are named for an eerie light emitted by the predatory grub stage, which dwells in leaf litter, as does the wingless, grublike adult female. This bioluminescence arises from a series of orange spots (Arnett 1960). We saw only the adult males in the Lost Pines and this only because they are winged and fly to blacklights at night. They are remarkable for their antlerlike antennae, jaws shaped like tongs, black wings largely unshielded by wing covers, and for the orange-red, wormlike body. The importance of artificial sources of ultraviolet light to a survey of animal biodiversity within the confines of a forest can hardly be overestimated.

Fig. 130. Two glowworm beetles (*Phengodes* spp.; males).

Distribution: The distribution of this species is unclear.

Remarks: Length 19 mm. Our identification of the glowworm is tentative because we found the published key difficult to understand. We based the decision upon apparently identical specimens we saw in the Texas A&M collection, also collected in Bastrop County. When restrained between the fingers, the beetle does not bite straight down but stretches its neck backward as if to bite its own back and feebly nips the handler's flesh with tonglike jaws.

Similar species: We have a few specimens of a second *Phengodes,* smaller in size, and with wings of a much lighter color. Similar specimens are housed in the Texas A&M insect collection, where they also remain unidentified. In a broad sense they are all from Central Texas localities: Stephenville, Kerrville, Austin, Lost Maples, Fort Hood, San Antonio, and Bastrop. The identification of *Phengodes* species requires male specimens, a microscope, and the proper identification keys (Wittmer 1975). The task is difficult under the best of circumstances. True glowworms are not to be confused with fireflies (lightning bugs), which are also beetles that emit light.

leaf-rolling weevil (fig. 131)
Homoeolabus analis

Biology: The brightly colored female takes position near the base of a young blackjack oak leaf, chews from the midrib vein to the edge on each side, folds the leaf with the midvein acting as the crease, and lays an egg near the tip. She then

Fig. 131. The leaf-rolling weevil (*Homoeolabus analis*), (A) adult; (B) adult female rolling blackjack leaf.

rolls up the leaf from tip to base and chews the petiole so that the leaf will soon dry and drop to the ground, where the grub will eat the leaf. This complicated behavior suggests that growing grubs eat drying leaves rather than fresh ones. Transformation to the adult stage occurs in the remains of the leaf or in the soil nearby (Edwards 1949). When adults are approached they roll off the leaf to the ground below and become very difficult to find despite their bright red and black color.

Distribution: From the Atlantic Ocean to a western limit somewhere in Texas.

Remarks: Length 6 mm. This robust weevil is brightly colored in red and black as if to warn potential predators of distastefulness, but for all we know the animal is bluffing, because oaks are not known as toxic host plants. Adults appear briefly in spring when oak leaves are tender. They are usually given the scientific name *Attelabus analis* rather than the name used here.

Similar species: None.

Carolina whirligig beetle
Dineutus carolinus

Biology: Adult whirligigs are omnivorous scavengers that skate across ponds and creeks in schools or swarms using short, oarlike legs. Each compound eye is split into an upper and lower half that allows the animal to look above and below the water's surface simultaneously. When the beetle is diving underwater, it carries a bubble of air on the belly. When disturbed while sunning themselves on logs, these beetles tumble into the water like tiny turtles. Adults are good fliers, but they never flew to our light traps. The grub stage is an aquatic predator that feeds upon other insects.

Distribution: From the Atlantic Ocean to a western limit in Texas, perhaps not far from the Lost Pines.

Remarks: Length 10 mm. These beetles are wary and difficult to catch from shore because they detect the motion of an outstretched net and skate quickly out of reach into open water. The common names "apple bug" and "sweet bug" refer to a defensive odor with the pleasant aroma of apples.

Similar species: This is the most common whirligig of the ponds and creeks and is unlikely to be confused with any other.

giant water scavenger beetle (fig. 132)
Hydrophilus triangularis

Biology: The big, shiny, convex adults are scavengers in ponds and creeks. The gilled, cannibalistic grubs are predators of animals as substantial as small fishes. Once the prey is captured they tear off and swallow "large chunks" (Edwards 1949). Adult females use structures resembling the spinnerets of spiders to make silken pouches for their eggs. The tiny larvae inside occasionally eat one another before they have a chance to escape from the waterproof case.

Fig. 132. Giant water scavenger beetle (*Hydrophilus triangularis*).

Distribution: From coast to coast within the United States.

Remarks: Length 36 mm. At more than one and one half inches, this is the largest aquatic beetle in the United States. It dwarfs the surface-dwelling whirligig but is less likely to be seen because it remains underwater except for occasional visits to the surface for air. Unlike the whirligig it does fly to lights at night. Adults bear a long sharp spine on the lower surface that can passively spear a careless handler.

Similar species: The lesser water scavenger is less than an inch in length (*see* species account), but a second relative, the ovoid water beetle (*Dibolocelus ovatus*), is nearly as large though not so narrow in shape. It occurs at least sporadically from the Atlantic Ocean to a western limit near the Lost Pines.

lesser water scavenger beetle
Hydrochara soror

Biology: The adults and the predatory grubs live in ponds. Grubs in particular dwell among aquatic plants and are difficult to see (Matta 1982). This species was described in 1980 and its biology remains largely unknown.

Distribution: The lesser water scavenger beetle occurs from the Atlantic Ocean to a western limit in Nebraska (Smetana 1980).

Remarks: Length 15 mm. We found this animal to be quite common in the ponds, where we captured adults with dip nets. They also fly to lights at night.

Similar species: The giant water scavenger beetle is much more than one inch in length but its color and habitat are similar to those of this smaller relative.

black turpentine beetle (fig. 133)
Dendroctonus terebrans

Biology: All stages of the life cycle live in concealment beneath the bark of loblolly pines. Adults colonize new trees by flying away from the host in which they developed as grubs. Black turpentine beetles usually attack weak, dying, and recently deceased trees, and they tend to mate and lay eggs in the bark near the base of the trunk. When the grubs hatch they eat their way through the inner bark and produce winding galleries as they go. This behavior makes them a pest of lumber.

Distribution: From the Atlantic Ocean to a western limit near Austin, Texas, just west of the Lost Pines.

Remarks: Length 6 mm. The presence of this bark beetle and others in an infested pine is often marked by "pitch tubes" resembling popcorn kernels. These are defensive secretions of resin oozing from entry wounds made by the parasites, and sometimes they deter or kill invaders.

Fig. 133. Black turpentine beetle (*Dendroctonus terebrans*).

Similar species: Many bark beetles are small and dark in color and in this they resemble the black turpentine beetle. Identification requires a microscope and the proper keys or at least prior experience with the same. The black turpentine beetle differs from the smaller engraver beetles by a lack of spines on the wing covers and by the ready visibility of its head when viewed from above. A much more serious pest is the southern pine beetle (*Dendroctonus frontalis*) which has not been reported from the Lost Pines. This fact is intriguing because the destructive species is known from the larger forest in eastern Texas.

six-spined engraver beetle
Ips calligraphus

Biology: Similar to that of the black turpentine beetle, though the pattern of galleries produced by the feeding grubs is different.

Distribution: From coast to coast within the United States.

Remarks: Length 5 mm. Our own experience suggests that this is the most common or at least the most apparent bark beetle enemy of the loblolly in the Lost Pines. Hundreds of adults, pupae, larvae, and eggs can often be found by peeling bark at waist level from dead and dying trees.

Similar species: The six-spined engraver beetle differs from the black turpentine beetle by the six spines located on the sloping rear end of each wing cover and by the near invisibility of the head when viewed from above. It differs from the four-spined engraver by the larger size, the presence of two additional spines on each wing cover, and by its darker color.

four-spined engraver beetle
Ips avulsus

Biology: Similar to that of the six-spined engraver beetle, though the galleries or tunnels have a different pattern and the adults tend to select trunks and branches at greater heights.

Distribution: From the Atlantic Ocean to a western limit in the Lost Pines of central Texas.

Remarks: Length 3 mm. This is a very small brown beetle that is easily over-looked.

Similar species: *See* six-spined engraver beetle.

pine bark weevil (fig. 134)
Cossonus corticola

Biology: Pine bark weevils are tiny black beetles that fly to loblolly pines when the trees are already dead or dying. They live beneath the bark in gregarious dozens but do not eat the decomposing wood itself. They eat the fungi growing on it.

Distribution: From the Atlantic Ocean to a western limit in or near the Lost Pines.

Remarks: Length 3 mm. The pine bark weevil has been reported from decomposing hardwoods elsewhere, but in this forest we have seen it only on pine.

Similar species: Weevils are notoriously difficult to identify. However, there do not appear to be any species in the Lost Pines similar enough to this one in appearance and habits to cause confusion.

metallic bark-gnawing beetle (fig. 135)
Temnochila virescens

Biology: The bright metallic green of the adult seems out of place among the typically drab beetles that live on and in the bark of trees. Metallic bark-gnawing

Fig. 134. Pine bark weevil (*Cossonus corticola*).

Fig. 135. Metallic bark-gnawing beetle; right (*Temnochila virescens*).

beetles frequent weak, dying, or dead loblollies, where the female lays her eggs in galleries made by woodboring beetles. When the grubs hatch, they prey upon the woodborer grubs after chasing them down through their own tunnels. Adults are also predatory. They eat adult woodborers as well as their grubs.

Distribution: From the Atlantic Ocean to a western limit in or near the Lost Pines.

Remarks: Length 14 mm. Adults escape capture by dropping from the tree trunk to the ground. They also inflict tenacious bites with powerful jaws. On one occasion we accidentally dropped an adult black turpentine beetle into the same vial with a metallic bark-gnawing beetle. The turpentine beetle's limbs were soon amputated.

Similar species: None.

cylindrical bark-gnawing beetle
Airora cylindrica

Biology: Similar in all respects to that of the metallic bark-gnawing beetle.

Distribution: From the Atlantic Ocean to a western limit in or near the Lost Pines.

Remarks: Length 10 mm. This animal is curious for its ability to survive for weeks in a freezer at temperatures that kill all of the other insects treated here.

Similar species: The dark brown color is very common among small tree-frequenting beetles, but this predator's nearly cylindrical shape and robust jaws are useful for identification.

Texas beetle (fig. 136)
Brachypsectra fulva

Biology: The remarkable predatory grub stage lives beneath the outer bark of loblolly pine and preys upon spiders, ants, other grubs, and the abundant pseudoscorpions. Prey are sometimes impaled with the spearlike tail and eaten while held above the head, as if being devoured from a spit. We did see one individual feeding on a beetle grub in a more conventional manner. Adult males fly to blacklights during a brief period in midsummer and are presumably seeking mates at this time. Neither we nor any others have reported a living female from the wild.

Distribution: The Texas beetle has also been reported from several western states. The Lost Pines record as established here marks the eastern boundary of its range.

Remarks: Length 5 mm. Loblolly pine was not known to harbor the grubs until we found what is widely considered to be a rare species beneath flakes of the tree's outer bark. Adults are a rarer sight and until now had not been reported from the wild since the species was first made known to science at the time of the American Civil War. Those few specimens (and ours) were males. The female was entirely unknown until we found a dead specimen at the base of a loblolly and raised two more in culture dishes from grubs collected in the field (Fleenor and Taber 1999, 2000).

Similar species: Nothing in the forest resembles the tiny, trilobitic Texas beetle grub. Adults bear some resemblance to small click beetles, but comparison with the photos presented here should be sufficient to ensure a correct identification.

Surinam carrion beetle (fig. 137)
Necrodes surinamensis

Biology: This large dark scavenger circles dead vertebrates from the air like a vulture before landing to strengthen the comparison by eating decomposing flesh and maggots. Males and females mate in the dead animal's skull or chest cavity, and the female lays her eggs on the surface of the soil (Ratcliffe 1972). When the grubs hatch they eat the same food as the adults. If a carcass dries out these larvae will crawl across a road to find fresh maggots and carrion. Adults find maggots by shaving the dead animal's fur with their jaws. Occasionally they carry their prey into low vegetation as a leopard carries its kill into a tree. When approached they can squirt a foul-smelling liquid, which hits its mark at distances of up to one foot.

Fig. 136. Texas beetle (*Brachypsectra fulva*), (A) larva on loblolly
pine bark; (B) adult.

Distribution: The Surinam carrion beetle is primarily an eastern insect with sporadic occurrence in the northwestern United States; it is absent from the desert
Southwest beyond the Big Bend of Texas. Its range, as the common name suggests, extends into South America.

Remarks: Length 25 mm. We encountered a single specimen. It flew or crawled
to a blacklight at night.

Similar species: None.

Fig. 137. Surinam carrion beetle
(*Necrodes surinamensis*).

CHAPTER 8

Grasshoppers and Crickets

The grasshoppers of the Lost Pines are notable for having among their number three of the nine Texas endemic insects known to us from the forest. Perhaps they are relics of an ancient prairie much smaller in extent than the grasslands of today.

American bird grasshopper (fig. 138)
Schistocerca americana

Biology: This is a very large, extremely abundant, and well-camouflaged shorthorned grasshopper that lives in grassy clearings and does not jump from danger but flies high into the trees instead. Its unusual escape strategy is both effective and startling because of the grasshopper's impressive size and the rattling noise made by its snapping wings, and because the animal launches itself into the air from a hiding place only a few feet in front of the advancing shoe or boot. When it lands high on a trunk or branch it is almost always out of reach. Then, like a squirrel, it scuttles from side to side to avoid being seen. Freezing temperatures do not put a stop to its activities (Blatchley 1920).

Distribution: From the Atlantic Ocean to a western limit in Trans-Pecos Texas.

Remarks: Length 47 mm. The bird locust was once called the "clickety bug" because of the sound its wings make when it flies. The modern common name reflects its invariable flight into the trees. Strangely enough, this is an exceptional escape strategy, and it is paradoxical that more grasshoppers do not employ it instead of merely hopping or flying several feet away each time they flee.

One authority believed that the American bird grasshopper is the same species

Fig. 138. An American bird grasshopper (*Schistocerca americana*) at night.

as the biblical plague locust (Dirsh 1974). This is probably not true, though the New World bird locust is a pest of crops in its own right.

Similar species: The large size, brown-mottled forewings, clear hind wings, abundance, and behavior, when taken together, easily distinguish this animal from all other grasshoppers in the forest.

obscure locust (fig. 139)
Schistocerca obscura

Biology: The young hoppers eat elm leaves and switch to grasses and herbs as they age (Duck 1944). We first encountered this species when a huge green female was seen laying eggs in the pure sand of a clearing. The limp abdomen was buried

Fig. 139. A juvenile obscure locust (*Schistocerca obscura*) on oak leaf.

vertically several inches in the ground and was extended well beyond its normal length. A clutch of several dozen reddish eggs had already been deposited when we came upon the scene. There would have been as many as one hundred and twenty if she had been allowed to finish. When young hoppers hatch underground they push their way up to daylight by alternately inflating and deflating a balloonlike structure just behind the head.

Distribution: From the Atlantic Ocean to a western limit in southern Arizona.

Remarks: Length 45 mm. Obscure locusts are about the same size as the big bird grasshopper but are not as common. They too are likely to fly into the trees when disturbed.

Similar species: The adult's dark green color combined with the female's large size help to distinguish this species from others. Confident identification requires the proper keys.

differential grasshopper (fig. 140)
Melanoplus differentialis

Biology: This is a large, yellow, and very destructive crop pest that feeds on grasses and other herbaceous plants in the Lost Pines. It also scavenges the remains of fellow grasshoppers that have died. Females insert the abdomen into the sandy soil and lay nearly two hundred eggs per clutch.

Distribution: From coast to coast within the United States.

Remarks: Length 34 mm. When resting at night in the tops of herbaceous vegetation, the differential grasshopper remains motionless and may be plucked off the plant by hand. Fishermen take advantage of this by collecting buckets of the bait before a rising sun restores vitality to the creature's limbs. Differential grasshoppers are particularly common in July. They fly from advancing feet in large numbers as the visitor wades through tall grass crowding the meadows of the Lost Pines.

Similar species: None.

crested grasshoppers
Arphia sulphurea, A. xanthoptera

Biology: Both species frequent mixed pine and oak forests. Males make a crackling noise in flight by snapping the hind wings, and on the ground they sometimes call to females by rubbing the hind legs against the wings as these are held at rest.

Distribution: Both hoppers occur from the Atlantic Ocean to western limits in Texas. *Arphia sulphurea* reaches its western limit near San Antonio, whereas *A. xanthoptera* ranges as far west as the Pecos River.

Remarks: Length of *A. sulphurea* 24 mm, *A. xanthoptera* 27 mm. *Arphia sulphurea*

Fig. 140. Differential grasshoppers (*Melanoplus differentialis*) mating on tree trunk.

usually has yellow on its hind wings, whereas the wings of *Arphia xanthoptera* appear bright orange in flight. The latter species grows to a larger size.

Similar species: None.

green band-winged grasshopper (fig. 141)
Chortophaga viridifasciata

Biology: This species occurs in low grass. Males call to females as they approach potential mates during courtship, and both sexes make crackling sounds in flight.

Distribution: From the Atlantic Ocean to Utah.

Remarks: Length 24 mm. The green band-winged grasshopper exists in a brown phase as well as the more distinctive green phase.

Similar species: None.

crested sand grasshoppers
Spharagemon cristatum, S. bolli

Biology: These hoppers occur in sandy meadows and powerline cuts. Boll's grasshopper in particular has an affinity for wooded areas. Males of both species make crackling sounds in flight as they court females. When on the ground they shake their hind legs instead.

Distribution: *Spharagemon cristatum* has two disjunct populations in the United States, one in the central part of the country from Louisiana to New Mexico and another in the southeast. Boll's sand grasshopper occurs from the Atlantic Ocean to Utah.

Fig. 141. Green band-winged grasshopper (*Chortophaga viridifasciata*).

Remarks: Length of *S. cristatum* 32 mm, length of *S. bolli* 28 mm. Boll's sand grasshopper has a smaller crest on its back than its close relative and a black band on the hind tibia that *S. cristatum* lacks.

Similar species: None.

broadhorned band-winged grasshoppers (fig. 142)
Psinidia fenestralis, P. amplicornis

Biology: Both species favor sandy soil, and *Psinidia amplicornis* also favors woodland. Males crackle softly when they fly, but females do not.

Distribution: *Psinidia fenestralis* occurs from the Atlantic Ocean to Texas with a new western record in the Lost Pines as established here. *Psinidia amplicornis* is a Texas endemic species, according to current data, and thus may be alternately known as the Texas broadhorned band-winged grasshopper.

Remarks: Length of *P. amplicornis* 24 mm, *P. fenestralis* 19 mm. We observed two *Psinida amplicornis* males displaying to a female by lifting their blue hind legs while raising their bodies on tiptoe. These grasshoppers are among the few shorthorned species attracted to blacklights at night.

Similar species: None.

Texas bush katydid
Scudderia texensis

Biology: Texas bush katydids feed on the foliage of oak trees and low vegetation. In the eastern United States they sometimes become a pest of cranberries (Rehn and Hebard 1914b). Males court females with "a soft sh-sh-sh" or "a zeet-zeet-zeet-zeet" (Dethier 1992). Mated females lay their eggs in the middle layer of a

Fig. 142. Male Texas broadhorned grasshopper (*Psinidia amplicornis*) displaying to a potential mate.

leaf. The bush katydid flies readily when approached, and its silent zigzag flight often takes it quickly into a distant oak, "a tree in which it delights to dwell" (Blatchley 1920).

Distribution: From the Atlantic Ocean to a western limit (in the southern United States) in Central Texas. In the northern United States the species occurs as far west as Montana.

Remarks: Length 25 mm. Both the scientific and the common name suggest some special affinity with Texas, perhaps endemicity, but despite the names this is a very widespread species.

Similar species: The Texas bush katydid resembles the thread-legged katydids in its green color but is stouter, has much shorter hind legs, flies faster and farther when disturbed, and is more common. Even closer relatives live in the forest so that microscopic examination and the proper keys should be employed if a confident identification is needed. For example, the fork-tailed bush katydid, *Scudderia furcata,* also occurs here and is best distinguished from the Texas bush katydid by tiny structures located at the tip of the male's abdomen.

fork-tailed bush katydid
Scudderia furcata

Biology: Much like that of the Texas bush katydid. Males sing to females with a "zeep zeep zeep" and the call is answered with a chirp produced when a listening female opens her wings (C. V. Riley in Blatchley 1920). When the female is ready to lay her eggs she chews the edge of a leaf, grips her egg-laying tube with her jaws, and lays up to about half a dozen eggs after inserting the tube between the layers of the leaf.

Distribution: From coast to coast within the United States.

Remarks: Length 19 mm. When disturbed this species does not fly as far as the Texas bush katydid (Blatchley 1920).

Similar species: *See* Texas bush katydid.

three-eyed conehead katydid (fig. 143)
Neoconocephalus triops

Biology: The powerful coneheads are distinctive in their diet because they feed on grass seeds, especially those of panic grass (Isely 1944), which grows abundantly in the forest. According to some reports, they escape capture by long zigzag flights, but other reports indicate that the species is loath to fly. Our own experience has seen a mixture of both. Other defenses include biting, and—strange as this seems for a grasshopper—they also escape underground by burrowing out of sight (Blatchley 1920). Three-eyed coneheads occur in two color

**Fig. 143. Left: Three-eyed conehead katydid (*Neoconocephalus triops*).
Right: Angular-winged katydid (*Microcentrum rhombifolium*).**

phases. Some are green and some are brown. Males sing to females with a loud "z-z-z-z-z" that reaches an intensity of 100 decibels (Greenfield 1990), and they often fly to blacklights at night. Mated females lay their eggs in grass stems rather than in the leaves, a habit that further distinguishes them from the bush katydids.
Distribution: From coast to coast within the United States.
Remarks: Length 32 mm. This animal has the usual pair of compound eyes but a black spot located on a beak above and between them appears at first glance to be a third eye, hence the scientific and common name.
Similar species: Several additional coneheads may occur in the Lost Pines, though we have seen only this one. Microscopic examination and the proper keys are required for confident identification.

angular-winged katydid (fig. 143)
Microcentrum rhombifolium
Biology: The angular-winged katydid presumably eats oak leaves and normally remains out of sight high in the trees. We found a single specimen that was drawn to a blacklight trap at night. Both sexes have large wings that are seldom used for flight. Males use their wings to sing on summer nights with a "tic-tic-tic-tic," and females reply by raising their own wings with a sudden upward jerk, producing a simpler song (Blatchley 1920). Mated females lay eggs in rows on twigs and leaves. They resemble small narrow pumpkin seeds.
Distribution: From coast to coast within the United States.

Remarks: Length 28 mm. This grasshopper prefers the heights of trees and is thus shielded from human contact and seldom collected.

Similar species: None.

long-spurred meadow katydid
Orchelimum silvaticum

Biology: Common in July in the lush vegetation growing along pond margins, this species is seldom if ever noticed elsewhere. Others have described the long-spurred meadow katydid as clumsy and easy to capture. We found males and females clinging to long stems and can agree with the latter characterization at least. In the eastern United States they are found high in post oaks as well as on corn and in lush grass, but we have not noticed them in trees in the Lost Pines. Meadow grasshoppers in general seem to be omnivorous, eating flowers, foliage, and other insects, such as moths, beetles, and sometimes one another (Blatchley 1920). The song is a soft chatter that is hard to describe in words. When the species was first made known to science the call was described as a series of "zips" and "zees" (McNeill 1891). Mated females chew holes in the stems of herbaceous vegetation and lay their eggs inside.

Distribution: The long-spurred meadow katydid occurs from Pennsylvania to the Pecos River area of West Texas.

Remarks: Length 21 mm. In life these attractive grasshoppers have striking orange-red eyes.

Similar species: Several meadow katydids occur in Central Texas, and the best way to distinguish one species from another is by a microscopic examination of the male's abdomen (Rehn and Hebard 1915).

Comanche thread-legged katydid (fig. 144)
Arethaea constricta comanche

Biology: Poorly known. We found the incredibly long-legged adults in powerline cuts and in meadows, where they presumably eat the foliage of herbaceous vegetation and perhaps oak leaves as well. Outside the forest they have been collected from mint (*Monarda citriodora*) and from grasses and huisache (*Vachellia farnesiana;* Hebard 1936). Mints are abundant in the woods but this hopper is seldom if ever seen clinging to them.

Distribution: The Comanche subspecies is found nowhere in the world but in Central and southern Texas. The entire species range extends from the grasslands of Nebraska to northern Mexico.

Remarks: Length 38 mm. We found the Comanche thread-legged katydid to be locally abundant in May when hundreds of adult males and females suddenly

Fig. 144. Comanche thread-legged katydid (*Arethaea constricta comanche*).

appeared in a small section of a powerline cut. Within a few weeks they vanished from sight. In some years they remain well into the summer in reduced numbers.

Similar species: This thread-legged katydid is smaller and much more common than the Texas thread-legged katydid (*see* species account), which we found only once.

Texas thread-legged katydid (fig. 145)
Arethaea grallator

Biology: So poorly known that even its diet is speculative (Isely 1941; Gangwere 1961). Leaves and flowers of herbaceous vegetation and the foliage of oaks are probably its normal foods. Females have a unique way of laying their eggs. They choose a *Gaillardia* wildflower or one of the *Hordeum* grasses and nibble a notch into the base of the stem. Then they lay an egg in the notch and cover it up with chewed stem material and mud.

Distribution: This katydid is a Texas endemic that occurs nowhere else in the world but in the east-central part of the state.

Remarks: Length 40 mm. We found a single specimen. It was perched on a blackjack oak leaf at the edge of a meadow, far from the site where we found the

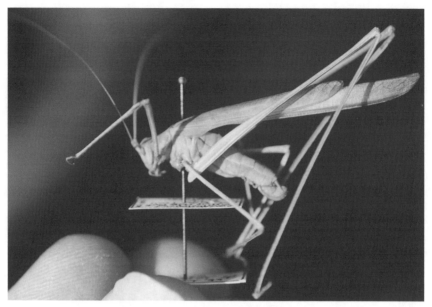

Fig. 145. Texas thread-legged katydid (*Arethaea grallator*).

Comanche subspecies in occasional abundance. When thread-legged katydids are approached they fly for a short distance with a slow flutter that appears to be a glide rather than powered flight because their outstretched wings have the appearance of a cape spread wide.

Similar species: *See* Comanche thread-legged katydid.

two-striped grasshopper
Mermiria bivittata

Biology: This big hopper seems to prefer little bluestem grass more than do the other large grasshoppers of the Lost Pines. When approached, individuals do not fly into the trees but soar a great distance across the meadow before landing once more on their favored food. In summer they often perch at the tips of the plant during the hottest hours of the day.

Distribution: From the Atlantic Ocean to Nevada.

Remarks: Length 40 mm. In other parts of the United States the two-striped grasshopper occasionally becomes a pest (Helfer 1953).

Similar species: The large size and preferred habitat in combination with the slanted face and oddly thickened antennae help to distinguish this hopper from all others in the forest. Confident identification requires the proper keys because at least one close relative may occur in the same area.

admirable slant-faced grasshopper
Syrbula admirabilis

Biology: This species occurs in low grass on dry soil. Males call to females with a song produced by rubbing the hind legs against the wings. Females sing too.

Distribution: From the Atlantic Ocean to Arizona.

Remarks: Length 31 mm. The admirable slant-faced grasshopper has one of the most complicated courtship rituals in the insect world (Otte 1981).

Similar species: None.

Stevenson's shieldback grasshopper (fig. 146)
Pediodectes stevensonii

Biology: Essentially unknown. One additional shieldback species occurs in the Lost Pines, and that one is clearly a predator. Nevertheless, the diet of Stevenson's shieldback must be left to speculation. Perhaps it shares the highly unusual fare of its close relatives, or perhaps it is omnivorous or even vegetarian. We *can* say that in the loblolly forest this animal is nocturnal. We plucked one female after dark from an oak leaf six feet above ground, and another walked to a blacklight near the edge of a pond. In West Texas, individuals were found in grasses and bushes (Tinkham 1944), but beyond our own experience there is no mention of life in the trees. Tinkham discovered that the female lays about forty eggs. We encountered no males of this species or of any other shieldback.

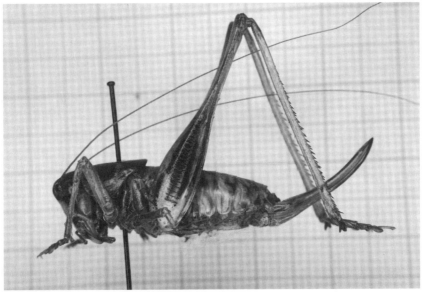

Fig. 146. Stevenson's shieldback grasshopper (*Pediodectes stevensonii*).

Distribution: The distribution of Stevenson's shieldback is difficult to determine at present due to past confusion over the identification of the species. It appears to be an animal of the central plains, ranging from an eastern limit near the Lost Pines to Colorado.

Remarks: Length 38 mm. This species and the other shieldback known to be predatory are extremely rare in the forest, whereas herbivorous grasshoppers sometimes go beyond mere abundance to plague proportions. The explanation for the contrast may be similar to the reason for the small numbers of big cats that prey upon enormous herds of African antelope, for the prey of the shieldback is often its fellow grasshopper. A single predator must take many meals, and this requires many prey items per predator. The predators cannot be expected to outnumber the individuals they eat, and the predatory species may well be restricted to small populations.

Shieldbacks received their common name because of an especially large plate or shield overlying the thorax. The wings of the two flightless Lost Pines species are so tiny, if they exist at all, that the shield partially or entirely hides the winglets from view. The scientific name *Pediodectes* means "biter of the plains," and individuals are liable to live up to their name when handled.

Similar species: Considering the intriguing biology of the shieldbacks, it is perplexing and disappointing to find that no reliable key exists for their identification (*see* Rentz and Birchim 1968). We found it necessary to sort out the situation ourselves, and after collecting all the available literature on the subject, we now believe that the identity of at least our two Lost Pines species can be assured in terms of currently favored names. Stevenson's shieldback is distinguished from Haldeman's shieldback by the peculiar white mask on its face. Haldeman's shieldback is bigger and more robust in shape, and it comes in green as well as the brown of Stevenson's species.

Haldeman's shieldback grasshopper (figs. 147, 148)
Pediodectes haldemanii

Biology: These are flightless predatory katydids that eat vegetation only when starved for meat. A sit-and-wait hunting strategy allows them to "snap off a leg of a passing grasshopper . . . or bite especially into the head region, holding the prey with their fore and middle legs" (Isely 1941). Males court females by singing with their otherwise vestigial wings. They are said to be alert, shy, and prone to chirp like a cardinal from high in the bushes (Hebard 1931; Isely 1944). In the Lost Pines Haldeman's shieldback is apparently active both night and day. We encountered two specimens, one a brown female that crawled to a blacklight placed at a treeline surrounding a large meadow and the other a green female that was exposed on the ground in a powerline cut during broad daylight.

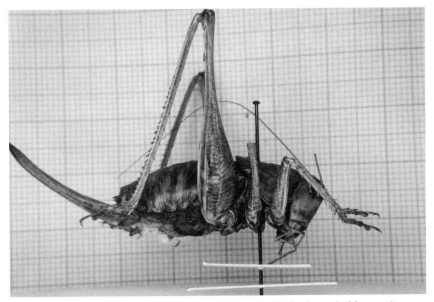

Fig. 147. Haldeman's shieldback grasshopper (*Pediodectes haldemanii*); brown phase.

Fig. 148. Haldeman's shieldback grasshopper (*Pediodectes haldemanii*); green phase.

In western Texas the species has been collected in bushes and trees (including mesquite) and is considered nocturnal. In captivity it kills and eats grasshoppers (Tinkham 1944), but it jumps away in nature when approached by humans and does not take an aggressive, mantislike fighting stance, as do some of its spectacularly combative relatives. Tinkham believed that Haldeman's shieldback (which he referred to as the American shieldback) is naturally herbivorous. Males sing to females with a soft "tsee-tsee-tsee-tsee" that carries up to forty feet, and they are silenced easily, waiting for some time until after a disturbance passes before resuming their song.

Fig. 149. Greater arid-land grasshopper (*Neobarrettia spinosa*); photographed at the Ottine Swamp in Gonzales County. This is the rarely observed female.

Distribution: In the United States this species probably occurs from at least as far east as Louisiana to western limits in the Great Basin.

Remarks: Length 60 mm. Illustrations of the predator's sharp teeth were said to show a resemblance to those of a tiger (Isely 1941, 1944). The behavior of our own specimens confirmed the warning that this katydid will bite when handled.

A carnivorous species much larger than either of the shieldbacks is the greater arid-land katydid (*Neobarrettia spinosa;* fig. 149), a spectacular grasshopper several inches in length that raises its wings and spiny legs like a praying mantis when provoked. It is not bluffing, for it delivers a painful bite too. This katydid occurs from Arizona to an eastern limit near the Lost Pines of Central Texas, and there are several published records from Bastrop County (Cohn 1965); we never saw it in the Lost Pines. The species is strongly associated with mesquite trees, opportunistic colonizers from the south that are uncommon within the confines of the forest.

We thank Dr. Theodore Cohn of San Diego State University for numerous emails that helped us identify the carnivorous katydids discussed here. The literature at the time of this writing was insufficient to identify most of them properly, and his nearly fifty years of experience proved invaluable.

Similar species: *See* Stevenson's shieldback.

Central Texas leaf katydid (fig. 150)
Paracyrtophyllus robustus

Biology: One male was found on a blackjack oak leaf and one female was found on the leaf of a shrubby post oak in a powerline cut. No others were seen. Oak leaves are presumably their favored food. The green color and amazingly leaflike wings provide such excellent camouflage that we almost overlooked both individuals, though each was perched on an exposed leaf in broad daylight. When

Fig. 150. Central Texas leaf katydid (*Paracyrtophyllus robustus*),
(A) male; (B) female on oak leaf.

handled the male rubbed its wings together and produced a squeaking chirp. The wings, though large, are apparently not used for flight by either sex. The egg-laying behavior of the female remains unknown, and the eggs themselves were unknown until now. The single female contained twenty-six eggs that are different from those of the other katydids in the forest. They are elongate and sharp at both ends rather than being shaped like pumpkin seeds, and they were black when dissected rather than yellow.

Distribution: This species is a Central Texas endemic and as such is found nowhere else in the world.

Remarks: Length 36 mm. An authority on the grasshoppers of the United States noted the highly disjunct distribution of this Texas species, which is disrupted because the animal is restricted to islands of oak surrounded by prairie (Hebard 1941). Hebard discovered that specimens are rare in collections, and even when searching for them in the field "individuals are very seldom happened upon." Yet at the time of this writing the Texas Forest Service had recently identified the culprit of a post-oak defoliation in Lee County as this very species. Lee County shares a border with Bastrop County, where much of the Lost Pines forest is located. Strangely, these individuals were brown, whereas the Lost Pines specimens we saw were green, and green is the color mentioned in the literature.

The Central Texas leaf katydid's closest relative is also a Texas endemic but is found only in the Big Bend country, where it is known as the "quonker" because of the male's peculiar song. The Lost Pines species has a remarkably different song that sounds more like a series of chirps than a *quonk*.

Similar species: The broad, strongly veined, leaflike wings when held at rest seem to form a rounded shell about the animal's body. Males have a peculiar red knob of unknown function that can be seen on top of the abdomen when the wings are pulled aside. The latter feature best distinguishes the Central Texas leaf katydid from the only other true katydid that occurs in the forest to our knowledge. That species, *Pterophylla camellifolia,* has similar wings, though it is seldom seen because it dwells in the tops of oak trees. In summer after dark and to a lesser extent even on hot afternoons, its song may be heard rasping down from the leaves overhead. The voice can be described as a kind of shuddering chatter with an occasional "katy-she-did," for which katydids were named.

round-winged katydids
Texas false katydid, *Amblycorypha huasteca,*
and western round-winged katydid, *A. parvipennis*

Biology: We found these two leaf- and flower-eating species crouched in small, shrubby oaks growing in powerline cuts through the forest. The smaller, rounder-winged *A. parvipennis* is a flightless species though both sexes have wings (Isely 1941). Males call to females day and night with a song that sometimes sounds like a repeated "chic-a-chee." At other times it sounds more like "tsip-i-tsip-i-tsip-i-tsip-i-tsip" (Blatchley 1920). One dissected female contained a small number of eggs that greatly resemble pumpkin seeds. These are laid in the soil rather than on or in vegetation. She bends forward, grips the egg-laying structure between her jaws, and guides it into the ground (Isely 1941). There appears to be less known about *A. huasteca*. According to Isely's paper, the two species are quite similar in their habits. One difference is the ability of the Texas false katydid to fly rather well. Another is the Texas false katydid male's nocturnal song, which has been described as a "t-t-t-t-t-tk" (Tinkham 1948).

Distribution: *Amblycorypha huasteca* is a creature of the central plains, occurring from Kansas in the north to at least Tampico, Mexico, in the south (Rehn and Hebard 1914b). In Texas it ranges from the Louisiana border to the western part of the state. *Amblycorypha parvipennis* is likewise an animal of the central prairies. It occurs from Arkansas in the north to the Gulf Coast of Texas in the south.

Remarks: Length of *A. huasteca* 42 mm, length of *A. parvipennis* 33 mm. Pink round-winged katydids have been reported elsewhere from time to time, but we never saw them in this forest.

Similar species: The antennae are inserted far apart on the head, and this feature immediately separates the round-winged katydids from the bush katydids, which they most closely resemble. In bush katydids the bases of the antennae are not separated by a broad gap.

short-tailed cricket (fig. 151)
Anurogryllus arboreus

Biology: Unusual for living in family groups in burrows. These consist of a female and her offspring but no adult males. In fact, a male that attempts entry will be repelled. If he persists, the female bites off his leg and eats it (West and Alexander 1963). There are some remarkable similarities to ant nests here. For example, burrows consist of tunnels and chambers. Some are used for retreat from danger, others for the storage of food and waste. A mound of soil marks the entrance to the nest. The entrance is plugged from within against specific disturbance and when the female has brood. Eggs are laid inside the nest, carried to an egg pile, and groomed and guarded there. Some of the eggs, again like those of many ants, are "trophic" in function. They do not hatch and are eaten by the young crickets instead. Females do not allow their young to eat the viable eggs. Hatchlings, as many as fifty-six, remain in the nest for some time under the mother's protection, and she will advance against a nest disturbance rather than flee from it. The

Fig. 151. Short-tailed cricket (*Anurogryllus arboreus*).

presence of nest symbionts or "houseguests" is a further similarity to the ant colony. These small arthropods live beside and even on their hosts. We found only two of these crickets. Both were males singing in broad daylight outside their burrows with a high-pitched trill, and each was found separately on a loblolly trunk near ground level at the edge of a meadow. Others have seen this cricket abroad only after dark (Weaver and Sommers 1969). According to an authority on American crickets, the male's song is the loudest in the United States (Hebard 1934).

A curious behavior is the habit of limited self-cannibalism or mutilation. They remove and eat their own hind wings within one day of becoming adults. Hence these wings are not used for flight but only for food. The same fate befalls the rest of the female's body when she dies. Her young consume her remains before leaving the nest.

Distribution: From the Atlantic Ocean to a western limit somewhere in Texas, perhaps near the Lost Pines.

Remarks: Length 16 mm. Short-tailed crickets are uncommon in the Central Texas forest but reach pest status in eastern states, where they consume cotton, potatoes, peas, strawberries, tobacco, and most notably of all, pine (Blatchley 1920). Vegetation that is not eaten is used to line the burrow.

Similar species: None.

black field cricket (fig. 152)
Gryllus of undetermined species

Biology: The omnivorous field cricket made many appearances at our blacklight traps, especially in fall. Those we saw were stout, black individuals that varied with respect to the length of their wings. Some have long wings that would be described as "normal," whereas others have very short wings that are useless for flight. Males sing to females by scraping the wings together, and the resulting song is unique to each species.

Distribution: Field crickets occur from coast to coast within the United States.

Remarks: Length 17 mm. Unlike many of the insects that are attracted to blacklight traps at night, black field crickets tend to be found on the ground nearby rather than within the bucket itself.

Similar species: It is difficult to identify field crickets precisely without recording and analyzing the male's song. All of the large black crickets of the Lost Pines are surely members of the genus *Gryllus*. There may be two or more species in the area.

tree crickets

four-spotted tree cricket, *Oecanthus quadripunctatus;* fast-calling tree cricket,
Oecanthus celerinictus; narrow-winged tree cricket, *Oecanthus niveus*

Biology: Tree crickets are small, delicate, greenish insects that live not only in trees, as their name suggests, but also in herbaceous vegetation. Their omnivorous

Fig. 152. Unidentified field cricket (*Gryllus* sp.; female).

diet includes plant lice, flowers, and fruit (Walker 1962, 1963). Males chirp or trill to attract a female who then mounts her mate and feeds on secretions from glands at the base of his wings while he transfers a spermatophore (sperm package) to her. She then selects a plant and lays her eggs in its tissues after biting and drilling into the stem.

The narrow-winged species favors the heights of deciduous trees, whereas the other two species prefer herbaceous vegetation.

Distribution: The four-spotted tree cricket ranges throughout the continental United States, and both the fast-calling tree cricket and the narrow-winged species occur from the Atlantic Ocean to Central Texas.

Remarks: Typical lengths for these species are 13 mm. The slender greenish animals are well camouflaged when clinging to little bluestem grass or members of the daisy family. Males are readily identified by their much wider wings.

Similar species: Several additional tree crickets undoubtedly occur in the Lost Pines. Most of these can be identified by the dark patterns near the base of their antennae, but some species cannot be separated without analyzing the male's song.

CHAPTER 9

Dragonflies, Damselflies, Stoneflies, and Mayflies

Most of the animals treated in this chapter provide a splendid example of how biodiversity can increase when humans modify wild habitats. In this case the abundance of species and individuals is due to the construction of artificial ponds within the forest. The same can be said for an increase in biodiversity following the creation of powerline cuts. Indeed, powerline cuts appear to harbor the greatest insect diversity in these woods. They are used as foraging grounds by dragonflies that cruise back and forth between the artificial open spaces and the artificial ponds where they breed. We were fortunate enough to capture and identify every dragonfly species we saw in the Lost Pines, with one exception, the comet darner (*Anax longipes*), which we only sighted. Total body length of each species is cited from *Dragonflies through Binoculars* (Dunkle 2000), which offers color photos and further information on all of the dragonflies of the forest.

white-tailed skimmer (fig. 153)
Libellula lydia

Biology: Males are unmistakable for their white abdomen and black-banded wings as they patrol ponds in search of prey and mates and in defense of territories held against competing males. They threaten one another by raising the distinctively colored abdomen like a flag (Dunkle 1989). Female white-tails are darker in color, not as conspicuous as the males, and are so unlike their mates in appearance that

Fig. 153. White-tailed skimmer (*Libellula lydia*), (A) male perched on American beautyberry leaf; (B) female perched on a twig.

they are likely to be mistaken for a different species altogether. Mating occurs on the wing, and over time the female deposits about one thousand eggs by dipping the tip of her abdomen at the surface of the pond while hovering above it. Her mate guards her against other males during the process but is helpless to prevent small fish from gulping down the eggs. We observed this on several occasions, and it appears that the fishes are attracted to the surface disturbances made by egg-laying females. Both sexes are sometimes found far from water (Walker and Corbet 1975).

Distribution: From coast to coast within the United States.

Remarks: Length 43 mm. It is said that males will sometimes perch on bystanders. We never experienced this; to the contrary, we found all dragonflies unapproachable during daylight hours beyond capture with a net.

The twelve-spotted dragonfly (*Libellula pulchella*) occurs in all forty-eight contiguous states and often flies alongside the white-tailed skimmer (Needham et al. 2000). We did not notice the twelve-spot in the Lost Pines, but the females of the two species are easily confused in the field.

Similar species: None.

slaty skimmer (fig. 154)
Libellula incesta

Biology: This species prefers muddy-bottomed ponds for the development of its young and is very much at home in the Lost Pines. Males are dark, slaty blue and are most active in the morning. They guard their mates while the females deposit eggs in the water (Dunkle 1989).

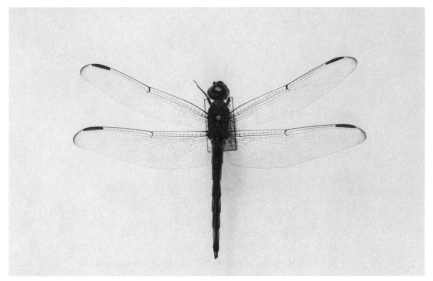

Fig. 154. Slaty skimmer (*Libellula incesta*).

Distribution: From the Atlantic Ocean to a western limit somewhere in Texas.
Remarks: Length 51 mm. This species, the white-tailed skimmer, and the roseate skimmer are the most common dragonflies of the forest.
Similar species: None.

roseate skimmer (fig. 155)
Orthemis ferruginea

Biology: The brightly colored males are territorial and fight until a single resident dominates a pond. The successful individual sallies from a favorite perch to battle his competitors, and after mating with a female he guards her from these other males. Females deposit their eggs by splashing the surface of the pond with the tip of the abdomen. This hurls the eggs onto the shore just above the waterline or onto emergent vegetation (Harvey and Hubbard 1987).
Distribution: In the United States the roseate skimmer occurs from coast to coast.
Remarks: Length 51 mm. The male's red to magenta color makes this species more visible from a distance than any other common dragonfly.
Similar species: None.

Fig. 155. Roseate skimmer (*Orthemis ferruginea*).

green darner (fig. 156)
Anax junius

Biology: Adults are common at artificial ponds, where males patrol territories and mate with less brightly colored females. The female typically lays her eggs in the tissues of submergent vegetation, often while still coupled to the male, and she sometimes submerges herself as she does so. This is in sharp contrast to the behavior of those species that simply deposit the eggs in water.

Like other dragonflies, green darners are diurnally active predators that consume huge numbers of mosquitoes and other small flying insects. There are two reports of attacks on hummingbirds (Dunkle 1989), and flocks of darners have been seen flying in pursuit of insect prey (Walker 1958). Juveniles, like those of all other dragonflies, are also predatory, but they catch their prey on the bottom of the pond rather than in the skies overhead. They are wingless and equipped with a complicated set of mouthparts known as the "mask," which flicks forward like a chameleon's tongue to catch passing animals as large as tadpoles. The structure and use of the mask have resulted in its comparison to a combination of hands, carving tools, and serving table (Needham and Westfall 1954). Shed skins of darner larvae can be seen in July above the waterline clinging to the stems of aquatic plants.

Distribution: The green darner occurs throughout the United States.

Remarks: Length 76 mm. This is one of the largest dragonflies in the country, though it is slightly smaller than the rarely seen swamp darner, which also occurs in the forest.

Fig. 156. Green darner (*Anax junius*), (A) male; (B) female roosting
at night on tree.

Similar species: The large size and blue and green colors, especially conspicuous
in the male, distinguish green darners from all other species in the Lost Pines.

plains clubtail (fig. 157)
Gomphus externus
Biology: The male plains clubtail rests on sandy ground with its abdomen el-
evated and its wings tilted down to touch the ground (Needham and Westfall

Fig. 157. Top left: Plains clubtail (*Gomphus externus*).
Top right: Banded dragonlet (*Erythrodiplax umbrata*).
Bottom: Widow skimmer (*Libellula luctuosa*).

1954). We confirmed this with our own observations in the sandy meadows of the Lost Pines. Females lay thousands of eggs by dipping the tip of the abdomen in pond water. We believe the juveniles of this forest develop in ponds rather than in large streams, as Needham and Westfall discovered elsewhere. They occur in groups, burrow in the mud like moles (Walker 1958), and when it is time to transform to the winged stage, they climb from the water and shed the nymphal skin on a tree stump.

Distribution: From Ohio to Utah.

Remarks: Length 53 mm. Clubtails are named for the dilation of the abdomen near its tip.

Similar species: None.

widow skimmer (fig. 157)
Libellula luctuosa

Biology: Widow skimmers range far from water much like the yellow-sided skimmer. The individual shown here was captured in a powerline cut at a great distance from the pond where it developed. Females are usually not guarded by males when they lay eggs, and when transforming to the winged adult stage, the nymphs crawl ashore to cast off their skins on grass near the pond (Needham and Westfall 1954).

Distribution: From coast to coast.

Remarks: Length 46 mm. When resting in clearings the widow can be approached quite closely before it takes flight.

Similar species: None.

banded dragonlet (fig. 157)
Erythrodiplax umbrata

Biology: Adult banded dragonlets are often seen in green vegetation around small ponds. Males are more likely to be noticed than females because of their territorial behavior and because females often rest in trees. Mating occurs on the wing, but the male does not guard the female when she lays her eggs in the water.

Distribution: In the United States the distribution is very limited, the species occurring only in Texas and Oklahoma.

Remarks: Length 43 mm. Young males do not have dark bands on their wings, and in this they resemble females. As males age the bands appear and become dark in color.

Similar species: None.

blue dasher (fig. 158)
Pachydiplax longipennis

Biology: This is a common, medium-sized, fast flyer with a wide habitat tolerance. It frequents still waters with or without fish, including ponds, marshes, bays, ditches, and swamps (Dunkle 2000). Perhaps the larval stage does not do well in acid waters, for it does not frequent bogs. When resting on a stem the territorial male raises its abdomen high in the air, thus performing a headstand.

Distribution: Coast to coast within the United States except for the Great Basin region.

Remarks: Length 40 mm. Blue dashers are common at artificial ponds in early May.

Similar species: Male eastern pondhawks bear a vague resemblance to the male blue dasher, but they lack the brownish patches on the distal half of the wing.

common baskettail (fig. 158)
Epitheca cynosura

Biology: This medium-sized species flies fast and erratically and includes winged termites in its diet (Dunkle 1989). It strays far from its native pond when foraging for prey. When at the pond the males patrol up to about thirty feet of shoreline

Fig. 158. Top left: Blue dasher (*Pachydiplax longipennis*). Top right: Common baskettail (*Epitheca cynosura*). Bottom: Greenjacket (*Erythemis simplicicollis*).

and mate with females in flight. The eggs are deposited in an unusual way, for they are not laid individually. Instead they are formed into a ball-shaped mass that unravels underwater as a gelatinous rope.

Distribution: From the Atlantic Ocean to Wyoming.

Remarks: Length 41 mm. The common name "baskettail" refers to the female's habit of carrying her eggs in a ball-shaped mass beneath her abdomen.

Similar species: None.

greenjacket (fig. 158)
Erythemis simplicicollis

Biology: This widespread dragonfly is voracious even for its kind and eats grasshoppers, damselflies, deer flies, butterflies, and other dragonflies (Walker and Corbet 1975; Needham and Westfall 1954; Dunkle 1989). It watches large animals, including humans, and uses them to flush its prey from vegetation (Dunkle 2000).

Mating usually occurs on a perch rather than in midair, and the females are sometimes guarded by their mates as they lay eggs in the water. Males confront each other aerially in a kind of circular treadmill display. One male hovers in front of the other for a moment before dropping down to yield the front spot to the second male, which soon reciprocates, restoring the original alignment.

Distribution: From the Atlantic Ocean to Arizona.

Remarks: Length 43 mm. We often searched for roosting dragonflies after dark but seldom found any. One greenjacket was plucked in this manner from a *Sesbania* leaf near the pond where it patrolled during the day. Voracious feeding behavior has given the greenjacket the alternate name of "pondhawk."

Similar species: This dragonfly vaguely resembles *Erythrodiplax umbrata*, but the face of the greenjacket is light green and the males become powdery blue with age. It can be confused with the plains clubtail because of its habit of resting on the ground and because of the slightly swollen tip of its abdomen. However, the two species have very different wing venation.

yellow-sided skimmer (fig. 159)
Libellula flavida

Biology: Both sexes forage in clearings located far from the nearest body of water. The behavior of the yellow-sided skimmer must be similar to that of the other members of its genus, but there appears to be little published on the subject. Its preferred habitats are said to be mucky or boggy spring seepages (Dunkle 2000), yet in the Central Texas forest it probably breeds in artificial ponds.

Distribution: From the Atlantic Ocean to a western limit in Texas just east of the Pecos River.

Remarks: Length 48 mm. The yellow-sided skimmer provides another example of the great differences between the sexes of some dragonflies. The blue male could easily be mistaken for a species different from the female.

Similar species: None.

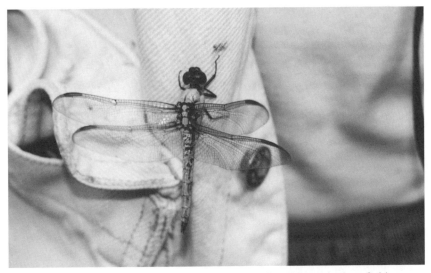

Fig. 159. Male yellow-sided skimmer (*Libellula flavida*) perched on field vest.

eastern amberwing (fig. 160)
Perithemis tenera

Biology: Amberwings have the most complicated courtship of any North American dragonfly. They also have a broad habitat tolerance: the larval stage can develop in rivers, ponds, or ditches. While the adult is perching it flexes its body and wings in a manner that suggests it is mimicking a wasp. The male selects an egg-laying site somewhere in the pond and leads a receptive female to the area. If the female decides to mate, the pair does so while perched on emergent vegetation. Then the female lays her eggs in the water while the male hovers over her as a guard against other males (Dunkle 1989). A curious feature is the explosion of the sinking egg mass (Walker and Corbet 1975), which may serve to disperse the individual eggs and decrease the likelihood of predation of the entire clutch by a single gulp from a predatory fish. Amberwings tend to fly closer to the water surface than do the high-flying dragonflies that might prey upon them (Needham and Westfall 1954).

Distribution: From the Atlantic Ocean to Arizona.

Remarks: Length 23 mm. At just under one inch this is one of the smallest dragonflies we encountered in the Lost Pines. Males are easily recognized by their orange wings with a few darker spots on each. Females have lighter wings with more spots or bands.

Similar species: None.

Fig. 160. Eastern amberwing (*Perithemis tenera;* male).

Fig. 161. Top left: Halloween pennant (*Celithemis eponina*).
Top right: Dwarf dragonlet (*Erythrodiplax minuscula*).
Bottom: Red-mantled glider (*Tramea onusta*).

Halloween pennant (fig. 161)
Celithemis eponina

Biology: In its fluttering flight and in its beautiful wing coloration this species is often compared to a butterfly. We found Halloween pennants at one large artificial pond and nowhere else. The female lays her eggs in the morning, in the water, and she does so while still in the grasp of her mate (Dunkle 1989). Halloween pennants fly in the rain and in strong wind (Needham and Westfall 1954).

Distribution: From the Atlantic Ocean to a western extreme in New Mexico.

Remarks: Length 38 mm. The common name is a good one, for the wings are entirely orange-yellow with the exception of the bands, which are dark brown rather than Halloween-black.

Similar species: None.

dwarf dragonlet (fig. 161)
Erythrodiplax minuscula

Biology: It is appropriate that this tiny species preys upon damselflies, for damselflies are small, fragile relatives of dragonflies. Mating takes place in the air or while the partners perch on vegetation, and males guard females while they lay their eggs in water (Dunkle 1989).

Distribution: From the Atlantic Ocean to a western limit in Texas near the Lost Pines.

Remarks: Length 25 mm. At a mere one inch in length, the dwarf dragonlet and the eastern amberwing are the smallest dragonflies we encountered in the Lost Pines. The dragonlet is likely to be overlooked as it hides in lush green vegetation along the edge of a pond. Its secrecy undoubtedly saves it from larger predatory relatives.

Similar species: None.

red-mantled glider (fig. 161)
Tramea onusta

Biology: The red-mantled glider prefers quiet waters such as those of artificial ponds. Males perch high in the trees as well as in the lower vegetation that is so commonly used by other dragonflies. They patrol large territories and mate with females while perched (Dunkle 1989). Mated females lay their eggs on algal mats alone or while still coupled to their mates. This species and its closest relatives are known as "dancing gliders" because of the dipping flight pattern they adopt. According to Dunkle, the dark red bands at the base of the hind wings provide shade on hot days, when the dragonfly droops its abdomen beneath the dark patches. These have given the species an alternate common name of "red saddlebags."

Distribution: From Indiana to the Pacific Ocean.

Remarks: Length 46 mm. This species was more difficult to catch than any of the other dragonflies except the comet darner. It cruises along in a bouncing flight, tends to stay farther from shore, and is prone to speed away from the pond entirely when the net swings and misses. Nor is it common to begin with.

Similar species: The violet-masked glider, *Tramea carolina,* may occur in the area. It has more red in the hind wing, and the outline of the dark wing pattern is not as jagged as that of the red-mantled glider.

great pondhawk (fig. 162)
Erythemis vesiculosa

Biology: Great pondhawks prefer ponds and other bodies of still water. They are known as voracious predators even among dragonflies and attack butterflies as well as their own kind (Needham and Westfall 1954). Males patrol sizable territories and mate with females while perched on vegetation. Females lay their eggs in the water by tapping the surface with the tip of the abdomen.

Distribution: The great pondhawk is a primarily tropical dragonfly that ranges into the southern United States, where it occurs mostly in Texas and Oklahoma, though there are isolated records in several other states.

Fig. 162. A great pondhawk (*Erythemis vesiculosa*) perched on purple marsh-fleabane.

Remarks: Length 61 mm. Before the largely grass-green adult matures, the small dark patch on the front edge of the wing near the wing tip is also green, an unusual exception to the shades of brown and black found in most dragonflies. Great pondhawks are wary of people and are difficult to catch.

Similar species: None.

swamp darner (fig. 163)

Epiaeschna heros

Biology: Similar to that of the green darner, which it slightly exceeds in size at nearly three and one half inches. It does seem to wander farther from the ponds than its close relative and is occasionally captured in buildings (Walker 1958). Adults feed in swarms on winged ants and termites and on other prey as large as cicadas (Dunkle 1989). Males do not defend territories. They mate with the female while hanging from a tree, and she does not lay her eggs while attached to the male as the green darner does. Nor does she lay her eggs below the waterline. Instead she chooses emergent vegetation or even the soil of a dry pond.

Distribution: From the Atlantic Ocean to a western limit in northern Texas and midwestern states to the north.

Remarks: Length 86 mm. Unlike the green darner, this big dragonfly loses its attractive colors shortly after death.

Similar species: None.

Fig. 163. Top left: Swamp darner (*Epiaeschna heros*). Top right: Neon skimmer (*Libellula croceipennis*). Bottom left: Eastern ringtail (*Erpetogomphus designatus*). Bottom right: Thornbush dasher (*Micrathyria hagenii*).

neon skimmer (fig. 163)
Libellula croceipennis

Biology: The male is a beautiful bright red dragonfly. We saw few individuals and none were females. One was patrolling a creek in mid-October, which is itself worthy of note because most of our dragonfly sightings were taken at ponds. Another staked a territory at the margin of a pond and returned again and again to a tree growing at the water's edge.

Distribution: In the United States the neon skimmer occurs from eastern Texas to California with a gap in southern New Mexico.

Remarks: Length 56 mm. The striking red color makes this the most beautiful of the Lost Pines dragonflies. According to one authority, the male actually seems to glow while perched (Dunkle 2000). It retains its beauty in the collection box.

Similar species: A second red species, *Libellula saturata*, may also occur in the forest. It is more thoroughly red than the species treated here, including the veins of the wings.

eastern ringtail (fig. 163)
Erpetogomphus designatus

Biology: Apparently poorly known. Our single specimen was a female captured near dusk while it perched on a grass stem in a meadow several hundred yards from a pond. In the net the dragonfly fluttered about as other species do, but when taken in hand it appeared to feign death and ceased all movement.

Distribution: From the Atlantic Ocean to New Mexico with isolated records farther west.

Remarks: Length 51 mm. Though male dragonflies were captured more often than females, we found no male of this species.

Similar species: None.

thornbush dasher (fig. 163)
Micrathyria hagenii

Biology: Thornbush dashers frequent rain ponds and ponds at the edges of forests (Paulson 1984). They fly early in the day, and at relatively low temperatures compared to other species, and are active in light so low that it is difficult to see them. Our single specimen was captured in a meadow at night.

Distribution: In the United States the thornbush dasher occurs only in Texas and in Arkansas; within this range its real home is the Rio Grande Valley (Dunkle 2000).

Remarks: Length 36 mm. This is a tropical animal that reaches its northern limit in the southern United States.

Similar species: None.

comet darner
Anax longipes

Biology: This big, uncommon species favors semipermanent, grassy ponds as long as there are few or no fish to prey upon its young (Dunkle 2000). We found the comet darner in precisely such a habitat. It feeds upon insects as large as medium-sized dragonflies. Males patrol territories that can extend to 150 feet in length, from morning to late afternoon. We saw two males engaged in this behavior, chasing one another through great expanses of air overhead while the other dragonflies, even the green darner, remained more closely tied to the extent of the pond itself.

Distribution: From the Atlantic Ocean to a western limit near Austin, Texas.

Remarks: The common name of "comet darner" was presumably given in recognition of the speed at which this attractive dragonfly streaks across the sky, or for its strikingly colored red tail. For the former reason, and because we saw it only once (in July, at the end of our work in the Lost Pines), we were unable to secure a specimen. In the standard work on Canadian dragonflies the authors describe the comet darner in one word: "magnificent" (Walker and Corbet 1975).

Similar species: Built like the green darner and similar in size, the male comet can be distinguished at a distance by its red abdomen.

firetail damselfly
Telebasis salva

Biology: The beautiful bright red males perch in low herbaceous vegetation near ponds. The reddish brown females do not drop their eggs into the water like so many of the dragonflies but insert them beneath the water line in the stem of a plant. Like all damselfies and dragonflies, the aquatic juveniles and the flying adults are predators of other insects. Damselflies are themselves preyed upon by their dragonfly relatives.

Distribution: This is one of the relatively few western insects of the forest, occurring from the Pacific Ocean to an eastern limit near the Lost Pines.

Remarks: Length 22 mm. Female firetails are brown and are thus easily mistaken for a different species.

Similar species: A second firetail, *Telebasis byersi,* reaches its western limit in Texas just as *T. salva* reaches its eastern limit in the same state. The males of both species are red and must be distinguished by microscopic examination of the tip of the abdomen.

blue-fronted dancer (fig. 164)
Argia apicalis

Biology: Dancers are named for their appearance in flight as they move from perch to perch along the shores of ponds and creeks. They rest in vegetation like other damselflies but are more prone than some to rest on the ground as well, including sidewalks (Westfall and May 1996). Males defend territories and will dart out to attack intruders. The female lays eggs in aquatic plants and wet logs while still attached to her mate (Dunkle 1990).

Distribution: From the Atlantic Ocean to Colorado.

Remarks: Length 35 mm. The blue head, thorax, and tail tip fade rapidly after death and can even change color with temperature when the animal is alive. Damselflies occasionally flew to our blacklights at night, but we never saw dragonflies doing the same.

Similar species: There are many dancer damselfly species in Texas, and their identification is difficult. The blue-fronted dancer is common at the artificial ponds of the Lost Pines.

golden stonefly
Neoperla clymene

Biology: The yellow-gold adults fly to blacklights in great numbers in spring and promptly begin mating in and on the light trap itself. They run rapidly when

Fig. 164. Blue-
fronted dancer
(*Argia apicalis*).

disturbed, often escaping on foot rather than on the wing. The juvenile or larval
stage lives on the bottom of ponds and feeds on fly maggots.

Distribution: From the Atlantic Ocean to a western extreme in or near the Lost
Pines with one disjunct population in Arizona.

Remarks: Length 16 mm. This is the only member of the stonefly order we encountered in the Lost Pines.

Similar species: None.

giant burrowing mayfly (fig. 165)
Hexagenia bilineata

Biology: The big adults appear at blacklight traps in spring but only in small
numbers. The juveniles or larvae live on pond bottoms or perhaps in the nearby

Fig. 165. Giant burrowing mayfly (*Hexagenia bilineata*).

Colorado River. Mayflies in general are unique among insects because there is a stage just before the adult that has wings, and this subadult sheds its flight organs with the rest of the exoskeleton as it passes to the final stage of development.

Distribution: Occurs sporadically from the Atlantic Ocean to a western limit in New Mexico.

Remarks: Length 30 mm. The small number of adults arriving at our lights is surprising considering that in the eastern United States they erupt in swarms large enough to stall traffic on bridges crossing the major rivers.

Similar species: None.

CHAPTER 10

Ant-lions, Owlflies, Dobsonflies, and Their Kin

The wings of these generally slender and soft-bodied insects have a complicated system of veins that suggests a network of nerves. This appearance gave rise to the name of the order Neuroptera. Some of the most interesting types are the larger ones rarely noticed in the Lost Pines or elsewhere. These include the dobsonfly, owlfly, and fishfly. We never saw a mantisfly in the forest, though they occur sparingly at porch lights in Austin, thirty miles northwest of the Lost Pines, and this despite the fact that in Central Texas the larvae are known to parasitize egg sacs of the green lynx spider (*Peucetia viridans*), which is abundant in the forest.

ant-lion (fig. 166)
Myrmeleon crudelis

Biology: The conical pit constructed in the sand by the ant-lion in its predatory larval stage ranks with the fire ant's mound as one of the most apparent insect homes in the Lost Pines. And the one is a predator of the other, for ants that blunder into the pit slide down its slippery slope and are seized in the huge jaws of the larva that lies hidden at the bottom. Thus the ant-lion is described as a "sit-and-wait" predator rather than one that searches out its prey. Prey are injected with toxin from the jaws and consumed below ground. If the ant evades the first strike and attempts to climb up the slippery slope, the ant-lion flips sand at it,

Fig. 166. Ant-lions, (A) adult of unidentified
species; (B) larva.

causing the quarry to slide once more into waiting jaws. The adult ant-lion is a
clumsy gray flier that resembles a damselfly or small dragonfly.

Distribution: From the Atlantic Ocean to the Pecos River region of west Texas.

Remarks: Adult length 25 mm. Some ants drop pebbles into the pit when an ant-
lion makes its home on a mound or nest.

Similar species: There are probably several ant-lion species in the forest that resemble *Myrmeleon crudelis* in the appearance of larva, adult, and pit. Microscopic
examination and the proper keys are required for confident identification. The
representative adult chosen here for illustration purposes has not been identified
to species.

lacewings (fig. 167)
Eremochrysa punctinervis and allies

Biology: Adult lacewings are small, nocturnal, weakly flying insects that flutter
through oak foliage on nights too cold for many insects to be on the wing. Most
are delicate green creatures that eat plant lice and release an unpleasant odor
when handled. The crawling larvae have the same diet and are important biocontrol
agents. They hatch from eggs suspended above a leaf or stem on long stalks that
give protection from one another as well as from other enemies.

Distribution: The species listed here occurs from the Atlantic Ocean to the western United States.

Remarks: Typical lengths including wings are 15 mm or less. Green lacewings in
particular are well camouflaged on foliage and are most likely to be seen while
flying.

Fig. 167. Eggs of a green lacewing.

Similar species: There are many green lacewings and there are brown ones too. Microscopic examination and the proper keys are required for a confident identification, which is difficult under the best of circumstances.

fishflies (fig. 168)
Chauliodes rastricornis, C. pectinicornis

Biology: The larval stage of the fishfly is an aquatic scavenger and predator that lives in ponds and resembles the dobsonfly hellgrammite in appearance and behavior. It eats copepods, algae, rotifers, and immature insects (Dolin and Tarter 1982), and when the time comes to transform into the adult stage, it crawls out of the water and metamorphoses beneath a sheltering rock or log.

Adult fishflies resemble adult dobsonflies, just as the larvae of the two relatives resemble one another. Very few of these primitive creatures flew to our blacklights over the years and we saw none during the light of day. In the eastern United States *Chauliodes rastricornis* appears first, at dusk in May and June, whereas *C. pectinicornis* appears at night in July (Dolin and Tarter 1982). In the Lost Pines we found both species that are known to occur in the United States, though according to a comprehensive work on the subject, *C. pectinicornis* should not have been expected nearly as far west as Central Texas (Hazard 1960).

Distribution: Fishflies occur from the Atlantic Ocean to a western limit in the Lost Pines of Texas as established here for *C. pectinicornis,* and in southwestern South Dakota for *C. rastricornis* (Johnson et al. 1997).

Fig. 168. Top: The fishflies *Chauliodes pectinicornis,* left, and *C. rastricornis,* right. Bottom: Owlfly (*Haplogenius appendiculatus*).

Remarks: Wingspan of *C. rastricornis* 80 mm, *C. pectinicornis* often a little less. The adult's diet, if it feeds at all, remains unknown.

Similar species: The jaws of the fishfly are much less imposing than the big, conspicuous mandibles of the dobsonfly. *Chauliodes pectinicornis* can be distinguished from the more common *C. rastricornis* by yellow marks on top of its head in place of dark or blackish marks.

owlfly (fig. 168)
Haplogenius appendiculatus

Biology: Adults are nocturnal predators that resemble ant-lions but are larger and much faster on the wing. The natural prey is unknown. Big robber flies, themselves highly predatory insects, are eaten under laboratory conditions. When resting during the day the owfly mimics twigs by gripping a branch or stem and by raising the long abdomen at an angle of nearly ninety degrees. Females lay their eggs on twigs in the shade of oak or juniper trees (Henry 1977). Larvae are similar to ant-lions but do not make pits in the sand. Instead they resemble a bit of oak leaf and rely on this camouflage while waiting for insect prey with jaws wide open. Prey are bitten, paralyzed with venom, and consumed. Afterwards the jaws are groomed clean.

Distribution: From the Atlantic Ocean to at least as far west as Arizona.

Remarks: Wingspan 71 mm. Owlflies have a musky odor that one of us detected when our single specimen was collected during the day while resting in the typical posture described.

Similar species: None.

dobsonflies (fig. 169)
Corydalus cornutus, C. luteus, ?C. texanus

Biology: The monstrous winged females lay their eggs at night on leaves that overhang running water, and when the larvae hatch they drop through the air into the current below. These juveniles are known as hellgrammites and are gilled bottom-dwelling predators that subsist upon aquatic insects including their own kind. Hellgrammites are best known as a popular fishing bait and for their ability to nip handlers with their powerful jaws. When the time arrives to transform to the adult stage, they crawl ashore and pupate in the soil beneath a stone or some other covering object. Adults live no longer than two weeks and are so specialized for reproduction that they appear to require no food at this stage of their lives. Under lab conditions they reject insect prey but will drink sweet liquids instead. The female's powerful jaws are inherited from the voracious hellgrammite stage and can draw blood should she bite a human handler.

The male's jaws could hardly be more different in size and shape. They are enormous sickles that are used to stimulate his mate (but perhaps not to grip her, as has sometimes been said). First he prods the female, then he lays the long jaws across her back. If a second male approaches, the two begin fighting. Big mandibles flail away and the female is likely to be knocked aside in the melee. Jaws are sometimes broken off in battle. Smaller males not only win on occasion but sometimes dislodge a larger male that has already rested its jaws on a female's back (Parfin 1952).

Distribution: The common dobsonfly *C. cornutus* occurs from coast to coast within the United States. For discussion of the remaining two species of the United States, see "Similar species."

Remarks: Wingspan 102 mm. This large and striking insect has a fierce, primitive aspect. Our few specimens were drawn to blacklights long after dark near the edge of a large pond in May, though the world authority on dobsonflies suggested that they probably flew in from the Colorado River one mile away, or perhaps from an associated creek. Unfortunately, the males with their spectacular jaws are known to be less attracted to lights than are females. Our experience confirms this generalization for we failed in our attempts to draw them in. This contrast is paradoxical because when there is a difference between the sexes of an

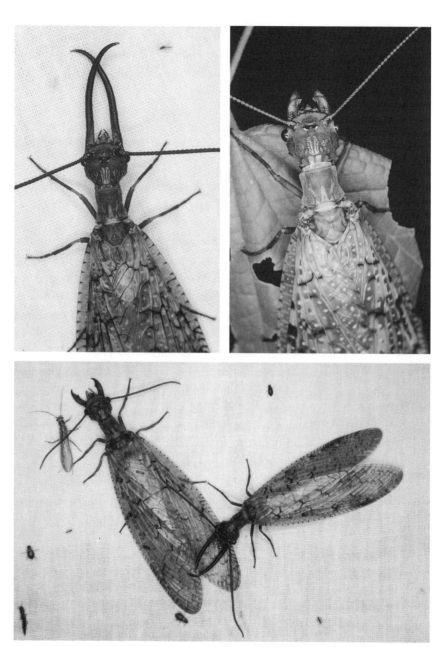

Fig. 169. Texas dobsonfly (*Corydalus texanus*), (A) male; (B) female;
(C) courting pair at blacklight at night (photographed in the
Ottine swamp of Gonzales County).

insect species, it is usually the male that flies to lights more readily than the female. The examples shown here were found in the Ottine swamp of Gonzales County and are specimens of the Texas dobsonfly.

Similar species: Three dobsonfly species occur in the United States and all three occur in Texas. The Texas dobsonfly (*C. texanus*) has a conspicuous dark ring surrounding each white spot on its wings, but it is not known to occur quite as far north as the Lost Pines (Contreras-Ramos 1998). On the other hand, the yellow dobsonfly (*C. luteus*) has been collected in the Central Texas forest but not by us. It lacks the conspicuous color pattern displayed on the head of *Corydalus cornutus*. The species most likely to be seen is the common dobsonfly (*C. cornutus*). It resembles the Texas species but does not have a dark ring around each white wing spot.

alderfly
Sialis unidentified species

Biology: The short-lived adults are black, day-flying insects that remain close to the water where they developed as larvae. Eggs are laid in masses of up to nearly a thousand on objects overhanging the water. In this behavior alderflies resemble their relatives the dobsonflies. Larvae crawl on muddy bottoms of ponds, streams, lakes, and rivers and prey on other small animals. Eventually they leave the water and transform into the winged adult stage (Arnold and Drew 1987).

Distribution: Undetermined because our single specimen is a female that cannot be identified even with a microscope and the standard key (Ross 1937).

Remarks: Wingspan 26 mm. Alderflies must be rather uncommon in the Lost Pines, for we saw a single specimen during years of study. It was resting several feet from the shore of a large artificial pond.

Similar species: Several alderflies occur in Texas, and the females of some species are too similar to be distinguished from one another. Our Lost Pines specimen could be *Sialis velata, S. itasca,* or *S. concava* (female unknown). The latter occurs from the Atlantic Ocean to at least as far west as Kerrville and is the only species specifically reported from Texas in the very old standard reference (Ross 1937). A search of the shorelines surrounding artificial ponds, preferably in mid-March, might turn up more specimens and allow a confident identification.

CHAPTER 11

Mantids, Walkingsticks, and Cockroaches

Mantids belong here with their relatives the cockroaches because they might have evolved from a roach or roachlike ancestor that switched from omnivory to an exclusively predatory diet. The origin of the exclusively herbivorous walkingsticks is not so obvious, but we treat them here because their shape, size, and manner of development are at least suggestive of the mantis condition.

Carolina mantis (fig. 170)
Stagmomantis carolina

Biology: Though seldom seen in the Lost Pines, the Carolina mantis is probably abundant in the strict sense of occurring in large numbers. The species is nearly invisible due to an apparent preference for the heights of trees rather than the open lowlands of meadows. Occasionally a Carolina mantis shows up at blacklights, and we did encounter one female after dark on a low-growing plant at the edge of a pond. This was the only specimen seen under natural conditions.

The Carolina mantis is a predator with a broad diet including flies, roaches, and other insects. In nearby Austin a male flew to a hanging hummingbird feeder and awaited the arrival of bees, but the females must walk or leap wherever they go because their wings are too small for flight. The egg cases that they leave on bark, fence posts of wood, and even on metal poles are instantly recognizable as

Fig. 170. Carolina mantis (*Stagmomantis carolina*); male on left, female on right.

tough brown pods with a braided appearance. In fact, these are more likely to be seen than the insects themselves.

Distribution: From the Atlantic Ocean to the Rocky Mountains and Arizona.

Remarks: Length 53 mm. Common names for mantids include "soothsayers," "mule killers," "devil's riding horses," and in the U.S. Southwest and Mexico, "campomoche."

Similar species: The Carolina mantis resembles the more famous praying mantis, but the latter does not occur in this forest. Large size, green and brown color, and a preference for the heights of vegetation distinguish the Carolina mantis from the small brown Scudder's mantis, which remains close to the ground. The northern grass mantis differs from both by its larger size, tiny wing flaps, and thickened antennae.

Scudder's stick mantis (figs. 171, 172)
Oligonicella scudderi

Biology: The wingless females of this tiny brown ground mantis race and leap across the sandy soil when they are not hiding or hunting in clumps of little bluestem grass, where their protective coloration makes them nearly invisible. Males are ready fliers that flutter to blacklight traps at night. The only records of this animal's prey seem to be our own observations of males devouring small flies, wasps, and caddisflies at blacklights after dark (fig. 171). Scudder's mantis will also drink water in captivity.

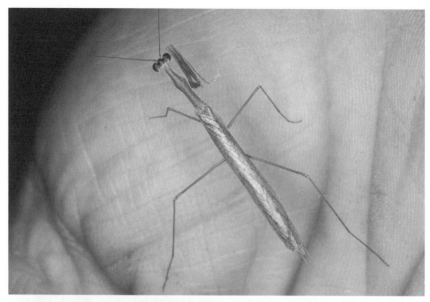

Fig. 171. Scudder's stick mantis (*Oligonicella scudderi*), (A) male on palm of hand; (B) male eating a wasp at night, with blacklight trap in the background.

Fig. 172. The previously unreported egg case of Scudder's stick mantis.

The egg case of Scudder's mantis was unknown until now. We obtained two specimens when each of two captured females produced the tiny structures and glued them to the sides of plastic collection vials (fig. 172).

Distribution: From the Atlantic Ocean to West Texas.

Remarks: Length 35 mm. Outside the Lost Pines this animal has been described as rare (Hebard 1943; Tinkham 1948). Within the forest it is abundant but difficult to see and must be sought by sweeping grass with a net. Early fall is a good time of year to observe Scudder's stick mantis.

Similar species: *See* Carolina mantis.

northern grass mantis (fig. 173)
Brunneria borealis

Biology: This large and attractive mantis is unique among the Lost Pines animals treated here because every individual is a female. The species exists without males and therefore without mating and without sexual reproduction. Females lay eggs protected by cases that are themselves remarkable among those produced by mantids because one end is drawn out into a little point through which all the tiny juveniles must escape when they hatch. When most mantids leave an egg case, each crawls out through its own individual escape hatch. Yet another striking feature is the reduction of the wings to tiny flaps that may have no function

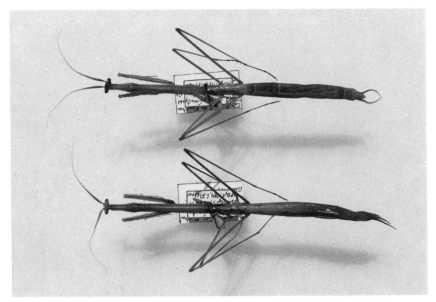

Fig. 173. Northern grass mantis (*Brunneria borealis*).

at all. Northern grass mantids can be classified as predators with complete confidence, but we could find no published records of their prey. In the Lost Pines they occur in meadows of little bluestem grass and nowhere else, as far as we know. Given this fact, and their considerable size, their diet may consist largely of grasshoppers.

Distribution: From the Atlantic Ocean to a western limit near the Lost Pines. We saw specimens in the Texas A&M collection that were captured in Brazos County, Comanche County, and Erath County, Populations are probably disjunct and sporadic.

Remarks: Length 77 mm. We found only two individuals of this intriguing but poorly studied species. They were caught minutes apart on the same night, well after dark, as we swept a little bluestem meadow with nets. In life they were light green but after death they soon turned wood-brown.

Nearly sixty years before our own study, an authority who encountered the northern grass mantis elsewhere in Texas reported that individuals tend to rest at a height of one foot above ground and climb higher into the grass when disturbed (Hebard 1943). Yet in our experience they were never seen during the day, and at night we saw them only in our sweep nets.

Similar species: *See* Carolina mantis.

Tamaulipas walkingstick (fig. 174)
Diapheromera tamaulipensis

Biology: This stick insect or walkingstick crawls about in hardwood trees and among the grasses of meadows and clearings and is unusual among our walking-sticks for not being restricted to one such habitat or the other. It feeds on leaves of blackjack oak and hackberry and on little bluestem grass, where we collected individuals with sweep nets. This is the first record of little bluestem as a food plant for the species.

Tamaulipas walkingsticks are active both day and night. Mating pairs are commonly seen during daylight hours in the hackberries that grow heavily along Central Texas fence lines. Females are gray or green, thicker than the slender brown males, and especially remarkable for the pair of "horns" borne on the head; males lack these altogether. The female's color makes her harder to see in grass habitats than the male, but the male's incredibly twiglike coloration and shape makes this sex more difficult to detect in the trees.

Distribution: Within the United States the Tamaulipas walkingstick occurs only in Texas, where it inhabits a narrow corridor stretching from the Pecos River in the west to an eastern limit near the Lost Pines.

Remarks: Length 90 mm. The presence of horns on the female's head and their absence from the male's head is baffling. When horns are present in one sex but not in the other it is usually the male that bears them, for he uses the weapons to fight other males in competition for mates.

Fig. 174. Female Tamaulipas walkingstick (*Diapheromera tamaulipensis*) on blackjack oak at night.

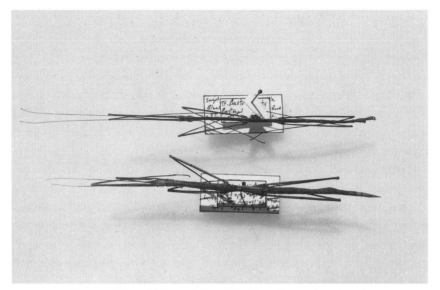

**Fig. 175. Thread-like walkingstick (*Pseudosermyle strigata*);
male at top, female at bottom.**

Similar species: This species is easily confused with the best known of North American walkingsticks, *Diapheromera femorata*. The problem is mitigated in the Lost Pines by the apparent absence of the latter species from this southern forest. The photographs provided here will aid in the identification of the four Lost Pines walkingstick species, but microscopic examination and the proper keys should be consulted when positive identification is important.

thread-like walkingstick (fig. 175)
Pseudosermyle strigata

Biology: In the Lost Pines this skeleton-like animal appears to feed on the leaves of little bluestem grass and on no other plant. This is the first report of little bluestem as a host for the species. Nearly sixty years before our own study the insect was found in nearby Flatonia, Texas, feeding on Texas bunch-grass (*Nolina texana;* Hebard 1943). That habitat was outside the forest and is located instead on the primordial grassland remnant known as the Fayette Prairie. Exceedingly slender and well camouflaged in the light brown color of dry grass, this animal is easily overlooked even when close at hand.

Distribution: From Alabama to a western limit in or near the Lost Pines.

Remarks: Length 60 mm. The male is the thinnest stick insect in the forest.

Similar species: *See* Tamaulipas walkingstick *and* Blatchley's walkingstick.

Blatchley's walkingstick (fig. 176)
Manomera blatchley

Biology: Contrary to the observations of others who believed the species to be more strictly nocturnal, we found this rare animal to be very active during the day. In fact, both sexes were fully exposed in a meadow, in the tops of little bluestem grass, at the hottest hour of the afternoon, and all this during the hottest August on record (1999) for the nearby city of Austin, Texas. The animal feeds on no other host plant, according to our experience. In the eastern United States a relative was found in piney woods habitat like that of the Central Texas forest (Blatchley 1920; Helfer 1953). Females are green on the upper surface and blend in well with living stems of the host plant. Males are thinner, browner, and strangely enough bear a greater resemblance to twigs than to grass, though we have never seen them on woody plants. In summer the two sexes are often seen mating on little bluestem beginning as early as June.

Fig. 176. Female Blatchley's walkingstick (*Manomera blatchley*)
on little bluestem grass.

Distribution: As far as we know this is the first report of the species from Texas. Its range as previously understood was limited to the eastern United States from the Atlantic Ocean to Oklahoma.

Remarks: Length 85 mm. The Lost Pines presents a splendid opportunity for the study of a variety of insects that are poorly known and that are clinging to remnants of an ancient little bluestem prairie. Blatchely's walkingstick is among their number.

Similar species: *See* Tamaulipas walkingstick.

giant walkingstick (fig. 177)
Megaphasma dentricus

Biology: This is a huge leaf-eating vegetarian, and previous records of its host plants include grape vines in the river bottoms of nearby Victoria, Texas (Caudell 1903), post oaks in the same area (Hebard 1943), and "shrubs and trees" (Somes 1916). We saw a single specimen, a male, and it was on a post oak trunk in July.

In Texas the giant walkingstick is "extremely local" in its appearance (Hebard 1943). Hebard and a colleague visited the site in Victoria where the walkingstick had been reported from river bottom grapevines, but a search of many hours ended in frustration without a single specimen. He suggested that night collecting with a flashlight or headlamp might meet with greater success.

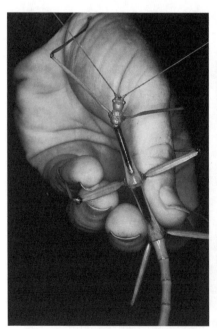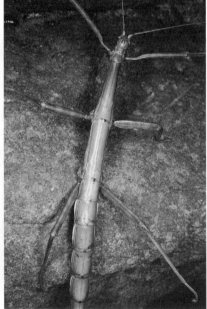

Fig. 177. Giant walkingstick (*Megaphasma dentricus*), (A) male; (B) female.

Fig. 178. Boll's sand cockroach (*Arenivaga bolliana*), male.

Distribution: The giant walkingstick has an unusual inland range from New Mexico in the west to Kentucky in the east.

Remarks: Reaching lengths of nearly seven inches, this animal is the longest insect in the United States. An early authority described it as more tropical in appearance than any of the other walkingsticks of the United States and noted that "the large size commands attention wherever seen" (Caudell 1903). The species is much more common in the Ottine swamp of Gonzales County south of the Lost Pines.

Similar species: None.

Boll's sand cockroach (fig. 178)
Arenivaga bolliana

Biology: The rarely seen female is a round, wingless, dark brown, tanklike roach that lives in rat burrows beneath mesquite trees (Hebard 1917). Males are sometimes seen after dark clinging to little bluestem grass, but they are most often encountered when flying to blacklights at night.

Distribution: Within the United States this species occurs only in Texas, and the Lost Pines is near the eastern limit of its range.

Remarks: Length 20 mm. Boll's sand cockroach is the largest and most commonly seen cockroach of the forest. It is smaller than some of the better known house pests (nearly all of which are exotics introduced into the United States), but none of those familiar pests has invaded these woods. All of the species we saw were natives.

Similar species: The Tonkawa cockroach (*A. tonkawa*) may occur in the Lost Pines. It resembles Boll's sand cockroach so greatly that males can be separated only by a microscopic examination of the reproductive structures (Hebard 1943). We performed these dissections and never saw the Tonkawa roach.

Pennsylvania wood roach (fig. 179)
Parcoblatta pensylvanica

Biology: This species is a denizen of grasslands as well as forest. It appears on pine trunks at night. In keeping with its reputation as the only roach of the forest that sometimes becomes a house pest (Helfer 1953), it has moved into the Depression era stone cabins of Bastrop State Park. Subfreezing weather does not prevent the insect from moving about (Blatchley 1920).

Distribution: From the Atlantic Ocean to San Antonio, Texas, not far west of the Lost Pines.

Remarks: Length 15 mm. Pennsylvania wood roaches were considered rare in Central Texas by one authority, but they are probably abundant in the isolated Lost Pines forest. The females are much more commonly seen than the males.

Similar species: Several close relatives are likely to occur in these woods. Confident identification requires microscopic examination and the proper keys.

Fig. 179. Female Pennsylvania wood roach (*Parcoblatta pensylvanica*)
with egg case, on loblolly pine at night.

Fig. 180. The beautiful pale-bordered cockroach
(*Pseudomops septentrionalis*), mating pair.

pale-bordered cockroach (fig. 180)
Pseudomops septentrionalis

Biology: This is the most beautiful roach in the forest, and our experience confirms the generalization that it tends to climb into low-growing herbaceous plants, unlike the other species treated here. We seldom saw it under different circumstances, and our sightings occurred during daylight hours. Almost nothing is known about its biology.

Distribution: In the United States the pale-bordered cockroach has long been thought to occur naturally only in Texas, from near the Louisiana border in the east to the Devils River area in the west. However, populations have been discovered in Alabama and Mississippi, suggesting either accidental introduction from farther west or natural range expansion (Schiff and Schieffer 1999). The bright colors of the pale-bordered cockroach suggest a tropical exotic, but this elegant creature is a Texas native.

Remarks: Length 12 mm. Pale-bordered roaches seem to prefer low areas near bodies of water; the few specimens we have seen were in a dry creekbed in Austin, at the edge of the Ottine swamp in Gonzales County, and along pond margins in

the Lost Pines. A better common name would be the "elegant roach."
Similar species: None.

dark wood roach
Ischnoptera deropeltiformis

Biology: Dark wood roaches are primarily ground dwellers that frequent leaf litter and logs. Males are unusual among cockroaches because they tend to fly rather than run when disturbed (Blatchley 1920). Females have reduced wings and cannot fly at all.

Distribution: From the Atlantic Ocean to a western limit in or near the Lost Pines.

Remarks: Length 14 mm. Dark wood roaches are said to prefer moist forests. If this is true, then the dry Lost Pines must be an exception and is perhaps a marginal habitat for the species.

Similar species: The dark color combined with the orange legs distinguish this slender roach from all others.

Texas cockroach
Chorisoneura texensis

Biology: The small yellow Texas cockroach lives in logs and flies to blacklights at night. Both sexes are fully winged. They have been collected elsewhere under leaves and in vegetation, especially in oak trees and bayberry, but we have never seen them in these situations.

Distribution: From the Atlantic Ocean to a western extreme near Del Rio, Texas.

Remarks: Length 8 mm. Boll's sand cockroach would be a better choice as a "Texas" species because in the United States it occurs nowhere else, whereas the tiny yellow species treated here is widely distributed in the southeastern states.

Similar species: This roach is much smaller than almost all of the other Lost Pines species, but confident identification requires microscopic examination and the proper keys.

Schwarz's cockroach (fig. 181)
Compsodes schwarzi

Biology: Poorly known. Schwarz's cockroach has been found elsewhere under stones and it was long ago predicted to occur under bark as well (Hebard 1943). We confirmed that prediction in the Central Texas forest.

Distribution: Unusual because the range is broken up into three regions not in contact with one another: southern Texas, southern Florida, and Arizona (Atkinson et al. 1991).

Fig. 181. The previously unreported egg case of Schwarz's cockroach
(*Compsodes schwarzi*); magnified view.

Remarks: Length 6 mm. As far as we know the little female has never been illustrated, and this is the first report of the egg case or ootheca (fig. 181; length 2 mm).

Similar species: Schwarz's cockroach is smaller than all others treated here, but it should be identified with a microscope and the proper keys.

CHAPTER 12

Termites, Earwigs, and Angel Insects

These small animals are likely to evade notice unless a search is made beneath bark, logs, or stones. All but the angel insect are considered pests when they occur beyond the wild.

arid-land subterranean termite (fig. 182)
Reticulitermes tibialis

Biology: This is an extremely common and readily observed termite occurring beneath the bark of decomposing logs and snags. Colonies must remain in contact with soil even when the workers tunnel indoors and become pests. Members of the soldier caste have a larger, darker head with more powerful jaws than those of the worker caste. The blackish winged sexuals erupt from the colony after rains for the nuptial or mating flight.

Distribution: This is one of the relatively few western animals of the Lost Pines, occurring from the Pacific Ocean to an eastern limit near Lake Michigan. In Texas its range stops just west of the Louisiana border.

Remarks: Length 4 mm (soldier). Nearly every decomposing loblolly seems to have a colony tunneling beneath its bark. In the forest the arid-land termite is beneficial because it reduces dead trees to nutrients that can be recycled by other animals and by plants.

Similar species: The lesser desert termite is smaller and much less common. It does not appear to make its colonies in logs, and its soldiers have sickle-shaped jaws.

Fig. 182. Soldiers and workers of the arid-land subterranean termite (*Reticulitermes tibialis*) on a decomposing loblolly pine log. Darker-headed individuals near center are soldiers.

lesser desert termite
Amitermes minimus

Biology: Lesser desert termites live beneath stones rather than within logs and feed on buried wood, whether this is in a natural setting or part of a telephone pole or fence post. Roots and cow chips are also eaten. Members of the soldier caste have a big head and sickle-shaped mandibles with a tooth near the base. Workers vibrate rapidly and dispense an alarm chemical when disturbed. The winged males and females feign death under similar circumstances.

Distribution: This is one of the relatively few western insects of the forest, ranging from the Pacific Coast to an eastern limit in the Lost Pines as established here.

Remarks: Length of worker 2 mm. Lesser desert termites are destructive pests in some parts of the western United States. They appear to be uncommon in the forest.

Similar species: *See* arid-land subterranean termite.

striped earwig (fig. 183)
Labidura riparia

Biology: This is an omnivorous, nocturnal, and very large introduced earwig that catches prey as fast and as wary as flies by snatching them with the distinctive forceps located at the tip of the abdomen. Striped earwigs are fine biocontrol

Fig. 183. The exotic striped earwig (*Labidura riparia*); male on left, female on right. Hindwings are open, expanded, and fully transparent.

agents because they kill more insects than they eat (e.g., twenty armyworms per night), and this toll includes a fellow exotic, the red imported fire ant queen. They are known to favor waterfronts, and in Central Texas we did indeed encounter them in greatest numbers along the shore of Lake Somerville east of the Lost Pines. Yet in the forest itself we never saw them along any of the shores of the artificial ponds. Our several specimens flew to blacklights placed in a meadow located more than one hundred yards from the nearest of these unnatural waters. This is especially interesting because striped earwigs are thought to make appearances at lights only rarely, and according to one report they were deemed incapable of flight in any event. During the day these exotics hide beneath stones, logs, and sundry debris. Females are remarkable for the parental care they provide, guarding their eggs in tunnels in the soil.

Distribution: Introduced into the United States and now occurring from the Atlantic Ocean to Texas, with a separate introduction into California.

Remarks: Length 26 mm. At more than one inch in length, this is presently the largest earwig in Texas, and it is the only species that we noticed in the Lost Pines. Striped earwigs are protected by an oily secretion that smells worse than carrion (Blatchley 1920). However, we did not notice this odor during our few encounters. They can give a painful nip with the distinctive forceps. There is no penchant for crawling into ears, as folklore maintains.

Similar species: None.

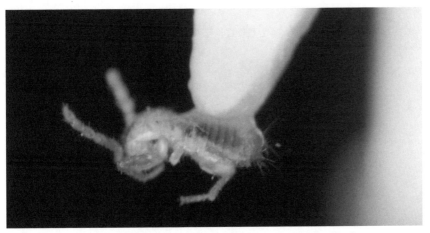

Fig. 184. A Hubbard's angel insect (*Zorotypus hubbardi*), from decomposing loblolly pine snag.

Hubbard's angel insect (fig. 184)
Zorotypus hubbardi

Biology: Hubbard's angel insect is a rare or at least rarely seen animal that resembles a termite and shares the same habitat of decomposing wood. These insects live in groups if not in colonies, and each sex exists in the form of both winged and wingless individuals. The wingless individuals are blind. Though angel insects live beneath bark, they eat the fungi growing on the wood, not the wood itself. Mites and dead colony members are consumed opportunistically.

Distribution: From the Atlantic Ocean to a western limit in the Lost Pines as established here.

Remarks: Length 2 mm. Hubbard's angel insect is the only member of the insect order Zoraptera that occurs in the United States outside Florida, where a second species also occurs. The origin of the common name "angel insect" is unclear.

Similar species: A comparison of the photos will serve to distinguish an angel insect from the termites that might surround its colony beneath the bark of a decomposing pine.

CHAPTER 13

Silverfish, Scorpionflies, Foot-spinners, Millipedes, and Centipedes

The insects of this chapter are distantly related to one another and to the more familiar insects that comprise each of the major orders. The many-legged millipedes and centipedes are of course not insects at all.

Texas pine silverfish (fig. 185)
Allacrotelsa spinulata

Biology: Pine silverfish are omnivorous scavengers. They are silvery, wingless insects that actively avoid light and must be sought beneath loblolly bark, where they are exceedingly abundant, and in the sandy leaf litter, where they may be more numerous still. Their enemies include the nocturnally active spitting spider (fig. 195).

Distribution: The pine silverfish was first discovered in Texas but is now known to occur from coast to coast within the United States.

Remarks: Length 14 mm. The Lost Pines would be a splendid field site for the study of this insect's nearly unknown biology. Every living loblolly seems to harbor them beneath its rough bark.

Similar species: None. The smaller, pestiferous silverfishes that chew on old books indoors do not occur in the Lost Pines.

Fig. 185. The Texas pine silverfish (*Allacrotelsa spinulata*) on loblolly pine bark.

scorpionfly (fig. 186)
Panorpa nuptialis

Biology: Adults are odd-looking red insects with long beaks and black and orange wings. They appear in fall and winter in small numbers to scavenge dead animals and sip nectar from flowers. On one occasion a group of seven was seen feeding on a dead frog (Byers 1954). Favored habitats are open areas along treelines and powerline cuts. We normally found them on the ground rather than on vegetation. Male scorpionflies bear a harmless structure at the tip of the abdomen that resembles a scorpion's sting but is used to grasp the female as the two prepare to mate. He also vibrates his wings and presents her with a gift in the form of a salivary secretion. Both sexes regurgitate a brownish substance when handled. They are clumsy fliers, and when disturbed they set down again after only a few seconds in the air. The bright colors of the body and wings warn potential enemies of distastefulness, or perhaps they only mimic animals that truly do taste bad or deliver a painful sting. Scorpionfly larvae resemble caterpillars. However, they do not live in vegetation or feed upon green leaves. They crawl in the soil and scavenge for food.

Distribution: From the Atlantic Ocean to the Austin, Texas, area just west of the Lost Pines.

Remarks: Wingspan 36 mm. According to one report, scorpionflies are becoming scarcer because red imported fire ants prey on the vulnerable soil-dwelling larval stage.

Similar species: None.

dark foot-spinner (fig. 187)
Oligotoma nigra

Biology: Foot-spinners are remarkable for spinning silk from their front legs as they construct tunnels in which they live as members of a loosely knit community. While spinning they resemble a boxer throwing punches, even to the swollen "gloves" near the tip of each forearm (fig. 187). Tunnels are built on plants, in lichens, under rocks, under logs, and even under cow chips. The diet is vegetarian. Males have wings but the females, which guard their eggs like earwigs, do not.

Distribution: This is an Old World exotic that occurs sporadically in the western United States and reaches an eastern limit near the Lost Pines.

Remarks: Length 9 mm. Our single foot-spinner encounter was with a male that flew to a blacklight trap at night. In its homelands of Pakistan, India, Egypt, and Iran, the dark foot-spinner lives on date palms, but in the Lost Pines its tunnels must be constructed elsewhere, for there are no palms in these woods. We never saw a native foot-spinner.

Similar species: Several native footspinners probably occur in the forest. Microscopic examination and the proper keys are required for confident identification.

giant millipede (fig. 188)
Narceus americanus

Biology: This is an attractive reddish brown animal that can exceed six inches in length. It usually remains hidden beneath logs during the day. On warm nights it

Fig. 186. Scorpionfly (*Panorpa nuptialis;* mating pair on leaf).

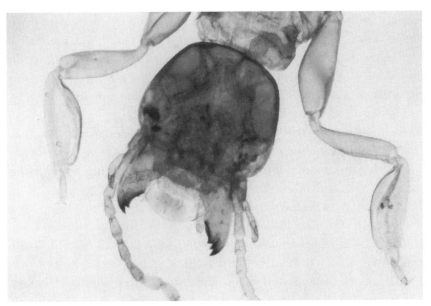

Fig. 187. The dark foot-spinner (*Oligotoma nigra;* male), showing swollen forelegs used to spin silk.

Fig. 188. The giant millipede (*Narceus americanus*) on eastern juniper.

emerges to crawl on the ground and on tree trunks in search of the dead plants and animals that it eats. The habitat affiliation is not so much with the pines of the Central Texas forest as with its oaks and hickories (Dowdy 1968), yet the closeup shown here features one of two individuals that crawled side by side up the trunk of an eastern juniper during a rare rainy spell in early autumn.

Molting occurs during dry periods, when the animal burrows into a log, seals itself off, and sheds its skin (Hopkin and Read 1992). Its eggs are laid in a curious manner. The female places each one in a wad of chewed leaf litter, passes it backward with many cooperating legs, and shapes it within the rectum before placing the egg in a pile with others (Levi and Levi 1987).

Distribution: From the Atlantic Ocean to a western limit near Georgetown, Texas, not far north of the Lost Pines.

Remarks: Giant millipedes do not bite or sting when handled, but they do dispense a yellow fluid, which stains the skin although doing no real harm.

Similar species: None. Several smaller millipedes are occasionally seen in these woods, usually hiding beneath rocks and logs but sometimes crawling on bark in the manner of the giant American millipede. They can be difficult to identify, and the world authorities themselves sometimes cannot provide an identification even when material is sent for examination. In one case we know nothing beyond the fact that the specimen was a female of the family Parajulidae, order Julida (Rowland Shelley, pers. comm.).

centipedes (figs. 189, 190)

Biology: All centipedes are carnivorous. They typically have fewer legs per segment than do millipedes and are flatter in form. We saw at least three species

Fig. 189. Margined centipede (*Hemiscolopendra marginata;* lighter color in life).

Fig. 190. Unidentified stone centipede.

from time to time beneath rocks and decomposing logs. The species featured here is the margined centipede, *Hemiscolopendra marginata*. There appears to be very little published information on its natural history. It lives under and within fallen pines (avoiding hardwoods), is sluggish compared to its speedy relatives, and is prone to enter buildings and bite the occupants (Hoffman and Shelley 1996).

Distribution: The margined centipede occurs from the Atlantic Ocean to the Big Bend area of West Texas.

Remarks: Length 60 cm. In nearby Austin, Texas, centipedes of a related species but of much greater size (five inches or so) turn up in buildings from time to time. We saw no individuals of such length in the Lost Pines. A second species, several inches long, brown, very sinuous, and with an enormous number of legs, was occasionally seen beneath and within rotting logs. Perhaps this is a soil centipede of the order Geophilomorpha. It remains to be identified. A third species, short, fast, and with very long legs that have an elbowed appearance, is the house centipede (*Scutigera coleoptrata*) that sometimes becomes a pest in homes. The Lost Pines is also home to a common but unidentified species of stone centipede (fig. 190). Perhaps it is a species of the genus *Lithobius*.

Similar species: No suitable key to identification of North American centipedes existed at the time of this writing, but Dr. Rowland Shelley of the North Carolina Museum of Natural Sciences was in the process of publishing one. We thank him for identifying the margined centipede.

CHAPTER 14

Spiders, Scorpions, and Other Arachnids

The spiders of the Lost Pines include among their number two species of medical importance. These are the brown recluse (*Loxosceles reclusa*) and the southern black widow (*Latrodectus mactans*). The widow's bite can be lethal and the bite of the much more abundant recluse can cause lingering wounds. A single scorpion species shares the woods with its spider relatives. It is abundant but not deadly. And though between us we visited the forest and its clearings more than a hundred times, we encountered a single tick and were seldom annoyed by chiggers (juvenile mites).

bowl-and-doily spider (fig. 191)
Frontinella pyramitela

Biology: This is a very small spider, conspicuous only for its distinctive web, which suggests a wispy bowl hovering above a silken saucer or doily. Webs are spun in trees and are often seen at chest height along hiking trails. They are especially apparent in the boughs of eastern juniper.

Distribution: From coast to coast within the United States.

Remarks: Length 4 mm. The tiny spider is easily overlooked in the large web, which often collects debris more conspicuous than the animal itself.

Similar species: None.

Fig. 191. Web of the bowl-and-doily spider (*Frontinella pyramitela*).

green lynx spider (fig. 192)
Peucetia viridans

Biology: The green lynx is a large, bright green, meadow-dwelling predator that blends into foliage near the tips of herbaceous vegetation such as little bluestem grass and various members of the daisy family. These spiders catch their prey, including red imported fire ants, without need of the highly reduced web, which females use instead to embrace their spiny egg sac. When the young hatch, the female guards them to the extent of spitting venom at intruders (Jackman 1997).

Distribution: From coast to coast within the United States.

Remarks: Length 16 mm. This is the most apparent spider of the forest during spring and summer months.

Similar species: None.

giant orb weaver (fig. 193)
Araneus bicentenarius

Biology: Big adult females appear briefly in spring when they seem to be everywhere, building the largest webs in the woods. These are nearly circular, sometimes several feet wide, and they span hiking trails at night in such densities that flashlights or headlamps are needed to avoid blundering into them. During the day the animal can be found hiding in a curled oak leaf (the "refugium") near one

Fig. 192. The green lynx spider (*Peucetia viridans*), (A) female with
Carolina red wasp prey; (B) male.

of the top edges of the web. A remarkable feature is the lichenlike pattern on the
abdomen, which is useful as protective coloration on the lichen-bearing oaks this
harmless species favors. The spider preys upon insects as large and heavily armored as the male ox beetle that we found hanging in pieces from a web. It had
flown into the trap during the previous night.

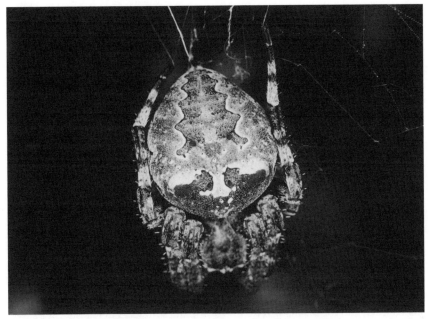

Fig. 193. Giant orb weaver (*Araneus bicentenarius*).

Distribution: From the Atlantic Ocean to a western extreme near Austin, Texas, not far from the Lost Pines.

Remarks: Length 25 mm. The literature describes this orb weaver as rare (Levi 1971). In the Central Texas forest it is briefly and seasonally common.

Similar species: None.

brown recluse spider (fig. 194)
Loxosceles reclusa

Biology: The brown recluse is an extremely abundant predator that occurs in numbers beneath the rough bark of nearly every loblolly pine, whether living or dead. It is particularly common under the loose, heavy shingles near the bases of trees. A dozen or more sometimes live side by side. When the bark is lifted from the underlying wood, a patch of white silk clings to both surfaces until the threads are finally pulled apart like a ball of medical cotton. The spider is the dark spot hiding within a quarter-sized patch of silk, and on its back is a darker pattern often compared to the shape of a violin. The brown recluse feeds on bark-dwelling insects.

Distribution: From Georgia to a western limit near the Lost Pines.

Remarks: Length 11 mm. Recluses are best known for turning up indoors in

Fig. 194. Brown recluse (*Loxosceles reclusa*).

folded linen and for the nasty bites they sometimes inflict. These result in a slow-healing, ulcerous wound.

Similar species: A close relative (*Loxosceles devia*) occurs west of the Lost Pines and perhaps within the forest itself. Microscopic examination and the proper keys are required for confident identification, which remains difficult under the best of circumstances (Gertsch and Ennik 1983).

spitting spider (fig. 195)
Scytodes undetermined species

Biology: This unique predator lives beneath bark in the same microhabitat as that of the brown recluse, but it is much less common. Spitting spiders earn their name with an unusual manner of capturing prey. They shoot a venomous substance from their fangs in a zigzag squirt that requires only a fraction of a second to do its work (McAlister 1960). This pins the prey to the wood surface and allows the spider to make its kill without a web and without biting its victim, though it often does that too. Here we show an adult specimen feeding on the Texas pine silverfish, *Allacrotelsa spinulata*. The camera's flash eventually drove the predator into the protection of its cavelike den within a decomposing snag.

Spitting is used successfully in defense against enemies as large as the bark scorpion. We saw one male and one female sharing a web in September. This female and others nearby were carrying egg sacs in their jaws. In summer we saw two males walking about and apparently competing in a female's web. In both cases the spiders were occupying the ends of decomposing oak logs.

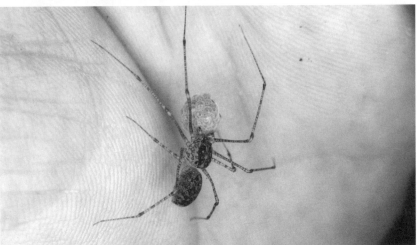

Fig. 195. The spitting spider (*Scytodes* sp.), (A) with Texas pine silverfish prey;
(B) with egg sac held by fangs.

Distribution: Unknown.

Remarks: Length 8 mm. Our inability to identify this interesting animal to the species level is due to a lack of published work on spitting spiders in general (Jackman 1997).

Similar species: The habitat and appearance of the harmless spitting spider predispose it for misidentification as a brown recluse. The photos provided here will obviate that problem.

garden spiders
Argiope aurantia, A. trifasciata

Biology: These are very large orb-weaving spiders that do not hide during the day in a retreat, as the giant orb weaver does, but remain in the center of the web. They occur on clumps of little bluestem grass in meadows, on shrubby oaks in powerline cuts, and along fencerows. The female golden garden spider (*A. aurantia*) produces a large, round egg sac, whereas the egg sac of the banded garden spider (*A. trifasciata*) is shaped like a kettle drum (Kaston 1978).

Distribution: Both garden spiders occur from coast to coast within the United States.

Remarks: Length 25 mm. These impressive spiders are not as common in the clearings of the forest as one might expect. Adult golden garden spiders have a wide dark band extending from front to back on the upper surface of the abdomen. The banded garden spider lacks this band but has a series of stripes on the abdomen that extend from side to side, and perhaps more obviously, it has more black bands on the legs.

Similar species: None.

orchard spider (fig. 196)
Leucauge venusta

Biology: Orchard spiders build an orb-shaped web that is unusual because it is tilted or even horizontal rather than vertical, like the more typical web of the giant orb weaver. This spider is more common among the trees than in the meadows.

Distribution: From the Atlantic Ocean to Texas, perhaps with a western limit not far from the Lost Pines.

Remarks: Length 7 mm. The beautiful orchard spider flaunts several patches of reflective "international orange" on the rear of the abdomen. At night these patches glare brightly in a flashlight's beam.

Similar species: None.

Fig. 196. The beautiful orchard spider (*Leucauge venusta*).

spinybacked orbweaver
Gasteracantha cancriformis

Biology: The large orb-shaped web of this small, spiny, hard-shelled, crablike spider spans hiking trails in summer and fall. The species is known to prefer wooded areas.

Distribution: From coast to coast within the United States.

Remarks: Length 10 mm. The color of the unmistakably shaped abdomen may be white, yellow, orange, or red (Jackman 1997). We saw white and yellow individuals in webs only a few feet apart on a trail. Whatever color the abdomen might take, it bears six dark, conspicuous spines.

Similar species: None.

southern black widow (fig. 197)
Latrodectus mactans

Biology: Black widows usually build irregular webs beneath logs, stones, boards, and metal sheets, but one large female was seen in broad daylight high up in the vegetation of a meadow. Males are much smaller and unlikely to be noticed. Females occasionally eat their mates, giving the species its common name. Black widows more typically eat insects, including the red imported fire ant.

Distribution: The southern black widow occurs from the Atlantic Ocean to a western limit somewhere in Texas.

Remarks: Length of female 11 mm. The black widow's bite is the most dangerous among all spiders in the United States, but individuals are more likely to retreat than attack when disturbed.

Similar species: We have seen only the southern black widow in the forest. Two others may occur there. These are the northern black widow (*L. variolus*) and the western black widow (*L. hesperus*). The shape of the red markings on the female's abdomen and the color of her egg sac are used to distinguish one widow species from another (Kaston 1978).

A fairly close relative of the black widows is the harmless and orange-red *Tidarren sisyphoides,* which we encountered on a single occasion. The specimen was a female hiding in a dried leaf refugium suspended from the top of a cobweb attached to a tree branch overhanging a dry creekbed, just as the literature reports for both behavior and hiding place. The species is especially interesting for its tiny male, which amputates one of its own appendages just before the last molt of its development (Levi and Levi 1987). *Tidarren sisyphoides* occurs from coast to coast in the United States. We thank James Cokendolpher for identifying this species.

Fig. 197. Southern black widow (*Latrodectus mactans*) with egg sac.

audacious jumping spider (fig. 198)
Phidippus audax

Biology: This is a large, hairy, black and white jumping spider that lives in cover beneath the loose bark of loblolly pine and exposed on herbaceous vegetation. Jumping spiders are active hunters that pounce on their prey and do not capture them in a web. In this species the males are distinguished from females by their bright green fangs. Females produce an egg sac that contains up to 218 eggs (Jackman 1997).

Distribution: From coast to coast within the United States.

Remarks: Length 14 mm. Not commonly seen in the forest but beneficial in fields, where they kill a variety of agricultural pests.

Similar species: None.

Johnson's jumping spider (fig. 198)
Phidippus johnsoni

Biology: Johnson's jumping spider occurs on herbaceous vegetation in meadows and powerline cuts and is similar in habits to the audacious jumping spider.

Distribution: This is one of the relatively few western animals of the Lost Pines. It occurs from the Pacific Ocean to an eastern limit somewhere in Texas.

Remarks: Length 13 mm. Johnson's jumping spider has a reputation for biting humans. The results are not serious (Kaston 1978).

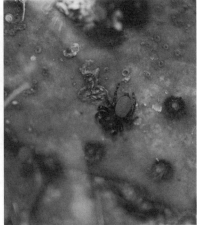

Fig. 198. Jumping spiders, (A) the audacious jumping spider (*Phidippus audax*); (B) Johnson's jumping spider (*Phidippus johnsoni*) on cactus pad.

Similar species: The cardinal jumping spider (*P. cardinalis*) is entirely red on top, whereas Johnson's jumping spider has a black cephalothorax and a mostly if not entirely red abdomen. The Apache jumping spider (*P. apacheanus*) is yellowish orange on top. Of these we saw only Johnson's species. *Phidippus clarus* (fig. 199; length 8 mm) has a mix of red and black on the abdomen. It is widely distributed in North America and does occur in the Lost Pines.

Chisos funnel-web spider (fig. 200)
Euagrus chisoseus

Biology: This spider resembles a very small tarantula. It prefers pine-oak-juniper forests and occurs mostly under rocks and logs, though there are records from caves farther west. Webs are constructed under cover and consist of two parts. Beneath the covering object is the flattened silk tube, which is the spider's retreat. Reaching into the exposed leaf litter is an extension that functions as a trap for the spider's prey. Female funnel-web spiders spin a cuplike container, deposit eggs inside, and cover the container with a silken lid (Coyle 1988).

Distribution: This species occurs from its easternmost limit in or near the Lost Pines forest to a western extreme in southeastern Arizona. It is known only from Texas, New Mexico, and Arizona.

Remarks: Length 15 mm. The Chisos funnel-web spider is often recorded from montane habitats, and the eastern extreme of the Central Texas forest may also represent the lowest altitude for the species.

Fig. 199. The jumping spider
(*Phidippus clarus*).

Similar species: The resemblance to a small tarantula and the long spinnerets protruding from the back end like a double tail distinguish this species from any other spider in the forest. Its closest relative is the better known species *Euagrus comstocki,* but in the United States that species occurs only in extreme southern Texas (Coyle 1988). Only once did we see a large, true tarantula. That individual was a battered male crawling up the trunk of a loblolly pine in broad daylight.

Fig. 200. Chisos funnel-web
spider (*Euagrus chisoseus*).

Fig. 201. Female crab spider (*Misumenoides formosipes*) among frostweed flowers.

crab spiders (fig. 201)
Misumenoides formosipes and others

Biology: Crab spiders are sit-and-wait predators that commonly perch in, on, or near flowers and prey upon visiting insects. They do not use webs to capture prey, but courting males of at least some species wrap their prospective mates loosely in silk (Levi and Levi 1987). The beautiful purple and white crab spider (*Misumenoides formosipes*) was found among the white flowers of frostweed. Females are much larger than the tiny males, and upon placing the two sexes together in a vial we watched the male scuttle about to position himself for mating on the female's abdomen. Our collection was made in November, though the previous records of which we are aware extend from May only to September.

An unidentified yellow species not shown here was seen from time to time on low-growing foliage in powerline cuts.

Distribution: *Misumenoides formosipes* occurs from coast to coast within the United States.

Remarks: Length 7 mm. The abdomen of the unidentified species not shown here bears a striking resemblance in size, shape, and color to a kernel of corn.

Similar species: The yellow spider may be a member of the genus *Misumenoides*. We noticed no other quite like it.

Fig. 202. Bark scorpion (*Centruroides vittatus*).

bark scorpion (fig. 202)
Centruroides vittatus

Biology: The bark scorpion is a nocturnally active predator that feeds on insects and spiders, which it captures with its claws and subdues with its sting. We have seen it hunting after dark at eye level on tree trunks and even crawling along branches high above ground. When not seeking prey it hides beneath logs and snags and under the loose bark of the same. When exposed to light it scurries beneath the closest available cover. The sting of this species is painful but not life-threatening, except perhaps to those few people who are allergic to the venom.

Distribution: From the Mississippi River to the Rio Grande near El Paso, Texas.

Remarks: Length 60 mm. This is the only scorpion in the forest, and it is extremely abundant. Another common name is the "striped scorpion."

Similar species: None.

harvestmen (figs. 203, 204)

Leiobunum vittatum, L. flavum, L. townsendi, Vonones sayi, Eumesosoma roeweri
Biology: Harvestmen, also known as "daddy-long-legs," are spiderlike in appearance. Depending upon the species, they are predators, scavengers, or a combination of both. We noticed five species in the Lost Pines. Three of these are large harvestmen with very long legs and body lengths of about 8 mm. One light-colored species, *Leiobunum flavum,* lacks the distinct dorsal stripe that is so prominent on *Leiobunum vittatum.* The former was encountered on several occasions at about eye level in the foliage of deciduous trees and once in a patch of frostweed plants, where some individuals had lowered their bodies into the white flowers, leaving little more than the long legs exposed. We saw only one specimen of the third long-legged species, *Leiobunum townsendi.* Its body is darker than those of the other two, and there are distinct white bands on the legs. The remaining two species have much shorter legs and bodies and frequent very different habitats. Say's harvestman (*Vonones sayi*) is a strikingly orange-red animal that we saw only beneath logs and rocks. In captivity Say's harvestman eats dead insects, living fruit flies, and fruits. The peak time for egg production is spring (J. C. Cokendolpher, pers. comm.). Roewer's harvestman (*Eumesosoma roeweri*) is more like the long-legged species in its grayish brown coloration, but like Say's harvestman, it has short legs and lives beneath logs.

Fig. 203. Striped harvestman (*Leiobunum vittatum*) on frostweed foliage.

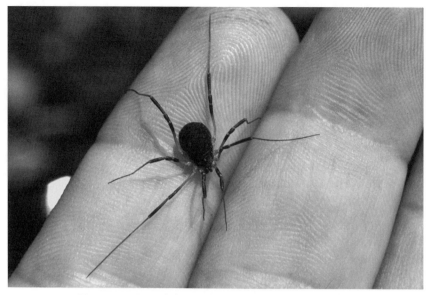

Fig. 204. Roewer's harvestman (*Eumesosoma roeweri*).

Distribution: All but one of the harvestmen treated here are eastern animals occurring from the Atlantic Ocean to a western limit in the United States somewhere near the biogeographical line that runs north-south through Texas. The exception is Townsend's harvestman, which is a western species occurring from Arizona to an eastern limit in Central Texas. It may be no coincidence that we saw a single specimen, because western animals are less common here than eastern species.

Remarks: These creatures resemble spiders but are more closely related to mites and are completely harmless.

Similar species: The identification of harvestmen is not a task for nonspecialists, partly because the keys needed for this purpose are either difficult to find or nonexistent. We thank James C. Cokendolpher for providing the identifications.

sun spider
Eremobates unidentified species

Biology: Sun spiders are not true spiders but are remarkable and rarely seen arachnids with huge jaws that are used to kill insect prey such as termites. In the laboratory they show themselves to be voracious predators. We saw them only twice and only at night. They were either attracted to our blacklight or to the insects that flew and crawled to it.

Distribution: Most sun spiders are creatures of arid western lands; the distribution of the Lost Pines species cannot be stated until it is properly identified.

Remarks: Length 15 mm. The first sight of a sun spider is likely to stun the observer because it looks so different from all other animals. When the arachnid's head, consisting mostly of jaws, is viewed at higher magnification with hand lens or microscope, it conjures thoughts of life from another world. Sun spiders are also known as "windscorpions" and "sunscorpions."

Similar species: As far as we know, we saw a single species in the forest. Perhaps there are others. We never saw the huge brown whipscorpion (*Mastigoproctus giganteus*)—well known from northern to southern Texas—in the Lost Pines.

pseudoscorpions (fig. 205)

Biology: Pseudoscorpions are tiny predators with claws resembling those of scorpions but with round abdomens that lack a tail or stinger. We encountered them in three situations in the Lost Pines. They are most common by far beneath the bark of loblolly pine, and only a few minutes of bark peeling are required before the first specimen makes an appearance. We also found them living as harmless hitchhikers on the bodies of large woodboring beetles and in the "fur" of the hairy bee-mimicking robber fly *Laphria macquartii*. When traveling on beetles,

Fig. 205. Unidentified pseudoscorpion from beneath wing cover of blind click beetle.

pseudoscorpions often hide beneath the wing covers; we saw them scramble out after their ride had been captured.

Distribution: The several species that we encountered must be identified by a specialist before their distributions can be determined.

Remarks: Typical lengths 2 or 3 mm. Pseudoscorpions are harmless animals that resemble tiny crabs about as much as they resemble scorpions.

Similar species: The identification of pseudoscorpions, like the identification of mites, is a difficult process. Keys are hard to find, difficult to use, or both. It is best to rely upon help from an authority on these little animals, but even that aid is unlikely to materialize.

CHAPTER 15

Molluscs and Earthworms

Molluscs and earthworms are soft-bodied invertebrates that require much moisture and thus are not as well represented in the rather dry ecosystem of the Lost Pines as are the insects and arachnids. The problem is exacerbated for snails because they also require calcium if they are to build their shells, and the sandy soils of the forest offer more silica than calcium. To illustrate the point, on a single hillside a mere thirty miles to the northwest of the Lost Pines, in the center of a populous city, we once saw the remains of more snails at a single glance than we saw during our entire study of the forest. The explanation is simple; the city of Austin was built on limestone soil and thus is rich in the calcium carbonate that is prime raw material for the construction of shells.

We found a total of seven molluscan species and two earthworm species. One of the molluscs is an unidentified freshwater clam found in fragments from time to time along the margins of artificial ponds. They were the inedible portions of a raccoon's meal and are not native to the hinterlands of the forest, though they probably made their way from the nearby Colorado River. It is also important to note that neither of the two earthworms identified here is native to the Lost Pines. We found them hours apart beneath logs and stones in an unusually wet November.

Fig. 206. Forest snails. Left: *Polygyra latispira*. **Right:** *Mesodon thyroidus*.

land snails (figs. 206, 207)
Mesodon thyroidus, Polygyra latispira, Rabdotus dealbatus

Biology: All three land snails occur beneath decomposing logs, branches, and leaf litter where at least the first two on this list feed upon fungi. None possesses the familiar lid with which to close the opening in time of need. Instead they prevent desiccation during dry spells by secreting a mucous film at the entrance to the shell. This "epiphragm" can be thought of as a temporary lid. Rains bring moisture that dissolves the epiphragm and revives the snail to activity.

Distribution: *Mesodon thyroidus* occurs from the eastern United States to a western limit near the Lost Pines. *Polygyra latispira* nearly made our list of Texas endemics but was bumped from appendix 1 when we discovered a record of this

Fig. 207. The snail *Rabdotus dealbatus*.

species from a single parish in westernmost Louisiana. *Rabdotus dealbatus* occurs from Georgia in the east to a western limit in Central Texas.

Remarks: The larger species are the round-spiraled *Mesodon,* growing to a diameter of more than one inch, and the elongate-spiraled *Rabdotus* (formerly known as *Bulimulus*), reaching a similar length. The round *Polygyra* grows no larger than about half that size.

Similar species: These are the only land snails we encountered.

slugs (figs. 208, 209)

Carolina slug, *Philomycus carolinianus,* and smooth black slug, *Deroceras laeve*

Biology: The Carolina slug lives beneath the cover of bark in forests and especially within the tunnels bored by insects. It feeds upon fungi growing on wood (Runham and Hunter 1970). Unlike garden snails and slugs, many of which are introduced exotics to begin with, this is one species that avoids urban and even agricultural settings. Strangely, we never saw it beneath bark or other covering objects. On a single occasion, on a hot afternoon, we spied one individual glistening on a rock in full sunlight.

The smooth black slug was seen at the close of an unusually rainy January when the woods were wetter than we had ever seen. Three individuals were crawling across the leaf litter, and at first glance one of us mistook them for leeches. These slugs have no external shell, but they do possess a small shell hidden beneath the skin. Their diet consists of a variety of flowering plants. When disturbed, the sleek, glistening animal exudes a defensive slime.

Fig. 208. The Carolina slug (*Philomycus carolinianus*) eating fungus.

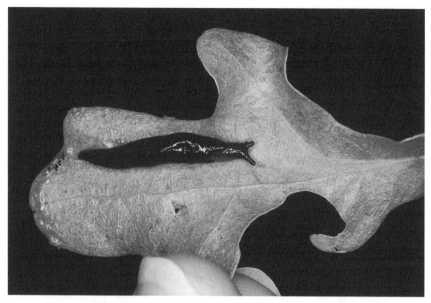

Fig. 209. The smooth black slug (*Deroceras laeve*) on oak leaf with characteristic clear slime trail.

Distribution: The Carolina slug is an eastern species that prefers humid forest and probably meets its western limit near the Lost Pines. In this regard it is notable that a checklist of slugs and snails occurring in Travis County just to the west of the forest does not contain reference to the Carolina slug (Neck 1994). The smooth black slug occurs throughout the United States.

Remarks: Length of the Carolina slug 75 mm, length of the smooth black slug 25 mm. The Carolina slug is clearly a native of the United States. Opinions differ as to whether the smooth black slug is a native species or an introduced exotic (Getz 1959; Burch 1962).

Similar species: A second black slug species may occur in the forest. The reticulated black slug (*Deroceras reticulatum*) exudes a milky slime when disturbed, whereas the smooth black slug exudes a clear slime.

water snail (fig. 210)
Physella virgata

Biology: Though a thoroughly aquatic species, this omnivorous snail does not have a gill. It must come to the surface periodically to replenish an air-filled cavity. Like the three land snails, it also lacks the familiar shell-closing lid that many aquatic snails bear on the muscular foot. Its most remarkable traits suggest the equipment and behavior of a molluscan spider. A snail on the bottom of a pond or ephemeral water-filled ditch releases its grip and rises by natural buoyancy to the surface, leaving a thread of mucus in its wake. When returning to the bottom it crawls back down this same thread or a neighboring thread made by another snail. Again like a spider, the snail recycles the thread by eating it. And reinforcing the analogy, by that time the strands of mucus have trapped small food particles in the water, just as a spider's silk serves to trap food. When a pool or pond dries out the adult snails burrow into the mud and await the return of rain.

Each snail has the organs of both sexes and is thus a true hermaphrodite. However, it does not fertilize itself as some plants do, and it does not play both roles in a single mating, as some other snails do. In a given mating each animal functions only as a male or as a female, often changing roles within a matter of days. We observed mating behavior in an ephemeral pool in late February.

Distribution: Occurs from the Pacific Ocean to the Mississippi River drainage system.

Remarks: Length 10 mm. Up to two hundred eggs are laid after mating, and though the snails often live in small, readily evaporated ditches, they require several months to reach adulthood. This species and its relatives are notable for their tolerance of polluted waters.

Similar species: None to our knowledge. Identification of small aquatic snails such as these can be difficult because it often requires the removal of the animal from its shell and a microscopic study of the soft anatomy.

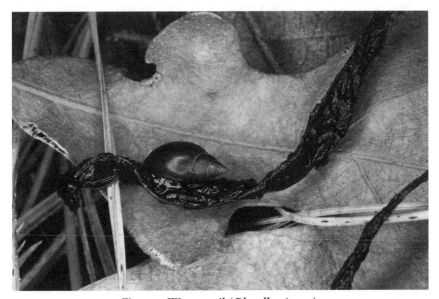

Fig. 210. Water snail (*Physella virgata*).

southern earthworm
Aporrectodea trapezoides

Biology: The southern earthworm does not reproduce sexually, and it may thus come as a surprise to find that the species retains the male sex despite the fact that males are sterile (Gates 1972; Reynolds 1977). Perhaps the male sex is evolving into oblivion, a fate already suffered by the males of the northern grass mantis. The southern earthworm presumably eats soil.

Distribution: This species now occurs on every continent except Antarctica. It is a native of the Old World and its presence in the Lost Pines is probably due to accidental introduction because of its popularity as angling bait. A map of forest earthworms occurring in the United States did not record the southern earthworm from as far west as the Lost Pines (Reynolds 1976).

Remarks: The southern earthworm reaches lengths of six inches and can regenerate its head if the front end of its body is cut off.

Similar species: The terminology required to identify earthworms is alien even to those versed in the identification of insects. It is best to send specimens to an authority. Our specimens were kindly identified by John Reynolds of the Oligochaetology Laboratory in Kitchener, Ontario, Canada.

dung earthworm
Microscolex dubius

Biology: The dung earthworm reaches several inches in length and apparently reproduces without sex though the males have not yet been lost to evolution. Its diet is remarkable because it seems to prefer animal waste over soil, including cow dung (de Mischis 1985).

Distribution: Like the southern earthworm, the dung earthworm is an exotic species accidentally introduced to various parts of the world because of its popularity as an angling bait. Southern South America is its native land (Gates 1972). As far as we know the species has not been reported from Texas until now.

Remarks: The dung earthworm has predatory natural enemies in the form of spiderlike harvestmen (de Mischis 1985).

Similar species: As indicated for the southern earthworm, these animals should be sent to a specialist because they are difficult to identify.

APPENDIX 1

Endemic Texas Insects Occurring in the Lost Pines

1. Texas rain beetle (*Scaptolenus ocreatus*); known only from Central and southern Texas.
2. Texas short-winged woodborer (*Methia constricticollis*); known previously from southern Texas only, with the Lost Pines now representing the northern limit of its range.
3. Texas long-lipped beetle (*Telegeusis texensis*); a new species endemic to Central Texas.
4. Texas water scorpion (*Ranatra texana*); endemic to Central and southern Texas. Not seen by us.
5. Central Texas leaf katydid (*Paracyrtophyllus robustus*); endemic to Central Texas.
6. Texas thread-legged katydid (*Arethaea grallator*); endemic to east-central Texas.
7. Texas broadhorned band-winged grasshopper (*Psinidia amplicornis*); sporadic records from Central to East Texas.
8. Texas bumblebee robber fly (*Laphria macquartii*); endemic to Texas, distribution uncertain.
9. Cole's robber fly (*Stichopogon colei*); endemic to Texas, known until now from only three counties (Bexar and Milam in Central Texas and Brewster in far West Texas). Bastrop County thus brings the total to four.

Future work may discover some of these species across the Rio Grande in northern Mexico.

APPENDIX 2

Exotic Animals Occurring
in the Lost Pines

1. Red imported fire ant (*Solenopsis invicta*); accidentally introduced from South America.
2. Tropical fire ant (*Solenopsis geminata*); possibly native, possibly Central or South American.
3. African dung beetle (*Onthophagus gazella*); intentionally introduced from Africa.
4. Striped earwig (*Labidura riparia*); accidentally introduced from the Old World.
5. Dark foot-spinner (*Oligotoma nigra*); accidentally introduced from the Old World.
6. Honey bee (*Apis mellifera*); intentionally introduced from the Old World.
7. Southern earthworm (*Aporrectodea trapezoides*); introduced from the Old World for use as fishing bait.
8. Dung earthworm (*Microscolex dubius*); introduced from southern South America for use as fishing bait.

Bibliography

Akre, R. D., A. Greene, J. F. MacDonald, P. J. Landolt, and H. G. Davis. 1981. *Yellowjackets of America North of Mexico.* USDA Agriculture Handbook no. 552.

Aldrich, J. M. 1926. American two-winged flies of the genus *Microphthalma* Macquart, with notes on related forms. *Proc. U.S. Nat. Mus.* 69 (13). 8 pp.

Allard, H. A. 1916. Some musical Orthoptera at Clarendon, Virginia. *Can. Ent.* 48:356–58.

Anonymous. 1990. Buescher State Park. Summary of representative plant communities. Unpub. ms. and plant lists. Resource Management Branch, Texas Parks and Wildlife Department, Austin.

Arnett, R. H. 1951. A revision of the Nearctic Oedemeridae (Coleoptera). *Amer. Midland Nat.* 45:257–391.

———. 1960. *The Beetles of the United States.* Washington, D.C.: Catholic University of America Press.

———. 1983. *Checklist of the Beetles of North and Central America and the West Indies.* Gainesville, Fla.: Flora and Fauna Publications.

———. 1985. *American Insects: A Handbook of the Insects of America North of Mexico.* New York: Van Nostrand Reinhold.

Arnett, R. H., N. M. Downie, and H. E. Jaques. 1980. *How to Know the Beetles.* Dubuque, Iowa: Wm. C. Brown Company.

Arnold, D. C., and W. A. Drew. 1987. A preliminary survey of the Megaloptera of Oklahoma. *Proc. Oklahoma Acad. Science* 67:23–26.

Ashmead, W. H. 1902. Classification of the fossorial, predaceous and parasitic wasps, or the superfamily Vespoidea. *Can. Ent.* 34:203–210.

Atkinson, T. H., P. G. Koehler, and R. S. Patterson. 1991. *Catalog and Atlas of the Cockroaches (Dictyoptera) of North America North of Mexico.* Entomol. Soc. Am. Misc. Pub. no. 78.

Baker, F. 1979. Soil survey of Bastrop County, Texas. USDA Soil Conservation Service in cooperation with Texas Agricultural Experiment Station, College Station.

Baker, W. L. 1972. *Eastern Forest Insects.* Misc. Pub. no. 1175. Washington, D.C.: USDA Forest Service.

Balduf, W. V. 1945. Bionomic notes on *Menecles insertus* (Say) (Hemiptera, Pentatomidae). *Bull. Brooklyn Entomol. Soc.* 40:61–65.

Beamer, R. H. 1929. Studies on the biology of Kansas Cicadidae. *Univ. Kansas Science Bull.* 18:155–63.

Berkman, A. H. 1928. The pH value of some Texas soils and its relation to the incidence of certain woody plant species. *Soil Science* 25:133–42.

Bilan, M. V., and J. J. Stransky. 1966. Pine seedling survival and growth response to soils of the Texas post-oak belt. *Bull. Stephen F. Austin State College of Forestry* 12:5–21.

Blatchley, W. S. 1910. *An Illustrated Descriptive Catalogue of the Coleoptera or Beetles (Exclusive of Rhynchophora) Known to Occur in Indiana.* Indianapolis: Nature Publishing Company.

————. 1920. *The Orthoptera of Northeastern America.* Indianapolis: Nature Publishing Company.

————. 1926. *Heteroptera, or True Bugs of Eastern North America.* Indianapolis : Nature Publishing Company.

Bohart, R. M., and A. S. Menke. 1976. *Sphecid Wasps of the World.* Berkeley: Univ. Calif. Press.

Bohls, S. W. 1944. *The Mosquitoes of Texas.* Austin: Texas State Department of Health. 100 pp.

Bomar, G. W. 1995. *Texas Weather.* 2d ed. Austin: University of Texas Press.

Borror, D. J., and R. E. White. 1970. *A Field Guide to the Insects of America North of Mexico.* Boston: Houghton Mifflin.

Bousquet, Y. 1984. Nomenclatural notes on Nearctic Pterostichini (Coleoptera: Carabidae). *Quaestiones Entomologicae* 20:1–5.

Bragg, L. H., and R. L. Neill. 1979. *The Herbaceous Flowering Plants of the Buescher Division.* University of Texas Environmental Science Park at Smithville, pub. no. 4. 120 pp.

Breland, O. P., and J. W. Dobson 1947. Specificity of mantid oothecae. *Ann. Entomol. Soc. Amer.* 40:557–75.

Bromley, S. W. 1933. Cicadas in Texas. *Psyche* 40:130

————. 1934. The robber flies of Texas. *Ann. Entomol. Soc. Amer.* 27:74–113.

Bryant, V. M., Jr. 1977. A 16,000 year pollen record of vegetation change in central Texas. *Palynology* 1:143–56.

Buchler, E. R., T. B. Wright, and E. D. Brown. 1981. Functions of stridulation by the passalid beetle *Odontotaenius disjunctus* (Coleoptera: Passalidae). *Animal Behaviour* 29:483–86.

Burch, J. B. 1962. *How to Know the Eastern Land Snails.* Dubuque, Iowa: Wm. C. Brown Company.

Bureau of Business Research. 1987. *The Climates of Texas Counties.* Natural Fibers Information Center. University of Texas at Austin in cooperation with the Office of State Climatologist, Texas A&M University.

Bureau of Economic Geology. 1974a. Austin Sheet. *Geologic Atlas of Texas.* University of Texas, Austin.

————. 1974b. Seguin Sheet. *Geologic Atlas of Texas.* University of Texas, Austin.

————. 1992. *Geology of Texas.* University of Texas, Austin.

Burgess, A. F., and C. W. Collins. 1917. The genus *Calosoma.* USDA Bull. no. 417.

Burke, H. R. 1976. The beetle *Zopherus nodulosus haldemani:* Symbol of the Southwestern Entomological Society. *Southwest. Entomol.* 1:105–106.

Byers, G. W. 1954. Notes on North American Mecoptera. *Ann. Entomol. Soc. Amer.* 47:484–510.

Campbell, L. 1995. *Endangered and Threatened Animals of Texas: Their Life History and Management.* Austin: Texas Parks and Wildlife Department.

Carlson, R. W. 1979. Family Stephanidae. Pp. 740–41 in *Catalog of Hymenoptera in America North of Mexico,* vol. 1: *Symphyta and Apocrita (Parasitica),* ed. K. V. Krombein, P. D. Hurd, Jr., D. R. Smith, and B. D. Burks. Washington, D.C.: Smithsonian Institution Press.

Carpenter, F. M. 1931a. The biology of the Mecoptera. *Psyche* 38:41–55.

————. 1931b. Revision of Nearctic Mecoptera. *Bull. Mus. Comp. Zool. Harvard* 72:205–77 + 8 plates.

Carr, A. 1952. *Handbook of Turtles: The Turtles of the United States, Canada, and Baja California.* Ithaca, N.Y.: Comstock Pub. Assoc.

Caudell, A. N. 1903. The Phasmidae, or Walkingsticks, of the United States. *Proc. U.S. Nat. Mus.* 26:863–85 + 4 plates.

———. 1905. Two interesting mantids from the United States. *J. New York Entomol. Soc.* 13:82–83.

———. 1911. Description of a new species of Orthoptera from Texas. *Can. Ent.* 43:137–38.

Chamberlin, W. J. 1939. *The Bark and Timber Beetles of North America North of Mexico.* Corvallis, Ore.: OSC Cooperative Association.

Chemsak, J. A. 1963. Taxonomy and bionomics of the genus *Tetraopes* (Cerambycidae: Coleoptera). University of California Publications in Entomology 30. Berkeley: University of California Press.

Childs, C. 2001. *The Secret Knowledge of Water: Discovering the Essence of the American Desert.* New York: Little, Brown.

Cohn, T. J. 1965. The arid-land katydids of the North American genus *Neobarrettia* (Orthoptera: Tettigoniidae): Their systematics and a reconstruction of their history. University of Michigan Museum of Zoology Misc. Pub. no. 126.

Cole, F. R. 1969. *The Flies of Western North America.* Berkeley: Univ. Calif. Press.

Contreras-Ramos, A. 1998. *Systematics of the Dobsonfly Genus* Corydalus *(Megaloptera: Corydalidae).* Lanham, Md.: Thomas Say Publications in Entomology, Entomological Society of America.

Corbet, P. S. 1999. *Dragonflies: Behavior and Ecology of Odonata.* Ithaca, N.Y.: Cornell University Press.

Correll, D. S. 1966. Pinaceae. In C. L. Lundell, *Flora of Texas I.* Renner: Texas Research Foundation.

Correll, D. S., and M. C. Johnston. 1970. *Manual of the Vascular Plants of Texas.* Renner: Texas Research Foundation.

Covell, C. V., Jr. 1984. *A Field Guide to the Moths of Eastern North America.* Boston: Houghton Mifflin.

Coyle, F. A. 1988. A revision of the American funnel-web mygalomorph spider genus *Euagrus* (Araneae, Dipluridae). *Bull. Amer. Mus. Nat. Hist.* 187:203–92.

Craddock, W. P. 1947. Aerial geology of the Carrizo Sandstone at Bastrop, Bastrop County, Texas. Master's thesis, University of Texas, Austin.

Craighead, F. C. 1950. *Insect Enemies of Eastern Forests.* USDA Misc. Pub. no. 657.

Cranfil, R. 1983. The distribution of *Woodwardia areolata. American Fern Journal* 73:46–52.

Creighton, W. S. 1950. *The Ants of North America.* Bull. Mus. Comp. Zool. Harvard 104.

Critchfield, W. B., and E. L. Little, Jr. 1966. Geographic distribution of the pines of the world. Misc. Pub. no. 991. Washington, D.C.: USDA Forest Service. 97 pp.

Cumley, R. W. 1931. A geologic section across Caldwell County, Texas. Master's thesis, University of Texas, Austin.

Danks, H. V. 1994. Regional diversity of insects in North America. *American Entomologist* 40(1):50–55.

Davis, J. R. 1996. The creeping water bugs (Hemiptera: Naucoridae) of Texas. *Southwest. Nat.* 41:1–26.

Davis, S. W. 1974. Hydrogeology of arid regions. Chapter 1 in *Desert Biology,* vol. 2, ed. G. W. Brown, Jr. New York: Academic Press.

Dethier, V. G. 1992. *Crickets and Katydids, Concerts and Solos.* Cambridge, Mass.: Harvard University Press.

Devereaux, W. L. 1877. *Tetraopes tetrophthalmus* Forst. *Can. Ent.* 9:143.

Deyrup, M., J. Trager, and N. Carlin. 1985. The genus *Odontomachus* in the southeastern United States (Hymenoptera: Formicidae). *Ent. News* 96:188–95.

Dillon, E. S., and L. S. Dillon. 1961. *A Manual of Common Beetles of Eastern North America.* Evanston, Ill.: Row, Peterson and Company.

Dirsh, V. M. 1974. *Genus* Schistocerca *(Acridomorpha, Insecta).* The Hague, Netherlands: Dr. W. Junk Publishers.

Dixon, J. R., N. O. Dronen, J. C. Godwin, and M. A. Simmons. 1990. The amphibians, reptiles, and mammals of Bastrop and Buescher State Parks: With emphasis on the Houston toad (*Bufo houstonensis*) and the short-tailed shrew (*Blarina* sp.). Final report in Texas Parks and Wildlife Department files, Austin.

Dodds, K. J., and F. M. Stephen. 2000. Partial age-specific life tables for *Monochamus titillator* in *Dendroctonus frontalis* infested loblolly pines. *Entomol. Exper. Appl.* 97:331–38.

Dolin, P. S., and D. C. Tarter. 1982. Life history and ecology of *Chauliodes rastricornis* Rambur and *Chauliodes pectinicornis* (Linnaeus) (Megaloptera: Corydalidae) in Greenbottom swamp, Cabell County, West Virginia, USA. *Brimleyana* 0(7):111–20.

Dougherty, V. 1980. *A Systematic Revision of the New World Ectrichodiinae (Hemiptera: Reduviidae).* Ph.D. diss., University of Connecticut, Storrs.

———. 1995. A review of the New World Ectrichodiinae genera (Hemiptera: Reduviidae). *Trans. Amer. Entomol. Soc.* 121:173–225.

Dowdy, W. W. 1968. An ecological study of some millipedes in two central Missouri communities. *Ann. Entomol. Soc. Amer.* 61: 1059–63.

Downie, N. M., and R. H. Arnett, Jr. 1996. *The Beetles of Northeastern North America.* Vol. 1. Gainesville, Fla.: Sandhill Crane Press.

Dozier, H. L. 1920. An ecological study of hammock and piney woods insects in Florida. *Ann. Entomol. Soc. Amer.* 13:325–80.

Drake, C. J., and H. M. Harris. 1934. The Gerrinae of the western hemisphere (Hemiptera). *Annals of the Carnegie Museum* 23:179–240.

Duck, L. G. 1944. The bionomics of *Schistocerca obscura* (Fabr). *J. Kans. Entomol. Soc.* 17:105–19.

Dunkle, S. 1989. *Dragonflies of the Florida Peninsula, Bermuda, and the Bahamas.* Gainesville, Fla.: Scientific Publishers.

———. 1990. *Damselflies of Florida, Bermuda and the Bahamas.* Gainesville, Fla.: Scientific Publishers.

———. 2000. *Dragonflies through Binoculars.* New York: Oxford University Press.

Dussourd, D. E., and T. Eisner. 1987. Vein-cutting behavior: Insect counterploy to the latex defense of plants. *Science* 237:898–901.

Eberhard, W. G. 1998. Sexual behavior of *Acanthocephala declivis guatemalana* (Hemiptera: Coreidae) and the allometric scaling of their modified hind legs. *Ann. Entomol. Soc. Amer.* 91:863–71.

Edwards, J. G. 1949. *Coleoptera or Beetles East of the Great Plains.* Ann Arbor, Mich.: Edwards Brothers.

Endrödi, S. 1985. *The Dynastinae of the World.* Boston: Dr. W. Junk Publishers.

Ferguson, K. 1986. *The Texas Landscape.* The Geographic Provinces of Texas. Austin: Texas Mosaics Publishing Company.

Fernald, H. T. 1934. *The North American and West Indian Digger Wasps of the Genus* Sphex *(Ammophila auct.).* Deland, Fla.: E. O. Painter Printing Company.

Fitzgerald, S. J., and B. C. Kondratieff. 1998. A new species of mydas fly (Diptera: Mydidae) from Mexico and a newly recorded species from Mexico. *Proc. Entomol. Soc. Wash.* 100:464–66.

Flamm, R. O., T. L. Wagner, S. P. Cook, P. E. Pulley, R. N. Coulson, and T. M. McArdle. 1987. Host colonization by cohabiting *Dendroctonus frontalis, Ips avulsus,* and *I. calligraphus* (Coleoptera: Scolytidae). *Environ. Entomol.* 16:390–99.

Fleenor, S. B., and S. W. Taber. 1999. Review of *Brachypsectra* LeConte with a new record of the Texas beetle (*B. fulva* LeConte; Coleoptera: Brachypsectridae). *Coleopterists Bull.* 53:359–64.

———. 2000. Discovery of the female Texas beetle and notes on the ephemeral appearance of adults. *Southwest. Ent.* 25:303–305.

———. 2001. A new long-lipped beetle from Texas and a review of the genus *Telegeusis* Horn (Coleoptera: Telegeusidae). *Coleopterists Bull.* 55:481–84.

Foster, J. H. 1917. The spread of timbered areas in central Texas. *Journal of Forestry* 15: 442–45.

Foster, J. H., H. B. Krausz, and A. H. Leidigh. 1917. General survey of Texas woodlands, including a study of the commercial possibilities of mesquite. *Bull. Agric. Mech. Coll. Texas,* 3d series 9(9):1–39.

Franklin, H. J. 1912. The Bombidae of the New World. *Trans. Amer. Entomol. Soc.* 38:177–486.

Freeman, B. 1996. Birds of Bastrop and Buescher State Parks, including Lake Bastrop: A field checklist. Natural Resource Program, Texas Parks and Wildlife Department, Austin.

Freitag, R. 1969. A revision of the species of the genus *Evarthrus* LeConte (Coleoptera: Carabidae). *Quaestiones Entomologicae* 5:89–212.

Gangwere, S. K. 1961. A monograph on food selection in Orthoptera. *Trans. Amer. Entomol. Soc.* 87:67–230.

Gardiner, L. M. 1957. Deterioration of fire-killed pine in Ontario and the causal wood-boring beetles. *Can. Ent.* 89:241–63.

Gassner, G. 1963. The biology and immature stages of the scorpionfly, *Panorpa nuptialis* Gerstaeker [sic]. Master's thesis, University of Texas, Austin. 105 pp.

Gates, G. E. 1972. *Burmese Earthworms.* Trans. Am. Phil. Soc., vol. 62, part 7. 326 pp.

Gaul, A. T. 1947. Additions to vespine biology III: Notes on the habits of *Vespula squamosa* Drury (Hymenoptera: Vespidae). *Bull. Brooklyn Entomol. Soc.* 42:87–96.

Gertsch, W. J., and F. Ennik. 1983. The spider genus *Loxosceles* in North America, Central America, and the West Indies (Araneae, Loxoscelidae). *Bull Amer. Mus. Nat. Hist.* 175:264–360.

Getz, L. L. 1959. Notes on the ecology of slugs: *Arion circumscriptus, Deroceras reticulatum,* and *D. leave. Amer. Midland Nat.* 61:485–98.

Glaser, J. D. 1976. The biology of *Dynastes tityus* (Linn.) in Maryland (Coleoptera: Scarabaeidae). *Coleopterists Bull.* 30:133–38.

Goddard, R. E., and C. L. Brown. 1959. Growth of drought resistant loblolly pines. Texas Forest Service Research Note no. 23. College Station, Texas.

Goodwin, J. T., and B. M. Drees. 1996. The horse and deer flies (Diptera: Tabanidae) of Texas. *Southwest. Entomol. Suppl.* 20. 140 pp.

Graenicher, S. 1927. On the biology of the parasitic bees of the genera *Coelioxys* (Hymen., Megachilidae). *Ent. News* 38:231–35, 273–76.

Gray, I. E. 1946. Observations on the life history of the horned passalus. *Amer. Midland Nat.* 35:728–46.

Greenfield, M. D. 1990. Evolution of acoustic communication in the genus *Neoconocephalus:* Discontinuous range, synchrony, and interspecific interactions. Pp. 71–97 in *The Tettigoniidae: Biology, Systematics and Evolution,* ed. W. J. Bailey and D. C. F. Rentz. Bathurst, Australia: Crawford House Press.

Gurney, A. B. 1938. A synopsis of the order Zoraptera, with notes on the biology of *Zorotypus hubbardi* Caudell. *Proc. Entomol. Soc. Wash.* 40:57–87.

———. 1950. Praying mantids of the United States, native and introduced. *Ann. Report Smithsonian Instit.,* 1950, pp. 339–62.

Halstead, T. F. 1972. Notes and synonymy in *Largus* Hahn with a key to United States species. *Pan-Pac. Entomol.* 48:246–48.

Hardy, A. R. 1975. *A Revision of the Genus* Pelidnota *of America North of Panama (Coleoptera: Scarabaeidae; Rutelinae).* University of California Publications in Entomology 78. Berkeley: University of California Press.

Harvey, A. W. 1981. A reclassification of the *Schistocerca americana* complex (Orthoptera: Acrididae). *Acrida* 10:61–77.

Harvey, I. F., and S. F. Hubbard. 1987. Observations on the reproductive behaviour of *Orthemis ferruginea* (Fabricius) (Anisoptera: Libellulidae). *Odonatologica* 16:1–8.

Hazard, E. I. 1960. A revision of the genera *Chauliodes* and *Nigronia* (Megaloptera: Corydalidae). Master's thesis, Ohio State University, Columbus.

Hebard, M. 1917. *The Blattidae of North America North of the Mexican Boundary.* Memoirs of the American Entomological Society 2. 284 pp.

————. 1931. The Orthoptera of Kansas. *Proc. Acad. Nat. Sci. Phil.* 83:119–227.

————. 1934. The Dermaptera and Orthoptera of Illinois. *Bull. Illinois Nat. Hist. Survey* 20:124–279.

————. 1936. Studies in Orthoptera which occur in North America north of the Mexican boundary. VI: A revision of the genus *Arethaea* (Tettigoniidae, Phaneropterinae). *Trans. Amer. Entomol. Soc.* 62:231–56 + 2 plates.

————. 1941. The group Pterophyllae as found in the United States (Tettigoniidae: Pseudophyllinae). *Trans. Amer. Entomol. Soc.* 67:197–219 + 2 plates.

————. 1943. The Dermaptera and Orthopterous families Blattidae, Mantidae and Phasmidae of Texas. *Trans. Amer. Entomol. Soc.* 68:239–319.

Helfer, J. R. 1953. *How to Know the Grasshoppers, Cockroaches and Their Allies.* Dubuque, Iowa: Wm. C. Brown Company.

Henry, C. S. 1977. The behavior and life histories of two North American ascalaphids. *Ann. Entomol. Soc. Amer.* 70:179–95.

Hinds, W. E. 1901. Strength of *Passalus cornutus* Fab. *Psyche* 12:9–262 + 1 plate.

Hoebeke, E. R., and K. Beucke. 1997. Adventive *Onthophagus* (Coleoptera: Scarabaeidae) in North America: Geographic ranges, diagnoses, and new distributional records. *Ent. News* 108:345–62.

Hoffmann, C. H. 1935. The biology and taxonomy of the genus *Trichiotinus* (Scarabaeidae— Coleoptera). *Entomol. Amer.* 15:133–209.

Hoffman, R. L. 1958. The subspecies of *Typocerus lunatus,* a cerambycid beetle. *Proc. Entomol. Soc. Wash.* 60:217–21.

Hoffman, R. L., and R. M. Shelley. 1996. The identity of *Scolopendra marginata* Say (Chilopoda: Scolopendromorpha: Scolopendridae). *Myriapodologica* 4(5):35–42.

Hook, A. W. 1988. Provisional checklist of Mutillidae (Hymenoptera) (wasps) of Brackenridge Field Station. www.utexas.edu/research/bfl/collections/mutil.html

Hopkin, S. P., and H. J. Read. 1992. *The Biology of Millipedes.* New York: Oxford University Press.

Hopping, R. 1921. A review of the genus *Monochamus* Serv. (Cerambycidae, Coleoptera). *Can. Ent.* 53:252–58.

Horn, G. H. 1881. Notes on Elateridae, Cebrionidae, Rhipiceridae, and Dascyllidae. *Trans. Amer. Entomol. Soc.* 9:76–90 + 2 plates.

Horsfall, W. R. 1941. Biology of the black blister beetle (Coleoptera: Meloidae). *Ann. Entomol. Soc. Amer.* 34:114–26.

Howden, H. F. 1951. Insect communities of standing dead pine (*Pinus virginiana* Mill.). *Ann. Entomol. Soc. Amer.* 44:581–95.

————. 1955. Biology and taxonomy of North American beetles of the subfamily Geotrupinae with revisions of the genera *Bolbocerosoma, Eucanthus, Geotrupes* and *Peltotrupes* (Scarabaeidae). *Proc. U.S. Nat. Mus.* 104:151–319 + 18 plates.

Howden, H. F., and O. L. Cartwright. 1963. Scarab beetles of the genus *Onthophagus* Latreille north of Mexico (Coleoptera: Scarabaeidae). *Proc. U.S. Nat. Mus.* 114:1–133 + 9 plates.

Hull, F. M. 1973. *Bee Flies of the World.* Washington, D.C.: Smithsonian Institution Press.

Hunter, M. L., Jr. 1990. *Wildlife, Forests, and Forestry.* Englewood Cliffs, N.J.: Prentice Hall.

Isely, F. B. 1941. Researches concerning Texas Tettigoniidae. *Ecol. Monographs* 11:457–75.

————. 1944. Correlation between mandibular morphology and food specificity in grasshoppers. *Ann. Entomol. Soc. Amer.* 37:47–67.

Jackman, J. A. 1997. *A Field Guide to Spiders and Scorpions of Texas.* Houston: Gulf Publishing.

Jensen, M. N. 2000. Silk moth deaths show perils of biocontrol. *Science* 290:2230–31.

Johnson, P. J., K. D. Roush, and X. Lin. 1997. A South Dakota record for *Chauliodes rastricornis* (Megaloptera: Corydalidae). *Ent. News* 108:57–59.

Kaston, B. J. 1978. *How to Know the Spiders.* 3d ed. Dubuque, Iowa: Wm. C. Brown Company.

Keeton, W. J. 1960. *A Taxonomic Study of the Milliped Family Spirobolidae (Diplopoda: Spirobolida).* Mem. Amer. Entomol. Soc. 17. 146 pp. + 18 plates.

King, E. A., Jr. 1961. Geology of northwestern Gonzales County. Master's thesis, University of Texas, Austin.

Kohlman, B. 1979. Some notes on the biology of *Euphoria inda* (Linné) (Coleoptera: Scarabaeidae). *Pan-Pac. Ent.* 55:279–83.

Kormilev, N. A. 1982. Records and descriptions of North American and Oriental Aradidae (Hemiptera). *Wasmann J. Biol.* 40:1–17.

Kovarik, P. W., and H. R. Burke. 1989. Observations on the biology and ecology of two species of *Eudiagogus* (Coleoptera: Curculionidae). *Southwest. Nat.* 34:196–212.

Kurczewski, F. E., and M. G. Spofford. 1986. Observations on the behaviors of some Scoliidae and Pompilidae (Hymenoptera) in Florida. *Florida Entomologist* 69:636–44.

Lago, P. K. 1988. North Dakota *Eleodes* (Coleoptera: Tenebrionidae). *Ent. News* 99:17–22.

Langston, R. L., and J. A. Powell. 1975. *The earwigs of California (Order Dermaptera).* Bull. Calif. Insect Survey no. 20. 25 pp.

Larkin, T. J., and G. W. Bomar. 1983. *Climatic Atlas of Texas.* Austin: Texas Department of Water Resources.

Larson, D. A., V. M. Bryant, and T. Patty. 1972. Pollen analysis of a central Texas bog. *Amer. Midland Nat.* 88:358–67.

Lawson, S. A., and F. D. Morgan. 1993. Prey specificity of adult *Temnochila virescens* F. (Col. Trogositidae), a predator of *Ips grandicollis* Eichh. (Col. Scolytidae). *J. Appl. Ent.* 115:139–44.

LeConte, J. L. 1881. Synopsis of the Lampyridae of the United States. *Trans. Amer. Ent. Soc.* 9:15–72.

Leng, C. W. 1902. Revision of the Cicindelidae of boreal America. *Trans. Amer. Entomol. Soc.* 28:93–186 + 3 plates.

Levi, H. W. 1971. The *diadematus* group of the orb-weaver genus *Araneus* north of Mexico (Araneae: Araneidae). *Bull. Mus. Comp. Zool. Harvard* 141:131–79.

Levi, H. W., and L. R. Levi. 1987. *Spiders and Their Kin.* New York: Golden Press.

Light, S. F. 1930. The California species of the genus *Amitermes* Silvestri (Isoptera). *Univ. Cal. Pub. Entomol.* 5:173–214.

———. 1932. Contributions toward a revision of the American species of *Amitermes* Silvestri. *Univ. Cal. Pub. Entomol.* 5:355–414.

———. 1934. The desert termites of the genus *Amitermes*. Pp. 199–205 in *Termites and Their Control,* ed. C. A. Kofoid. Berkeley: University of California Press.

Linsley, E. G. 1962. *The Cerambycidae of North America.* part 3. University of California Publications in Entomology 20. Berkeley: University of California Press.

Linsley, E. G., and J. A. Chemsak. 1976. *The Cerambycidae of North America.* Part 4, no. 2: *Taxonomy and Classification of the Subfamily Lepturinae.* University of California Publications in Entomology 80. Berkeley: University of California Press.

———. 1984. *The Cerambycidae of North America.* Part 7, no. 1: *Taxonomy and Classification of the Subfamily Lamiinae, Tribes Parmenini through Acanthoderini.* University of California Publications in Entomology 102. Berkeley: University of California Press.

———. 1995. *The Cerambycidae of North America.* Part 7, no. 2: *Taxonomy and Classification of the Subfamily Lamiinae, Tribes Acanthocinini through Hemilophini.* University of California Publications in Entomology 114. Berkeley: University of California Press.

———. 1997. *The Cerambycidae of North America.* Part 8: *Bibliography, Index, and Host Plant Index.* University of California Publications in Entomology 117. Berkeley: University of California Press.

Little, E. L. 1971. *Atlas of United States Trees.* Vol. 1: *Conifers and Important Hardwoods.* Misc. Pub. no. 1146. Washington, D.C.: USDA Forest Service.

Lodwick, L. N., and J. A. Snider. 1980. The distribution of *Sphagnum* taxa in Texas. *Bryologist* 83:214–18.

Luginbill, P., Sr., and H. R. Painter. 1953. May beetles of the United States and Canada. USDA Tech. Bull. 1060. 102 pp. + 78 plates.

Lutz, F. E. 1935. *Field Book of Insects.* New York: G. P. Putnam's Sons.

Lythe, A. L., Jr. 1949. Reklaw Formation in western Bastrop County, Texas. Master's thesis, University of Texas, Austin.

McAlister, W. H. 1960. The spitting habit in the spider *Scytodes intricata* Banks (Family Scytodidae). *Texas Journal of Science* 12:17–20.

McBryde, J. B. 1933. The vegetation and habitat factors of the Carrizo sands. *Ecol. Monographs* 3:249–97.

McCafferty, W. P., C. R. Lugo-Ortiz, and G. Z. Jacobi. 1997. Mayfly fauna of New Mexico. *Great Basin Nat.* 57:283–314.

McDermott, F. A. 1910. Note on the light-emission of some American Lampyridae. *Can. Ent.* 42:357–64.

McNeill, J. 1891. A list of the Orthoptera of Illinois. Part 2. *Psyche* 6:21–27.

Macgown, J., and M. Macgown. 1996. Observation of a nuptial flight of the horned passalus beetle, *Odontotaenius disjunctus* (Illiger) (Coleoptera: Passalidae). *Coleopterists Bull.* 50:201–203.

MacRoberts, B. R., and M. H. MacRoberts. 1956. Floristics of xeric sand hills in east Texas. *Phytologia* 80:1–7.

Manogaran, C. 1975. Actual evapotranspiration and the natural range of loblolly pine. *Forest Science* 21:339–40.

Matos, J. A., and D. C. Rudolph. 1985. The vegetation of the Roy E. Larsen sandylands sanctuary in the Big Thicket of Texas. *Castanea* 50:228–95.

Matta, J. F. 1982. The bionomics of two species of *Hydrochara* (Coleoptera: Hydrophilidae) with descriptions of their larvae. *Proc. Entomol. Soc. Wash.* 84:461–67.

Matthews, E. G. 1972. A revision of the Scarabaeine dung beetles of Australia. I: Tribe Onthophagini. *Australian J. Zool.,* Suppl. no. 9.

Maxwell, J. A., and D. K. Young. 1998. A significant range extension for *Eleodes tricostatus* (Say) (Coleoptera: Tenebrionidae). *Coleopterists Bull.* 52:90–92.

Maxwell, R. 1970. *Geologic and Historic Guide to the State Parks of Texas.* Guidebook 10. Bureau of Economic Geology, University of Texas, Austin.

Menke, A. S. 1963. A review of the genus *Lethocerus* in North and Central America, including the West Indies (Hemiptera: Belostomatidae). *Ann. Entomol. Soc. Amer.* 56:261–67.

———. 1979. Family Belostomatidae. Pp. 76–86 in *The Semiaquatic and Aquatic Hemiptera of California (Heteroptera: Hemiptera).* Bull. Calif. Insect Survey no. 21.

Michener, C. D., R. J. McGinley, and B. N. Danforth. 1994. *The Bee Genera of North and Central America (Hymenoptera: Apoidea).* Washington, D.C.: Smithsonian Institution Press.

Milliger, L. E. 1965. Some soil algae from Bastrop State Park, Texas. Master's thesis, University of Texas, Austin.

———. 1969. Some soil algae from Bastrop State Park, Texas. *Texas Journal of Science* 20:221–35.

de Mischis, C. C. 1985. The earthworms (Annelida, Oligochaeta) from the Pampa de Achala (Córdoba, Argentina). *Megadrilogica* 4(5):130–31.

Mitchell, J. D. and W. D. Pierce. 1912. The ants of Victoria County, Texas. *Proc. Entomol. Soc. Wash.* 14:667–76.

Mitchell, R. J. 1964. A quantitative assessment of the perennial vegetation of Bastrop State Park, Texas. Master's thesis, University of Texas, Austin.

Moody, J. V., and O. F. Francke. 1982. *The Ants (Hymenoptera: Formicidae) of Western Texas.* Part 1: *Subfamily Myrmicinae.* Graduate Studies, Texas Tech University, no. 27. Texas Tech University, Lubbock.

Morley, C. 1917. On the proctotrupid genus *Gonatopus,* Ljunch. *Entomologist* 50:222–27.

Morrow, M. B. 1931. Correlation between plant communities and the reaction and micro-flora of the soil in southcentral Texas. *Ecology* 7:497–507.

Neck, R. W. 1994. Land snails of Travis County. Pp. 146–51 in *Birds and Other Wildlife of South Central Texas,* ed. E. A. Kutac and S. C. Caran. Austin: University of Texas Press.

Needham, J. G., and M. J. Westfall, Jr. 1954. *A Manual of the Dragonflies of North America (Anisoptera).* Berkeley: University of California Press.

Needham, J. G., M. J. Westfall, Jr., and M. L. May. 2000. *Dragonflies of North America,* rev. ed. Gainesville, Fla.: Scientific Publishers.

Nixon, E. S. 1985. *Trees, Shrubs, and Woody Vines of East Texas.* Nacogdoches, Tex.: Bruce Lyndon Cunningham Productions.

Nutting, W. L. 1969a. The desert termites. *Pest Control* 37(9):11–20.

———. 1969b. Distribution and flights of rare North American desert termites of the genus *Amitermes. Pan-Pac. Entomol.* 45:320–25.

———. 1969c. Flight and colony foundation. Pp. 233–83 in *Biology of Termites,* vol. 1, ed. K. Krishna and F. M. Weesner. New York: Academic Press.

Ode, P. E. 1980. Milkweed beetles (*Tetraopes* spp.) on common milkweed (*Asclepias syriaca*) in the northeastern USA. *Melsheimer Entomological Series* 0(29):43–47.

Oliveira, P. S. 1985. On the mimetic association between nymphs of *Hyalymenus*-spp. Hemiptera Alydidae and ants. *Zool. J. Linn. Soc.* 83:371–84.

Olmi, M. 1984. *A Revision of the Dryinidae (Hymenoptera).* Mem. Amer. Entomol. Inst. 37, part 2.

Otte, D. 1981. *The North American Grasshoppers.* Vol. 1: *Acrididae, Gomphocerinae and Acridinae.* Cambridge, Mass.: Harvard University Press.

Painter, R. H. 1926. A review of the genus *Lepidophora* (Diptera, Bombyliidae). *Trans. Amer. Entomol. Soc.* 51:119–27.

———. 1962. The taxonomy and biology of *Systoechus* and *Anastoechus* bombyliid predators in grasshopper egg pods. *J. Kans. Entomol. Soc.* 35:255–69.

Painter, R. H., and E. M. Painter. 1962. Notes on and redescriptions of types of North American Bombyliidae (Diptera) in European museums. *J. Kans. Entomol. Soc.* 35:2–164.

Parfin, S. I. 1952. The Megaloptera and Neuroptera of Minnesota. *Amer. Midland Nat.* 47:421–34.

Parker, S. (ed. in chief). 1989. *McGraw-Hill Dictionary of Scientific and Technical Terms*, 4th ed. New York: McGraw-Hill.

Parks, H. B., V. L. Cory, et al. 1938. *Biological Survey of the East Texas Big Thicket Area.* [No publisher credited in this 51-page pamphlet, which appeared as a reprint in 1971.]

Paulson, D. R. 1984. Odonata from the Yucatan Peninsula, Mexico. *Notulae Odonatologicae* 2:33–38.

Polis, G. A., and W. D. Sissom. 1990. Life history. Pp. 161–223 in *The Biology of Scorpions*, ed. G. A. Polis. Stanford, Calif.: Stanford University Press.

Proceedings of the Brooklyn Entomological Society. 1914. Vol. 9, p. 65 (minutes of meeting).

Rasmussen, W. C. 1949. Sands of the Texas gulf coast: A review. *Texas Journal of Science* 1:84–96.

Ratcliffe, B. C. 1972. The natural history of *Necrodes surinamensis* (Fabr.) (Coleoptera: Silphidae). *Trans. Amer. Entomol. Soc.* 98:359–410.

Readio, P. A. 1927. Studies on the biology of the Reduviidae of America north of Mexico. *Univ. Kansas Science Bull.* 27:5–291.

Rehn, J. A. G. 1919. A study of the orthopterous genus *Mermiria* Stål. *Proc. Acad. Nat. Sci. Phil.* 71:55–120 + 3 plates.

Rehn, J. A. G., and M. Hebard. 1904. The Orthoptera of Thomas County, Georgia, and Leon County, Florida. *Proc. Acad. Nat. Sci. Phil.* 56:774–802.

———. 1914a. A revision of the Orthopterous group Insarae (Tettigoniidae, Phaneropterinae). *Trans. Amer. Entomol. Soc.* 40:37–184.

———. 1914b. Studies in American Tettigoniidae (Orthoptera). I and II. *Trans. Amer. Entomol. Soc.* 40:271–344 + 4 plates.

———. 1914c. Studies in American Tettigoniidae (Orthoptera). III. *Trans. Amer. Entomol. Soc.* 40:365–413 + 2 plates.

———. 1915. Studies in American Tettigoniidae (Orthoptera). IV: A synopsis of the species of the genus *Orchelimum*. *Trans. Amer. Entomol. Soc.* 41:11–83 + 4 plates.

———. 1916. Studies in the Dermaptera and Orthoptera of the coastal plain and piedmont region of the southeastern United States. *Proc. Acad. Nat. Sci. Phil.* 68:87–314 + 3 plates.

Rehn, J. A. G., and J. W. H. Rehn. 1936. On new or redefined genera of Nearctic Melanopli (Orthoptera: Acrididae, Cyrtacanthacrinae). *Trans. Amer. Entomol. Soc.* 62:1–30 + 2 plates.

Rentz, D. C., and J. D. Birchim. 1968. *Revisionary Studies in the Nearctic Decticinae.* Memoirs of the Pacific Coast Entomological Society vol. 3. 173 pp.

Reynolds, J. W. 1976. Un aperçu des vers de terre dans les Forêts Nord-Américaines, leurs activités et leurs repartition. *Megadrilogica* 2(9):1–11.

———. 1977. *The Earthworms (Lumbricidae and Sparganophilidae) of Ontario.* Life Sciences Misc. Pub. Toronto, Canada: Royal Ontario Museum.

Ribble, D. W. 1965. A revision of the banded subgenera of *Nomia* in America (Hymenoptera: Halictidae). *Univ. Kansas Science Bull.* 45:277–359.

Rice, M. E. 1988. Natural history observations on *Tetraopes* and other Cerambycidae (Coleoptera) from the Great Plains Ecosystem. *J. Kans. Entomol. Soc.* 61:412–19.

Richards, O. W. 1939. The British Bethylidae (S. L.) (Hymenoptera). *Trans. Royal Entomol. Soc. London* 89:185–344.

Ridley, W. S. 1955. Geology of the northwest corner of the Smithville quadrangle, Bastrop County, Texas. Master's thesis, University of Texas, Austin.

Riegel, G. T. 1963. The distribution of *Zorotypus hubbardi* (Zoraptera). *Ann. Entomol. Soc. Amer.* 56:744–47.

———. 1987. Order Zoraptera. Pp. 184–85 in *Immature Insects,* vol. 1, ed. F. W. Stehr. Dubuque, Iowa: Kendall/Hunt Publishing Company.

Riegel, G. T., and M. B. Ferguson. 1960. New state records of Zoraptera. *Ent. News* 71:213–16.

Riskind, D. H., and J. Moreland. 1973. The woody vegetation of the Buescher Division. University of Texas Environmental Science Park at Smithville, Pub. no. 2. 52 pp.

Rodgers, J. P. 1947. Sedimentary petrology of the Carrizo sand outcrop east of Bastrop, Bastrop County, Texas. Master's thesis, University of Texas, Austin.

Ross, E. S. 1940. A revision of the Embioptera of North America. *Ann. Entomol. Soc. Amer.* 33:629–76.

———. 1970. Biosystematics of the Embioptera. *Ann. Rev. Entomol.* 15:157–71.

———. 1984. A synopsis of the Embiidina of the United States. *Proc. Entomol. Soc. Wash.* 86:82–93.

Ross, H. H. 1937. Studies of Nearctic aquatic insects. I. Nearctic alder flies of the genus *Sialis. Bull. Illinois Nat. Hist. Survey* 21:57–78.

Ruckes, H. 1941. Note on the feeding habits of *Brochymena carolinensis* (West.) in Florida. *Bull. Brooklyn Entomol. Soc.* 36:27–28.

Runham, N. W., and P. J. Hunter. 1970. *Terrestrial slugs.* London, England: Hutchinson and Company.

Saunders, W. 1874. On some of our common insects. 18: The spotted pelidnota—*Pelidnota punctata,* Linn. *Can. Ent.* 6:141–42.

Savely, H. E., Jr. 1939. Ecological relations of certain animals in dead pine and oak logs. *Ecol. Monographs* 9:321–85.

Schaupp, F. G. 1883. Cicindelidae. *Bull. Brooklyn Entomol. Soc.* 6:73–108 + 5 plates.

Schiefer, T. L. 1998. Disjunct distribution of Cerambycidae (Coleoptera) in the Black Belt and Jackson Prairie in Mississippi and Alabama. *Coleopterists Bull.* 52:278–84.

Schiff, N. M., and T. L. Schiefer. 1999. New Blattodea records from Mississippi and Alabama. *Ent. News* 110:240–42.

Schlinger, E. I., R. van den Bosch, and E. J. Dietrick. 1959. Biological notes on the predaceous earwig *Labidura riparia* (Pallas), a recent immigrant to California [Dermaptera: Labiduridae]. *J. Econ. Entomol.* 52:247–49.

Schmidt, J. O., and M. S. Blum. 1977. Adaptations and responses of *Dasymutilla occidentalis* (Hymenoptera: Mutillidae) to predators. *Ent. Exp. Appl.* 21:99–111.

Schuh, R. T., and J. A. Slater. 1995. *True Bugs of the World (Hemiptera: Heteroptera).* Ithaca, N.Y.: Cornell University Press.

Schultz, R. P. 1997. *Loblolly Pine: The Ecology and Culture of Loblolly Pine* (Pinus taeda L.). Agricultural Handbook 713. Washington, D.C.: USDA Forest Service.

Schultz, T. D. 1989. Habitat preferences and seasonal abundances of eight sympatric species of tiger beetle, genus *Cicindela* (Coleoptera: Cicindelidae), in Bastrop State Park, Texas. *Southwest. Nat.* 34:468–77.

Scott, J. A. 1986. *The Butterflies of North America.* Stanford, Calif.: Stanford University Press.

Scudder, S. H. 1894. A preliminary review of the North American Decticidae. *Can. Ent.* 26:177–84.

———. 1896. Index to the Mantidae of North America, north of Mexico. *Can. Ent.* 28:207–15.

Sharp, F. 1894. Collecting in the "Lone Star State." *Ent. News* 5: 307–309.

Shelley, R. M., and W. D. Sissom. 1995. Distributions of the scorpions *Centruroides vittatus* (Say) and *Centruroides hentzi* (Banks) in the United States and Mexico. *J. Arachnol.* 23:100–10.

Sites, R. W., and J. T. Polhemus. 1994. Nepidae (Hemiptera) of the United States and Canada. *Ann. Entomol. Soc. Amer.* 87:27–42.

———. 1995a. The *Pelocoris* (Hemiptera: Naucoridae) fauna of Texas. *Southwest. Nat.* 40:249–54.

———. 1995b. The identity of *Pelocoris biimpressus* Montandon and synonymy of *Pelocoris* species in the southwestern United States (Heteroptera: Naucoridae). *Proc. Entomol. Soc. Wash.* 97:654–58.

Slater, J. A., and R. M. Baranowski. 1978. *How to Know the True Bugs.* Dubuque, Iowa: Wm. C. Brown Company.

Smeins, F. E., and D. D. Diamond. 1983. Remnant grasslands of the Fayette Prairie, Texas. *Amer. Midland Nat.* 110:1–13.

Smetana, A. 1980. *Revision of the Genus* Hydrochara *Berth. (Coleoptera: Hydrophilidae).* Memoirs of the Entomological Society of Canada no. 111. 100 pp.

Smith, D. R. 1989. The sawfly genus *Arge* (Hymenoptera: Argidae) in the Western Hemisphere. *Trans. Amer. Entomol. Soc.* 115:83–205.

Smith, R. L., and E. Larsen. 1993. Egg attendance and brooding by males of the giant water bug *Lethocerus medius* (Guerin) in the field (Heteroptera: Belostomatidae). *J. Insect Behav.* 6:93–106.

Somes, M. P. 1916. The Phasmidae of Minnesota, Iowa and Missouri (Orth.). *Ent. News* 27:269–71.

Spieth, H. T. 1941. Taxonomic studies on the Ephemeroptera. II: The genus *Hexagenia. Amer. Midl. Nat.* 26:233–80.

Stahle, D. W. 1996. Tree rings and ancient forest relics. *Arnoldia* 56(4):2–10.

Starbuck, T. J. 1984. The vascular flora of Robertson County, Texas. Master's thesis, Texas A&M University, College Station.

Taber, S. W. 1998. *The World of the Harvester Ants.* College Station: Texas A&M University Press.

———. 2000. *Fire Ants.* College Station: Texas A&M University Press.

Tinkham, E. R. 1944. Biological, taxonomic and faunistic studies on the shield-back katydids of the North American deserts. *Amer. Midland Nat.* 31:257–328.

———. 1948. Faunistic and ecological studies on the Orthoptera of the Big Bend Region of Trans-Pecos Texas, with especial reference to the orthopteran zones and faunae of midwestern North America. *Amer. Midland Nat.* 40:521–663.

Todd, T. W. 1956. Comparative petrology of the Carrizo and Newby sandstones, Bastrop County, Texas. Master's thesis, University of Texas, Austin.

de la Torre Bueno, J. R. 1906. Life histories of North American water-bugs. *Can. Ent.* 38:242–52.

Townes, H. 1949. The Nearctic species of the family Stephanidae (Hymenoptera). *Proc. U.S. Nat. Mus.* 99:361–70 + 1 plate.

Triplehorn, C. A. 1972. A review of the genus *Zopherus* of the world (Coleoptera: Tenebrionidae). Smithsonian Contributions to Zoology no. 108.

Tuskes, P. M., J. P. Tuttle, and M. M. Collins. 1996. *The Wild Silk Moths of North America.* Ithaca, N.Y.: Cornell University Press.

Tyler, H. 1975. *The Swallowtail Butterflies of North America.* Healdsburg, Calif.: Natuuregraph Publishers.

Van Duzee, E. P. 1904. Annotated list of the Pentatomidae recorded from America north of Mexico, with descriptions of some new species. *Trans. Amer. Entomol. Soc.* 30:1–80.

Vines, R. A. 1977. *Trees of East Texas.* Austin: University of Texas Press.

Walker, E. M. 1953. *The Odonata of Canada and Alaska.* Vol. 1. Toronto, Canada: University of Toronto Press.

———. 1958. *The Odonata of Canada and Alaska.* Vol. 2. Toronto, Canada: University of Toronto Press.

Walker, E. M., and P. S. Corbet. 1975. *The Odonata of Canada and Alaska.* Vol. 3. Toronto, Canada: University of Toronto Press.

Walker, T. J. 1962. The taxonomy and calling songs of United States tree crickets (Orthoptera: Gryllidae: Oecanthinae). I: The genus *Neoxabea* and the *niveus* and *varicornis* groups of the genus *Oecanthus. Ann. Entomol. Soc. Amer.* 55:303–22.

———. 1963. The taxonomy and calling songs of United States tree crickets (Orthoptera: Gryllidae: Oecanthinae). II: The *nigricornis* group of the genus *Oecanthus. Ann. Entomol. Soc. Amer.* 56:772–89.

Walter, H., and E. Stadelmann. 1974. A new approach to the water relations of desert plants. Chapter 5 in *Desert Biology,* vol. 2, ed. G. W. Brown, Jr. New York: Academic Press.

Ward, W. L. 1957. Geology of the Barton's Creek area, Bastrop and Fayette Counties. Master's thesis, University of Texas, Austin.

Warner, S. R. 1926. Distribution of native plants and weeds on certain soil types in eastern Texas. *Botanical Gazette* 82:345–72.

Waterhouse, D. F. 1974. The biological control of dung. *Sci. Amer.* 230(4):100–109.

Weaver, J. E. 1995. Life history, habits, and control of the cicada killer wasp in West Virginia. Circular 161, Agricultural and Forestry Experiment Station, West Virginia University, Morgantown.

Weaver, J. E., and R. A. Sommers. 1969. Life history and habits of the short-tailed cricket, *Anurogryllus muticus,* in central Louisiana. *Ann. Entomol. Soc. Amer.* 62:337–42.

Weber, N. A. 1972. *Gardening Ants: The Attines.* Philadelphia: American Philosophical Society.

Welch, J. L., and B. C. Kondratieff. 1990. A new species of *Nemomydas* (Diptera: Mydidae) from Texas. *J. Kans. Entomol. Soc.* 63:643–45.

Werner, F. G. 1969. Two flights of *Scaptolenus* (Coleoptera: Cebrionidae). *Coleopterists Bull.* 23:26–27.

West, M. J., and R. D. Alexander. 1963. Sub-social behavior in a burrowing cricket *Anurogryllus muticus* (De Geer). *Ohio J. Sci.* 63:19–24.

Westfall, M. J., Jr., and M. L. May. 1996. *Damselflies of North America.* Gainesville, Fla.: Scientific Publishers.

Wheeler, W. M. 1900. A study of some Texas Ponerinae. *Biol. Bull.* 2:1–31.

———. 1910. *Ants.* New York: Columbia University Press.

White, R. E. 1983. *A Field Guide to the Beetles of North America.* Boston: Houghton Mifflin.

Wittmer, W. 1975. The genus *Phengodes* in the United States (Coleoptera: Phengodidae). *Coleopterists Bull.* 29:231–50.

———. 1980. Remarks on a few species of *Malthinus* Latreille (Coleoptera: Cantharidae: Malthinini) from the United States. *Coleopterists Bull.* 34:271–79.

Wolcott, A. B. 1922. North American predaceous beetles of the tribe Tillini in the United States National Museum. *Proc. U.S. Nat. Mus.* 59(2370): 269–90 + 1 plate.

Wood, D. L., and R. W. Stark. 1968. The life history of *Ips calligraphus* (Coleoptera: Scolytidae) with notes on its biology in California. *Can. Ent.* 100:145–51.

Wood, S. L. 1982. *The Bark and Ambrosia Beetles of North and South America (Coleoptera: Scolytidae): A Taxonomic Monograph.* Great Basin Naturalist Memoirs no. 6.

Woods, R. D. 1934. Petrographic examination of some sections of the Carrizo Formation in central Texas. Master's thesis, University of Texas, Austin.

Worthley, H. N. 1924. The biology of *Trichopoda pennipes* Fab. (Diptera, Tachinidae), a parasite of the common squash bug. *Psyche* 31:7–16, 57–75, + 4 plates.

Yanega, D. 1996. *Field Guide to Northeastern Longhorned Beetles (Coleoptera: Cerambycidae).* Illinois Natural History Survey Manual no. 6. Champaign.

Youngman, A. L. 1965. An ecotypic differentiation approach to the study of isolated populations of *Pinus taeda* in south central Texas. Ph.D. diss., University of Texas, Austin.

Zaragoza, S. C. 1986. El genero *Distremocephalus* Wittmer en Mexico (Coleoptera: Phengodidae). *An. Inst. Biol. Univ. Nac. Auton. Mex.* 56:189–202.

Zobel, B. J., and R. E. Goddard. 1955. Preliminary results on tests of drought hardy strains of loblolly pine (*Pinus taeda* L.). Texas Forest Service Research Note no. 14. College Station.

Index

ISBN 1-58544-236-4

90000